THE AUTHOR Robert Cole is Professor of Modern British and European History at Utah State University in America and a Fellow of the Royal Historical Society. He has lectured at British colleges and universities and has travelled extensively in Europe. His writings include *A Traveller's History of France*, *A Traveller's History of Paris*, *Britain and the War of Words in Neutral Europe, 1939–1945*, *A.J.P. Taylor: The Traitor within the Gates*, and a number of articles on propaganda and historiography. He also has written and presented several scripts for radio.

SERIES EDITOR Professor Denis Judd is a graduate of Oxford, a Fellow of the Royal Historical Society and Professor of History at the London Metropolitan University. He has published over 20 books including the biographies of Joseph Chamberlain, Prince Philip, George VI and Alison Uttley, historical and military subjects, stories for children and two novels. His most recent books are the highly praised *Empire: The British Imperial Experience from 1765 to the Present* and (with Keith Surridge) *The Boer War*. He has reviewed and written extensively in the national press and in journals and is an advisor to the BBC *History* Magazine.

Other Titles in the Series

THE TRAVELLER'S HISTORY SERIES

Reviews of Individual Titles

A Traveller's History
of Germany

A Traveller's History of Germany

ROBERT COLE

Series Editor   DENIS JUDD
Line Drawings   *PETER GEISSLER*

Interlink Books
An imprint of Interlink Publishing Group, Inc.
New York • Northampton

First American edition published in 2004 by
INTERLINK BOOKS
An imprint of Interlink Publishing Group, Inc.
46 Crosby Street, Northampton, Massachusetts 01060-1804
www.interlinkbooks.com

Text copyright © Robert Cole, 2004
Preface copyright © Denis Judd, 2004
Line drawings Peter Geissler
Maps by John Taylor

The front cover shows the skyline of Dresden. © Morton Beebe/CORBIS

ISBN 1-56656-532-4   *3 117 7941*   *¹¹/₀₄*

Printed and bound in Great Britain

To order or request our complete catalog
please call us at **1-800-238-LINK** or write to:
Interlink Publishing
46 Crosby Street, Northampton MA 01060-1804
e-mail: info@interlinkbooks.com
www.interlinkbooks.com

Contents

Preface

Of all great Western nations, it is Germany that has suffered most from a turbulent history and a failure to achieve a lasting unity. It is only a hundred and thirty years since the various German states seemed to have been finally united under Prussian leadership at the end of the triumphant war with the France of Napoleon III. But by 1919 the First Reich had collapsed and Germany's western and eastern frontiers had been redrawn. Another fourteen years, and the coming to power of Hitler began a frenzied period of expansion and conquest only ended by the humiliation of Germany's unconditional surrender and partition in 1945. Even today, over a decade after German reunification, Germany is simply a part – though an enormously significant and influential part – of an expanding and continually redefining European Union.

If anything, what came before the establishment of what is recognisably modern Germany in 1871, was even more uncertain and confusing. The Romans, failing to subdue the fiercely independent German tribes, washed their hands of the place. Thereafter, German identity – apart from the language and some culture was lost amid a shifting, tumbling circus of principalities, bishoprics, electorates, empires and leagues. Germany was the classical 'geographical expression'.

Worse still, Germany was situated at the epicentre of powerful and often opposing European forces. To its east were the Slav people; to the west and south-west were the increasingly powerful nation states of France, Spain and England. When the reformation was set in motion by a German priest, Martin Luther, Germany was split into a roughly Protestant north and an overwhelmingly Catholic south. Subsequently no nation suffered more than Germany during the sectarian, ferociously waged Thirty Years War that ended in 1648. All of this, and much more, meant that Germany was awkwardly caught as the country in middle. One of the enduring puzzles for Germany's leaders was which way to face? Towards the untidy 'barbaric', 'backward' east, or to the 'progressive' but highly organised and competitive west? It was Hitler's momentous decision to choose the *lebensraum* of the east in 1941 having only partially subdued the west, that gave Britain and her allies the breathing space to regroup and begin the long fight back that ended in total victory in 1945.

Germany's uncertain place in the balance of European power, its confusion over identity and purpose, perhaps led to the rigidity and love of order that is still the object of some mocking caricature. It also helps to explain why German unity in the nineteenth century could only be achieved under the disciplined militaristic leadership of Bismarck's Prussia.

Professor Cole, the author of the bestselling volume *A Traveller's History of France* in this admirable series, explains in this new book the roots of modern Germany with his usual scholarly accuracy and sheer readability.

As a consequence, as well as the darker side, the complexity and genius of the German character are made manifestly plain: the extraordinary flowering of culture, especially in music; the romanticism and the revolutionary philosophies; the early social welfarism and the current 'green' politics; the commercial and technological skills that make Volkswagen and BMW hallmarks of excellence; the quality of Germany beer and wine and a great deal more.

As Germany, reunited and at last at ease with itself and its neighbours, enters the twenty-first century, it is attracting record numbers of tourists. Bob Cole's wonderfully informative book should be in every visitor's pocket.

Denis Judd
Tarn-et-Garonne
France

CHAPTER ONE

The Germans and Germany to 800

There were Germans long before there was Germany, in Western, Central and Eastern Europe. They shared similar yet not identical language, culture and ethnicity, fought and argued over matters political, territorial, ethnic, religious, economic and ideological including whether they should be ruled by a centralist king-emperor or a collection of quasi-independent territorial principalities and city-states, all the while pushing the envelope of intellectual, artistic and technological advancement. They formed a German nation only in 1871 under a Prussian king who was named German emperor. Even then the Germans remained what they had always been: a collection of tribes.

The Land

The German climate is damp, foggy and cold, though it escapes the excessive extremes of northern Russia; the damp contributes to the forests that spread across western and southern Germany. The land is bordered in the north by the North and Baltic Seas, and in the south by the Alps, which run along the country's southernmost edge. Germany's highest Alpine peak, the Zugspitze, is 2,963 metres, well below France's Mont Blanc and Switzerland's Matterhorn, both well over 4,000 metres. Garmisch-Partenkirchen, Germany's most famous ski resort, is virtually on the border with Switzerland. An Alpine foreland stretches north to the Danube River and is characterized by such ice-age glacial lakes as the Bodensee, which Germany shares with Switzerland, and forested massifs, most famously the Schwarzwald (Black Forest), the Schwäbische Alb, Fränkische Alb and the Böhmerwald.

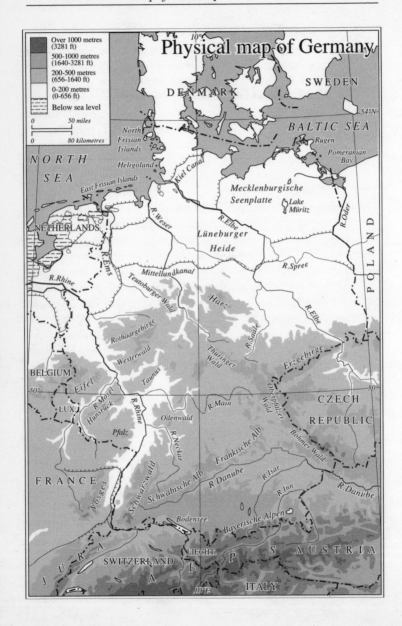

North of its Alpine border, Germany is marked by hilly regions and the great plain stretching from the Ural Mountains to the North Sea that was a roadway over thousands of years for tribal migrations, and in the Middle Ages for German expansion eastward to the frontiers of Russia. There Prussia took root and expanded, its economy always more agricultural than mercantile owing to the large deposits of wind-blown dust that created excellent soil for growing wheat, sugar beets and barley. An urban economy developed in the west, made possible by Germany's river system and its connection to the Baltic and North Seas.

RIVERS

The river system is nothing if not complex. For centuries it served as both pathways and barriers to migration, and as demarcation lines for tribal, ducal, princely and imperial regions. The Rhine was the boundary beyond which the Roman Empire never took root. Germany's rivers flow in all directions save south. The Nieman empties into the Baltic in what was East Prussia, the Vistula flows through former West Prussia to enter the Baltic at Gdansk (Danzig) in Poland, and the Oder, fed by the Neisse and Warta, runs to the Baltic through Brandenburg and Pomerania. Germany's longest northern rivers, the Elbe and Rhine (with the much shorter Weser) empty into the North Sea. The Rhine is fed by the Main and Ruhr, and the Elbe by the Spree, upon the banks of which the city of Berlin had its beginnings centuries before it was the German capital. Only the Danube flows eastward from its source in the German Alps, passing through Bavaria, Austria, Hungary and Romania to end finally at the Black Sea. Over 1,800 miles long, it is the longest German river by far, and second in Europe only to the Volga in Russia.

The river system contributed to the development of German trade and small semi-independent principalities by providing easily accessible venues for the transportation of trade goods over long distances. It added to Germany's beauty as well. The regions through which the Rhine and the Main flow are exceptionally beautiful and fertile; and medieval castles dot the wooded heights of the Rhine valley where the Lorelei once sang (or so German mythology has it) from Mainz south to Switzerland.

The People

The first inhabitants of German lands were Palaeolithic Indo-Europeans who migrated north from the Mediterranean basin 80,000 years ago. Over the millennia, they moved across Germany leaving traces of their presence and culture, which included ceremonial burials and totemic rituals, on pieces of bone, ivory, slate, horn and the walls of caves. They probably were the first permanent inhabitants of the Schleswig-Holstein area.

NEOLITHIC

Indo-Europeans were settled all across German lands by 7000 BC, the beginning of the Neolithic age. They now were skilled at crafting dug-out canoes, weapons – fish hooks, arrow heads and axe blades – and cooking pots. They also had begun domesticating plants and animals for food, and used dogs for hunting and herding. The first examples of hand-built dwellings date from this era, such as the wooden huts of the Swiss Lake Dwellers which rested on piles driven into the bottom of waters near the lake shore. Burials were in dolmans, passage graves and stone cists, the latter being a form of coffin, and were ritualistic, as suggested by the amber amulets and necklaces that commonly decorated the deceased. Such burials and related cultural habits were characteristic across southern Scandinavia, Schleswig-Holstein and northwestern Germany, and by 3000 BC had spread into Thuringia, Saxony, Austria, Hungary, Romania and the southern Russian steppes. Which brings us to the first Germans.

EARLY MIGRATIONS

Between 2000 and 1200 BC North Europeans separated into distinct tribes including some that can be called Germanic – a matter of language, not race. These likely were limited to Jutland and the southern tip of Sweden, for German lands then were largely occupied by Celts. However, by 200 BC the Celts were gone, driven out by the Germanic tribes that had emerged over the preceding millennium: Goths, Burgundians, Alemanni, Langobards ('long beards'), and Teutons and Suevians, the main carriers of an evolving Germanic culture. Some came from the east via the Great Plain, and others from Jutland and Schleswig-Holstein in the northwest. Their movement was part of a tribal *wanderlust* that went on for centuries, prompted by population increase, intertribal quarrels, rivalries and all-out war, and almost certainly by climatic changes. Early Scandinavian lore includes, for example, the tale of the 'winter when the frost giants ruled.' By the end of the pre-Christian era Germanic tribes and their varieties of Germanic culture were well established along the Rhine and the Danube. The runic alphabet emerged in this era, the basis of a written language then largely limited to inscriptions on weapons and monuments.

The Germans

Romans left the earliest written records regarding the Germans. They were, wrote the Romans, a people of fair complexion with reddish-blond hair, tall and powerfully built. Ausonius described most poetically his Suevian slave girl, Bissula: 'golden her hair, her eyes of blue colour; ... adorned by nature with charms which defy all artificial tricks. Well may other maidens use powder or rouge, her face does not owe its rosiness to the deftness of her fingers.' Men and women were similarly attired in sleeveless undergarments, breeches or trousers, a cloak made of wool or linen, often adorned with fur and held in place by a brooch, and necklaces and other adornments made of metal, glass or amber. Shoes were of leather and fastened around the ankle with a string. Weapons were bows and arrows, swords and short javelins, hatchets and huge shields that apparently also could be used as sleds to slide down icy mountain slopes.

DAILY LIFE

Germans dined on beer, wine, bread, vegetables and meats, the latter including both hunted fowl, boar and venison and domestically produced beef, pork and horse. Woman's work was cooking, sewing, spinning and weaving, and motherhood. Marriage was highly regarded, and women were expected to be virtuous far more than were men. An offended husband could whip and even kill an adulterous wife. Men's work was largely tilling crops (with horse-drawn ploughs, by Roman times), doing battle, and sometimes engaging in the amber trade. The early Germans kept slaves, and there were strict rules prohibiting slaves and freemen from marrying. If the latter married the former, their offspring automatically were slaves.

GODS AND GODDESSES

Religion and mythology were important aspects of early Germanic culture. The most reliable sources for what and how, are archaeological remains and old Icelandic sagas. There is also the North German Edda from the eighth century AD, but it is thought to have been influenced by Christianity. Germanic gods were perceived as superhuman and powerful, with whom tribesmen had a very personal relationship of mutual trust, service and loyalty – except, of course, when particular gods were duplicitous, selfish and cruel. The tribes also conceived of a cosmic race of giants separate from the gods, and with whom the gods made a war that eventually culminated in their destruction in the *Götterdämmerung* (twilight of the gods). This was a central theme in Richard Wagner's Ring Cycle operas. Gods and giants were 'beyond good and evil,' to borrow a phrase from Friedrich Nietzsche, Wagner's contemporary, but were neither eternal nor omnipotent. They were awe-inspiring, however, and the tribes approached their worship in an appeasement mode that sometimes included human sacrifice, often but not always prisoners of war. Among the Cimbri, white-clad priestesses supervised the ritual of suspending the victims over a large bronze cauldron, cutting their throats and letting the blood flow into the vessel. Human sacrifice also included drowning young girls.

The most important German deities were Wodan, the chief god, Thor and Freya. Wodan was the perpetrator of discord; Thor was the god of both prosperity and war; Freya was the earth mother goddess, in imagery much like Cybele, the mother of the gods in early Greek mythology. Both heaven and earth were populated with nymphs, spirits, elves, goblins, witches and werewolves ranging from the friendly to the hostile, and the spirits of the dead were believed to live on in trees and waters near the locales where they had dwelt in life. German tribes had no clear answer to life or death, and like the ancient Greeks, attached limitations to divinity that reflected the human condition itself.

THE ROMANS

Romans first encountered Germans probably in the second century BC. From then through the age of Augustus Caesar they regularly invaded Germanic lands and did battle with Germans who had invaded the north of Italy. Both sides won and lost, as when Teutons and Cimbri defeated Roman legions between 109 and 105 BC, and Roman general Marius annihilated these tribes in 102 and 101. On both occasions the Germans lived up to their reputation as fierce warriors with a strong sense of honour, backed by women who encouraged them by singing and shouting. Warriors preferred death in battle to being taken by the Romans as slaves. The women too; when captured by Marius' soldiers, they asked to become Vestal Virgins in order to protect their virtue, and when the request was denied, they killed their children and committed suicide. The Germans fascinated the Romans, who coined the phrase *Furor Teutonicus* to describe their battlefield presence. Sometimes they were recruited to serve in the Roman army.

Strabo, Pliny, Julius Caesar, Plutarch and Tacitus, among others, wrote accounts of Germanic wars and Germanic climate, terrain, customs and rituals. Their accuracy is debatable.

THE RHINE BOUNDARY

In AD 9 a German prince, Hermann, 'wielder of the Terrible Two-Handed Sword' ('Arminius' to the Romans), defeated three Roman legions at the Teutoburg forest just beyond the Rhine. Hermann was an Imperial army veteran and well understood Roman tactics. He led a temporary coalition of several German tribes. The defeat weakened Rome's reputation in the north, and a significant western German region free of Roman rule ensued. Thereafter the Rhine was a sort of border between Germany and the Roman Empire; even so, Rome established a provincial culture along its eastern banks protected by the *limes*, a frontier wall stretching to the Danube and into Austria and Hungary. Some of Germany's oldest cities emerged from this Roman cultural borderland: Strasbourg, Mainz, Cologne (Köln), Augsburg, Regensburg and Vienna (Wien), all linked by a system of Roman-built highways. This borderland produced improved agriculture, extended trade, and Roman construction: aqueducts, irrigation canals, palaces, baths, temples and portals, the remains of some of which still exist. Those involved in trade included Jews recently expelled from Palestine by the Romans.

Later Migrations

In the fourth century AD Germanic 'kingdoms' were formed by tribes that had settled in particular regions: Franks and Alemanni along the Rhine, Saxons, Angles, Jutes and Frisians along the North Sea coast into Denmark, Vandals on the upper Oder, Langobards between the Oder and the Vistula, Burgundians in the Main–Neckar region, Thuringians south of the Aller, and Goths – now Visigoths and Ostrogoths – across southern Europe from the Balkans to Spain.

Settled but still restless. The Langobards moved south into Italy and gave their name to Lombardy. The Ostrogoths also entered Italy where they remained until eliminated by the Byzantine Empire, while the Visigoths, pushed out of Gaul by the Franks, remained in Spain until driven out by the Moors. The Vandals moved through Spain and Italy and into North Africa where they too were done in by the Byzantines. The Jutes, Angles and Saxons established themselves in the British Isles, driving the Celts westward into Cornwall and Wales. The Franks, meanwhile, spread east and west from the Rhine, laying the foundations of an empire that would dominate western Europe for more than 300 years and from which would emerge both France and western Germany.

In the middle of all this were the Huns, who migrated from Asia into Europe in the fourth and fifth centuries. They overcame the Alans and Ostrogoths, drove the Visigoths westward, and came close to con-quering both the eastern and western empires. But only close. The Huns failed to take Rome even under their most feared leader, Attila (406–453). He was opposed by a coalition of Romans and Germans and defeated by them in 451 at Châlons. Pope Leo I (400?–461) made Attila back off from sacking Rome and eventually he was stabbed to death by Ildico, a German woman whom he had made his slave – or so tradition has it. Attila likely was the inspiration for King Etzel in the Germanic folk epic *Das Nibelungenlied*.

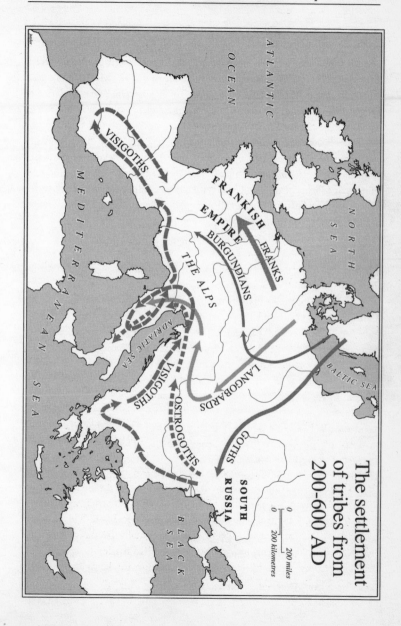

The settlement
of tribes from
200-600 AD

Christianity and the Germans

Many Germans became nominally Christian, having encountered Christianity soon after Constantine the Great (274?–337) made it the official religion of the Roman Empire. In 312, on the eve of a decisive battle with Maxentius over who would hold the imperial throne, Constantine claimed to have seen in the sky a cross and the words *in hoc signo vinces*, which meant that if he followed the cross he would be victorious. He was, and became both Roman Emperor and a Christian. This set Church leaders on a path that would lead to Rome being the centre of Christianity, complete with a power structure appropriate to that role. The latter was especially important because in 285, Emperor Diocletian had moved the imperial seat from Rome to Milan.

ARIANISM

During Constantine's reign, Christians were at odds over whether Arianism (denial of the divinity of Christ) or Athanasianism (that Christ and God were equally divine) was the true Christian doctrine. In 325, Constantine summoned the ecumenical Council at Nicaea to decide the issue. The Council backed Athanasianism (preferred in Rome) and thus reaffirmed the primacy of Rome within Christianity. Constantine preferred Arianism, as did Constantinople, the city he had built on the site of Byzantium at the entrance to the Black Sea; in 330 he made Constantinople the Imperial capital, which act affirmed Arianism. Rome stuck with Athanasianism, however, and the Council of Nicaea produced the Nicene Creed, which proclaimed the Athanasian-based concept of the Trinity (Father, Son and Holy Ghost). Eventually this became the credo of both the Western and Eastern Churches; but for the moment, Rome faced the possibility of losing its position as the centre of Christianity to Constantinople, just as it had its role as the centre of the Empire.

All the same, within a half century the Roman Church was asserting more authority and independence than ever. For example, in 390, on the orders of Bishop Ambrose of Milan, Emperor Theodosius did penance for the massacre of 7,000 Thessalonican insurrectionists. That was the good news; the bad was that migrating German peoples spreading across Europe and into Italy targeted the Church generally and Rome specifically. These Germans largely had embraced Arianism.

BISHOP ULFILA

Prior to the fifth century, there was little contact between Christians and German pagans outside of the Empire, and no serious effort to promote Christianity among them. A rare exception was the brief correspondence, ca. 397, initiated by Queen Fritigil of the Marcommani with Bishop Ambrose. The only significant missionary effort was that launched in 341 by Bishop Ulfila (311–382) among his fellow Visigoths. They were the first German tribe to become Christian, and it was Arian Christianity because Ulfila had been educated in Constantinople. Arianism soon spread from the Visigoths to the Ostrogoths, and then to the Vandals, Burgundians and others. Germanic Arians were tolerant of Roman Catholics, but at the same time felt no compunction against marauding in lands that embraced the western Church. Early Christian intellectual St Jerome wrote in 396: 'Bishops live in prisons, priests and clerics fall by the sword, churches are plundered, altars are turned into feeding troughs.' Of course, not all Germans were Arian invaders. Some had settled in the western Empire and become defenders of it against marauding Germans. For example Stilicho (359–408), the Roman general who confronted Alaric the Visigoth in Thessaly and the Peloponnesus was at least half German.

Arianism was dominant in these kingdoms while they lasted; Roman Catholicism took over as they were conquered by Franks and others, and by the seventh century had replaced Arianism altogether in German kingdoms.

The End of the Roman Empire

Western Roman emperors had disappeared by 476, replaced by *Patrici* (protectors) such as Goths Odovacar and Theoderic, who were nominally subservient to the eastern Empire. Meanwhile, Italian towns, agricultural lands and Rome itself were in serious economic and political decline. In the sixth century, Emperor Justinian tried but failed, to restore the Imperial system in Italy after driving the Goths out.

Soon Italy was comprised of regional fiefdoms run by military leaders and landowners who ruled independent of any central authority. Rome followed suit, with the papacy emerging as not only spiritual leader of the Catholic Church, but temporal leader of a Roman state. It was a perilous time: there were no guarantees that secular rulers, particularly Germans, would respect either the independence of Rome or papal authority. When the Lombards came to Italy, they adopted Italian as their language and embraced Roman Catholicism, but continued to tolerate Arianism. It was to the Franks, who embraced Athanasianism from the start, that the papacy turned for an ally upon whom it could depend.

The Franks

This tribe was composed of the Salian, 'Salt-Sea,' and Riparian, 'River,' Franks whom the Salians absorbed over time. The names indicate that some had contact with the North Sea while others connected primarily to such inland river valleys as the Rhine. There is little archaeological – but considerable mythological – evidence for exactly when and how they emerged. The earliest written records of their existence are third-century Roman commentaries on Frank raids along the English Channel coast, and far inland into Gaul along the river systems.

Clearly, these raids impressed the Romans. In 284 Emperor Diocletian revitalized a decaying Roman army by passing over 'the drones and cutthroats of the regular legions' and conscripting foreign mercenaries, including Franks who had been defeated by his army. When not serving in the Roman army, they were half-free *laeti*, agricultural settler-workers in northern Gaul. In due course, Franks formed their own regiments within the Roman army. By the fourth century many imperial commanders such as Silvanus, Charietto, Merobaudes and Bauto, among others, were of Frank origin, and the *Notitia Dignitatum,* a fifth-century list of Roman commands and posts, included many Franks. Then in the early sixth century the Frank tribes were unified under a recent convert to Christianity, Clovis (Chlodovech).

CLOVIS

Clovis (466–511) was the son of Childeric (437–481?) and the grandson of Merovich (?–456), the first Frank known to be regarded as a king and from whom the Merovingian dynasty took its name. Virtually nothing is known about Merovich (save for the legend that he was the offspring of a sea monster), and little more about Childeric except that he had extensive wealth and power. Clovis is better known. Under his rule a great Frank kingdom was formed that stretched from the Weser to the Pyrenees. Under Clovis the Franks made war against the Gallo-Roman King Syagrius, whom they defeated at Soissons in 486, the Alemanni and Visigoths, crushed respectively in 496 and 507 and then absorbed into Frankish culture in the sixth century, the Burgundians, who allied with the Franks to drive the Visigoths out of Gaul and into Spain, and the Thuringians, whom they fought more or less to a draw.

A nineteenth-century statue of Clovis the Merovingian king

The Franks developed an administrative and social system that reflected elements of the western Roman Empire. Their kingdom was centralized as never before, with Clovis as absolute monarch – Caesar, if you will. Military leaders, or *herzogë* (dukes) who were his loyal and subservient followers, replaced traditional tribal rulers. Under the dukes were *grafen* (counts) who oversaw administration and law in particular regions within tribal lands. All were directly responsible to the king, and were rewarded with grants of land, or fiefs, which technically remained royal property. These fiefs were worked by peasants who became tied to the land just as the lords were tied to the king. Thus began feudalism in Germany, which with additions that occurred in the late eighth and early ninth centuries, emerged as the dominant socio-economic system of the Middle Ages.

AFTER CLOVIS

The century after Clovis began a downhill slide for the Merovingians. True, some Saxons, the Frisians, Thuringians and Bavarians were added to the list of German tribes tributary to the Franks; but there was fighting between rulers and pretenders, rebellious subjects, rulers given over to debauchery, gluttony and other forms of degeneracy that undermined royal prestige, and widespread crime and general corruption. Many kings were deposed and sent off to monasteries. In the early seventh century the kingdom divided into Neustria (France), Burgundy which would eventually be part of France, and Austrasia, which included Alsace, Lorraine and the easternmost parts of the Frank kingdom. Each region had its own king and chief minister, the latter called the Mayor of the Palace *(maior domus)*. Unity was restored in 687 under Pepin of Heristal (635–714), a former mayor of Austrasia, which effectively ended the Merovingian dynasty. After Pepin the mayors were in charge, including Charles Martel (688?–741), who stopped the Muslim advance into the Frankish kingdom at Tours and Poitiers in 732 and whose son, Pepin the Short (714–768), became sole king of the Franks in 751 after sending his brother Carloman to a monastery.

At this point the Franks ruled the Gallo-Romans in what would become France, but failed to replace Gallo-Roman cultural traditions with their own. In the eighth century *langue d'oil,* the ancestor of modern French, emerged as the primary language of that region. The Franks continued speaking Germanic dialects, struggling mostly with 'sound shifts' that eventually would work out as the difference between High German (the south) and Low German (the north and east). Germanic law also prevailed, though Roman law was often allowed for those whose traditions were Roman. The essentials of Germanic law were set down in the Salic Law which dates from the last years of the reign of Clovis.

GERMANS UNDER THE FRANKS

The Frank Empire over time came to include Saxons, Frisians, Thuringians and Bavarians, who gave their names to German kingdoms, principalities and provinces of modern times including Franconia, a name derived from the Franks themselves. Frank rule was extended to the Frisians of the North Sea coast in the sixth century, just south of Denmark, who were politically weak on their own and culturally influenced by the Franks. The Frisians had long been so overshadowed by the greater power of the tribes around them that many sought their fortunes elsewhere, such as in the British Isles. Still, Friesland remains by name a region in modern Germany (though somewhat culturally isolated from the rest of the country) located next door to Holstein. Interestingly, the black and white milk cow breed known in the United States as 'Holstein' is called in Britain, 'Frisian.'

The Thuringians and Bavarians lay between the Elbe and the Danube. The former was a distinct tribe by the fourth century, and a formidable force by the fifth. The latter were unknown so far as a written historical record was concerned until the end of the sixth century. Their origins are vague at best: one theory is that they originated in Bohemia and moved from there to south of the Danube, which was their homeland when they confronted the Franks; the other is that they simply formed out of other groups already in that region. The Thuringians made war against the Franks during and after the reign of Clovis, but could not outfight them. After about 530, their influence in decline, some moved south with the Lombards into Italy, while others were absorbed by the Bavarians. Only their name on a map survived the epoch of the Franks.

Not so the Bavarians. They evolved a strong sense of separate identity, cooperated with such tribes as the Lombards for their own advancement and/or security, and finally made a deal with the Franks in the late sixth century for protection from the Avars, who had invaded Europe from Turkey. Childebert II (567–595) made Bavaria a dukedom, and at least nominally subordinate to the Frank kingdom. Even so, Bavarians continued to set their own course until the eighth century when they were subjected to what was by then a Frank Empire. Subjected, but not absorbed: the Bavarians remained conscious of their cultural heritage and maintained a sense of Bavarian identity – and a degree of self-governance – into the twentieth century.

The Saxons were between the Rhine and Elbe where they remained a strong presence. They were war-like and loosely organized politically, and were the last Germanic people to succumb to the Franks, in the eighth century under Charles the Great (742–814) who was known to the French as 'Charlemagne,' and embrace Christianity in the process. Along with other north Germans, Saxons acquired a keen interest in Britain and began invading that island in the fifth century. In fact, many Germans were in Britain even before then, employed as soldiers by Roman Britons, just as Romans employed Germans on the European continent. By the end of the seventh century most of Roman-Celtic Britain had been taken over by Saxons, Angles, Jutes and others. Kent, for example, first conquered by the Jutes, derives its name from the Germanic *cantware*. There are extensive Anglo-Saxon archaeological remains in East Anglia from as early as the fifth century, and Anglo-Saxons are a major presence in the chronicles of Gildas and the Venerable Bede in the sixth and eighth centuries. Saxons also moved into Gaul in this period, where they served as soldiers for the Frank king Chilperic and for the Breton princess Fredegund, who, ironically, deployed them in battle *against* the Franks.

The Triumph of Christian Rome

Roman Catholicism emerged as the dominant religion among the Germans, beginning more or less when Clovis married Burgundian Princess Clotilda, a Roman Catholic who won him – nagged, as

Edward James described it – over to the Roman Church. Whether Clovis had been a pagan or an Arian Christian is not clear, since there were Arians among the Franks just as there were among other German tribes. Clovis was baptized with 3,000 other Franks on Christmas Day in 496; thereafter the Frank kingdom formed strong ties with Rome.

'ST CLOVIS'

As the strong right arm of the Church Clovis naturally had its support in extending his dominions. Indeed, of all the kingdoms established by Germanic tribes and their Celtic and Slavic allies, only the Kingdom of the Franks endured, in part because of this connection. Byzantine Emperor Anastasius appointed Clovis a Roman consul, while the Roman Church virtually canonized him for his support. Gregory of Tours, a leading propagandist for Rome, recorded that miracles were a regular part of Clovis' experience: he was anointed with holy chrism contained in a vial brought from heaven by a white dove; a mysterious white light guided his army to their victory over Alaric II, the Visigoth; and a white doe showed his army where to ford the River Vienne. But Clovis was hardly a saint; he made war constantly, and murdered his relatives for fear that they might conspire against him for the throne – and then built a church in memory of each of them.

CONVERSION

Bringing Germans into the Roman Church was not easy. Arianism was a barrier, of course, but even more, rural Germans insisting on continuing ancient pagan rituals even after converting to Christianity. When Bishop Eligius of Noyon-Tournai preached that drunkenness and dancing were sins against God, his rural Frank audience repudiated him, saying 'you will never uproot our customs, but we will go on with our rites as we have always done, and we will go on doing so always and forever.' Roman historian Procopius wrote that 'these barbarians, though they have become Christians, preserve the greater part of their ancient religion; for they still make human sacrifices and other sacrifices of an unholy nature. . . .' Gregory of Tours described the 'barbarians' of Cologne as having a temple where they made offerings and gorged

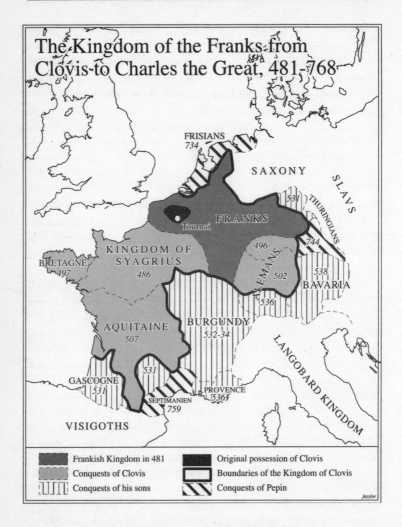

The Kingdom of the Franks from Clovis to Charles the Great, 481–768

FRISIANS
734

SAXONY

SLAVS

531

THURINGIANS

FRANKS

Tournai

KINGDOM OF
SYAGRIUS
486

496

744

ALEMANS

BRETAGNE
497

502

538

BAVARIA

536

AQUITAINE
507

BURGUNDY
532-34

LANGOBARD KINGDOM

GASCOGNE
531

531

PROVENCE
536

SEPTIMANIEN
759

VISIGOTHS

Frankish Kingdom in 481	Original possession of Clovis
Conquests of Clovis	Boundaries of the Kingdom of Clovis
Conquests of his sons	Conquests of Pepin

jtaylor

themselves on meat and wine 'until they vomited.' Bringing Germans into the Church was further retarded by the relative scarcity of religious centres where baptism could be properly administered. The conversion of Rhenish (Rhineland) Franks was still being pursued in the late seventh century, and some other Germans were still pagans into the eighth and ninth centuries.

The first missionaries spreading western Christianity among the Germans clearly were Romans, and even later when bishops and cardinals appeared bearing German names it was no guarantee that they actually were Germans. Irish and Anglo-Saxon monks were among the most successful Roman Christian missionaries, such as St. Columbanus, who arrived from Ireland about 590 and founded monasteries in the Frankish kingdom, and Wilfrid of York, who sought to convert Frisians.

WYNFRITH

The most famous Anglo-Saxon missionary was Wynfrith of Wessex (680?–754) who worked among the Frisians, Hessians, Thuringians and Bavarians. He was made a bishop in 722 and took the name Boniface. As Boniface he came to be known as the 'great organizer' and perhaps in that sense the creator of the Frankish-German Church. He preached to the unconverted, organized ecclesiastical discipline, and established abbeys and bishoprics. With regard to the latter, Boniface went further than any predecessor because he made a point of using sites that had been centres of pagan practices. That this did not always go down well with the Germans is made clear by the fact that in 754, he and fifty-two of his fellow missionaries were killed by pagan Frisians to whom he was preaching at the time. Boniface was ordained an archbishop in 732, and in 738 became Primate and Papal Nuncio of Germany. He founded the Abbey Fulda, and his remains lie in the crypt of Fulda Cathedral. In due course Boniface was canonized and became St Boniface, 'the Apostle of the Germans.' And for this reason, Fulda became and remains, the site for German bishops meeting in annual convention.

PEPIN

By the eighth century power was in the hands of mayors of the palace. Charles Martel was recognized and accepted as the most powerful man in the kingdom following his victories over the Muslims at Tours and Poitiers in 732. Had this happened in Clovis' reign, Martel likely would have been murdered as a potential rival for the throne. But now the Merovingian kings were useless, and it would have been natural for 'the most powerful man in the kingdom' simply to take the throne. For whatever reasons, Martel passed that aspiration on to his son, Pepin the Short (714–768), to whom the Frank Assembly gave regal power in 751. Of course, technically the Merovingians still were kings of the Franks, which meant that Pepin had to find some 'legitimation of his kingship by an authority, recognized by the entire people, which would carry more weight than the mere possession of royal blood.' Who better than Pope Stephen II (?–757)? Pepin had developed a close relationship with Boniface who, in addition to missionary work, served as papal representative and sought a tighter link between the papacy and German bishoprics. Moreover, in the year of Pepin's 'elevation,' the Lombards took control of the Imperial (Byzantine) province of Ravenna in central Italy which deprived the papacy of its traditional protector.

Needing an ally, Pope Stephen II crossed the Alps in the winter of 753–754 and met with Pepin. He pleaded for help; Pepin asked whether it was a good thing that there should be kings with no power in the land of the Franks; he replied that whoever exercised royal power should also hold the royal title – and that was that. Boniface, acting on the Pope's behalf and with the approval of the most powerful nobles, anointed and crowned Pepin as King of the Franks. Pepin thereupon attacked the Lombards and forced them to surrender Ravenna, Spoleto and Benevento to the papacy. This marked the foundation of the Papal States that would survive until they became part of a unified Italy in 1870. Stephen rewarded Pepin by conferring upon him the title 'Patrician of the Romans.'

FRANK–ROME ALLIANCE

Thus began an alliance between Rome and the Franks that would last for centuries. The 'donation of Pepin' as it came to be known – giving to the Church the lands Pepin took from the Lombards – was the founding of a Carolingian protectorate of the Roman Church; and the coronation of Pepin by Boniface began the tradition by which all European monarchs, German as well as others, had their royal powers symbolically bestowed upon them by God acting through His earthly representatives, the princes of the Roman Catholic Church. Rome had triumphed; but so too had the Franks, for there would be no greater liaison between Church and State after Pepin than that which came to pass between his son, Charles the Great, and Pope Leo III (?–816).

Charles the Great

Upon Pepin's death the Assembly divided the Frank kingdom between Charles and his brother Carloman. Neither liked the arrangement, and when Carloman died (of natural causes, it is assumed) in 771 the Frank Assembly elected Charles king of all of the Franks, as required by Salic Law. Charles refused to give Carloman's sons their father's portion, and their mother fled with them to Lombardy where she sought the protection of King Desiderius. Charles read this as a threat, went to war with Lombardy, to the delight of Pope Hadrian I (?–795) who regarded the Lombards as Rome's mortal enemies, and forced Desiderius to abdicate. Charles placed the Lombard crown on his own head and officially took the title 'King of the Franks and Lombards and Patrician of the Romans.' This was the first step on the 'path of conquest' that would expand his kingdom into an empire, and make him 'Charles the Great.'

CHARLES AT WAR

Charles saw the security of the Frank state as his primary concern, which meant unifying all of the German tribes under Frankish rule. The immediate problem was the Saxons. Some had come to his side but many others, particularly east of the Rhine, clung fiercely to their pagan traditions and independence. He made war against them almost continuously from 774 until 804. Charles' biographer Einhard (770–840) described these Saxons as a determined and 'faithless' enemy, 'given to the worship of devils, and hostile to our religion' who raided monasteries and killed priests as well as committing other acts of defiance against the kingdom and the Church. Charles' war with the Saxons was long, brutal and relentless, and included the destruction of the Saxon god Irminsûl who was either a carved tree trunk or according to one source, a statue of the Hermann (Arminius) who had done battle against the Romans centuries before. The most telling battle was near

Verden on the Aller in 782, in which some 4,000 Saxons were slaughtered after having been betrayed by members of their own nobility. Their leader, the 'Sachsenführer' Widukind (743–807), submitted to Charles and in 785 was baptized with Charles standing as his godfather. Many Saxons repudiated Widukind, and the war dragged on for another twenty years. Finally Charles prevailed, and though the Saxons embraced Frank rule, the Christian faith, and became among Charles' most loyal subjects, they never forgot the brutality of his conquest.

Meanwhile, Tassilo III of Bavaria (?–794?) was encouraged (as if he needed it) by his father-in-law, King Desiderius of Lombardy, to defy Charles. Tassilo did, but was defeated, dethroned and forced to enter a monastery. Bavaria became a province of the Frank kingdom. Charles also fought a war with the Welatabians, and then with the Avars of Hungary, whom he crushed finally in 799. He also had to confront the Vikings, who menaced Europe throughout the ninth and tenth centuries. When news first came to Aachen that they were on the shores of his empire, Charles is supposed to have said, tears in his eyes: 'Know ye my faithful servants, wherefore I weep thus bitterly? I fear not these wretched pirates, but I am afflicted that they should dare to approach these shores, and sorely do grieve when I foresee what evil they will work on my sons and on my people.'

And, a war of another sort: in 792 'proud, arrogant and cruel' Queen Fastrada humiliated a Thuringian noble while Charles was away. The noble had pledged his daughter to wed a Frank, but refused to send the girl when the time came. Fastrada publically threatened that he and his supporters would be guilty of treason if they did not produce the girl. Resentful of this, the nobles conspired to overthrow the king and replace him with Pepin Hunchback, Charles' son by one of his early concubines. The plot failed, of course, the nobles were punished, and Pepin spent the rest of his life in the monastery at Plüm.

RONCESVALLES

In 778 Charles went to Spain to liberate Christians from the Muslims. Suleiman ibn Arabi guaranteed that Saragossa would be open to the

Franks when they arrived. It was not, and the Franks besieged the city, hoping to starve its defenders into submission. However, supplies were smuggled into the city and resistance continued. Then news came that the Saxons were again on the rampage. Charles abandoned what had become a fruitless campaign and ordered his army to head for home. Along the way, he also ordered that the walls of the Basque city of Pamplona, which earlier had welcomed the Franks, be torn down. The army then headed across the Pyrenees through the pass of Roncesvalles. Roland (Hroutland), Count of Breton and related to Charles, brought up the rear.

The Basques attacked this rearguard, slaughtering it to the last man. As there were no survivors, and as portraying fallen warriors as heros was a staple of folklore, a heroic legend was born: that Roland fought heroically, refusing to summon aid by blowing his horn, Olifant, for fear that it would endanger Charles, and breaking his sword, Durandel, so that it would not fall into enemy hands. This was the essence of *Chanson de Roland* written in the eleventh century, followed in 1170 by the German version, *Rolandslied*. Ironically, the Basques were among the Christians whom Charles had gone to Spain to liberate.

CHARLES AS EMPEROR

Charles built a centralized feudal state with himself as absolute a monarch as was possible in that era, over both secular and ecclesiastical orders. The social structure was based on serfdom and tenancy of peasants bound to the land and vassals and sub-vassals holding land granted to them by those higher up the social ladder and a nobility reflecting the needs of regional governance. A chancellor oversaw, in Charles' name, the administration of finance and interior organization, while an arch-chaplain carried out the king-emperor's orders regarding the rituals and rules of conduct applied to the clergy. Imperial representatives called *missi dominici* enumerated the duties of all the imperial subjects based upon their class and estates. Clovis had created dukes and counts, to which Charles added *margrafen* (marcher lords) assigned to govern and protect the imperial borderlands. The medieval concept of the army as a system of vassals, professional soldiers and warriors, all provided by landed aristocrats as part of their arrangement with the

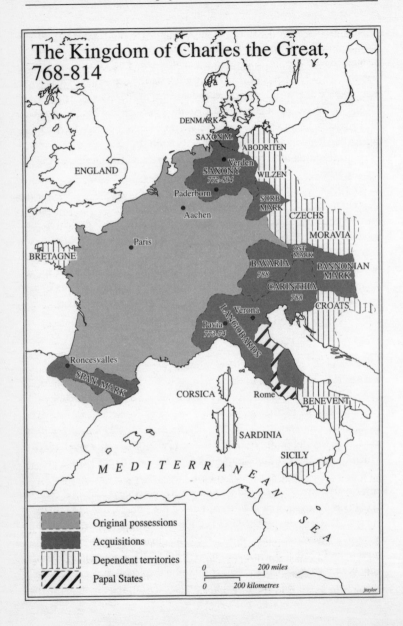

The Kingdom of Charles the Great, 768-814

DENMARK

SAXON M.

ABODRITEN

ENGLAND

SAXONY
772-804

Verden

WILZEN

Paderborn

SORB MARK

Aachen

CZECHS

Paris

MORAVIA

BRETAGNE

OST MARK

BAVARIA
788

PANNONIAN MARK

CARINTHIA
788

CROATS

Verona

LANGOBARDS

Pavia
773-74

Roncesvalles

SPAN. MARK

CORSICA

Rome

BENEVENT

SARDINIA

SICILY

M E D I T E R R A N E A N

S E A

Original possessions

Acquisitions

Dependent territories

Papal States

0   200 miles

0   200 kilometres

jtaylor

king-emperor, also evolved in Charles' era. It would dominate Germany as in Europe for half a millennium.

Meanwhile, free peasants formed protective associations called 'gilds,' in which each member swore an oath to aid one another in times of crisis and danger. This was a precedent for the merchant and artisan 'guilds' that were characteristic of medieval cities. And a monetary system of sorts emerged in Charles' time, the most basic unit of which was the *pfennig* (penny).

Fortification was characteristic of the European Middle Ages which was an epoch of more or less constant warfare. Germany was no exception; castles, by their nature military fortifications, were the residence of anyone from regional prince to minor feudal noble; kings lived in palaces, but they were surrounded by towns, which were surrounded by walls from which they could be defended in case of attack. In medieval Germany, both *burg* (castle) and *stadt* (town, city) indicated a fortified place. The names of many German cities indicate their origins in this regard, such as Marburg, Hamburg and Freiburg. Meanwhile, a German city that ends with *berg*, such as Bamberg or Freiberg, was named after a mountain rather than a fortified place.

The Carolingian Renaissance

Einhard noted that the king built the great basilica of the Holy Mother of God in Aachen as well as seeing to the repair and care of other sacred edifices throughout the Empire. He also built a half-mile long bridge over the Rhine at Mainz, and great palaces in Aachen, Ingelheim and Nijmegen. Meanwhile, Charles laboured to fulfil his perceived role as a Christian prince devoted to establishing the City of God (as elucidated in his favourite book, St Augustine's *De Civitate Dei*) by spreading Roman Christianity among the Germans and founding monasteries. It was in Charles' time that Romanesque became the architectural standard for church building throughout the Empire, Aachenmünster being a classic example. Also, builders decorated, in the words of the *Libri Carolini*, 'with the most precious of objects and materials the places which are dedicated to the divine service.' The Gregorian Chant also came into its own in the Carolingian age.

The cathedral in Aachen built by Charles the Great

LEARNING

Charles was keen to encourage the revival of classical learning and to promote religious studies and education among both boys and girls – ironic, in the sense that, again according to Einhard, Charles was himself only marginally literate. He began with the 'School of the Palace,' which set the standard for monastic schools throughout the empire. It was headed after 782 by the noted English monk Alcuin of York (735–804), who emphasized teaching based on the seven liberal arts of the classical curriculum: the *Trivium* (grammar, rhetoric, dialectics) and the *Quadrivium* (arithmetic, geometry, music, astronomy). Charles also organized a Court Academy which included both men and women of the inner circle. Each member of the Academy took a symbolic biblical or classical name: for example, Charles was David of the Old Testament, Alcuin was Horatius Flaccus and Einhard, a talented architect as well as chronicler, was Beseleel, builder of the Jewish tabernacle. The Academy accompanied Charles on his journeys around the empire, and during meals would join with him in discussing, always in Latin, readings from classical literature and from the writings of Church leaders.

Charles the Legend

'The king,' wrote Einhard, 'who excelled all the princes of his time in wisdom and greatness of soul, did not suffer difficulty to deter him or danger to daunt him from anything that had to be taken up or carried through, for he had trained himself to bear and endure whatever came, without yielding in adversity, or trusting to the deceitful favours of fortunes in prosperity.' True enough; but Charles extended the Frankish state and Roman Christianity through conquest, which sometimes meant killing thousands. Nor was he a devoted husband. He divorced his first wife, Lombard princess Desiderata, in favour of Swabian princess, Hildegard, who died and was followed by Fastrada and then Liutgard. Admittedly, save for Desiderata Charles remained with these wives until they died in office, so to speak, but all the while concubines were a regular part of his existence and he fathered children with them as well as with his wives. His mother, Berthrada (Bertha Big Foot), may have had something to do with this. She understood that royal marriage had little to do with love and affection and everything to do with politics. The company of a concubine, on the other hand, had only one purpose, at least among the Franks.

CHAPTER TWO

Medieval Germany,
800–1300

On Christmas day in the year 800, Charles attended mass at St Peter's in Rome, dressed as a Roman patrician. Pope Leo III sat on the bishop's throne. The Gospel was read, and Charles knelt in prayer at the high altar. Leo went to him, placed the crown of the Caesars on his head, and bowed before him. The congregation then shouted: 'To Charles Augustus, crowned by God, the great and peace-giving Emperor, be life and victory!'

The First Empire

Thus was born the 'Holy Roman Empire.' Was this famous coronation serious, or was it, as one historian wrote scathingly, 'a comedy improvised by a handful of antiquarian-minded ecclesiastics'? One point was to make Charles heir of the Caesars and 'defender of the faith,' roles which he accepted. Another was to reaffirm the principle laid down in 754 when Boniface crowned Pepin (only with more ceremonial hoopla) that temporal power rested upon a spiritual foundation; which meant that the pope ultimately was superior to the emperor. Popes and emperors would dispute this issue for centuries, just as territorial princes would dispute imperial centrism. The empire survived for a millennium, but not quite as 'created.' Under Charles it included both the Romanic west and the Germanic east; but under Otto the Great, it excluded France and was irrevocably the possession of German rulers.

THE ROOTS OF PARTICULARISM

Meanwhile, wars plagued the empire and encouraged territorial dissidence. Norsemen in the west (frequently referred to in *The Annals of*

The Carolingian empire
at the treaty of Verdun, 843

0   200 miles
0   200 kilometres

SAXONY

THURINGIA

Aachen

AUSTRASIA

Verdun

Strasbourg   BAVARIA

NEUSTRIA   SWABIA

CARINTHIA

AQUITAINE   BURGUNDY   LOMBARDY

GASCONY   PROVENCE   ITALY

SPANISH MARCH

Rome

■ East Frankish Kingdom
(Louis the German)

■ Middle Kingdom (Lothair)

■ West Frankish Kingdom (Charles the Bald)

jtaylor

Fulda) and Magyars in the east seemed more interested in plunder and looting than conquest and occupation, and fighting them off became the concern of tribal dukes and princes more than of emperors. The result was rising particularism: claims of territorial rights in opposition to subordination to imperial authority. Indeed, Charles the Fat was deposed by territorial nobles in 887 largely because he reunited the

Carolingian Empire that the Treaty of Verdun in 843 had divided into three parts: a Romanic kingdom (Neustria) west of the Rhine under Charles I, the Bald (823–877), a Germanic kingdom east of it under Louis II, the German (804–875), and a northern Italian kingdom under Lothar I (795–855). The effect of Verdun, in historian Kurt Reinhardt's words, was to make the Empire 'a disorganized mass of regional units.' Historian Robert-Hermann Tenbrock was kinder, arguing that out of this particularism grew such national states as France – and eventually Germany, of course.

THE FRENCH–GERMAN DIVIDE

Tenbrock has a point. Verdun reflected a divide that was linguistic as well as political. At Strasbourg in 842 Charles and Louis had sworn loyalty to each other in defiance of Lothar's claims to the imperial throne. Their oath was then presented to their respective armies in both Old French and Old High German. Over time, Franks west of the Rhine and Moselle had embraced French, a language derived from Gaulic and Latin, while those to the east continued to speak their hereditary German dialects. From this separation comes 'Germany' in English and 'Germanie' in French, both derived from the Latin *Germania*, and 'Deutschland' in German, which derives from the Old High German *diutskland*.

The German Kingdom

The German kingdom east of the Rhine emerged in the tenth century as the heart of the Empire. Its first distinctly 'German' as opposed to Carolingian monarch was Conrad I, duke of Franconia (?–918). He soon learned that particularism was alive and well. When he tried to rule in the centralist manner of Charles the Great, the dukes of Saxony, Bavaria and Swabia turned against him. All the same he was able to sidestep Salic Law which required the election of kings regardless of lineage, and impose the dynastic principle. When Conrad was near death, he chose his own successor with the act of sending the symbols of kingship – lance, robe, crown and sword – to the Saxon Henry I, 'the Fowler' (876–936), via his own brother. The electors concurred.

St Michael's church, Hildesheim

Henry founded the Saxon line of king-emperors. He also took the first step since Charles the Great to minimize Church influence over the imperial throne by refusing to be crowned by the archbishop of Mainz. Henry also diluted the particularist problem by claiming to be only *primus inter pares* (first among equals) and worked collaboratively with the dukes of Bavaria, Swabia, Lotharingia, Franconia, Saxony and Lorraine. In exchange for their feudatory submission, Henry sought their advice on internal and external policy. Success in war did no harm to this relationship, either. Henry did well against the Wends, Danes and Magyars – during a truce with the latter he crossed the Elbe and took the Slav encampment of Brandenburg in what would become West Prussia – and, in alliance with the duke of Bavaria, defeated Duke Wenceslaus I of Bohemia (?–929). Wenceslaus then acknowledged German supremacy, paid tribute and converted to Christianity. He paid the price, however; the pagan Czechs overthrew and murdered him in 929. On the other hand, he was recognized as the first Bohemian Christian martyr.

Henry's son, Otto I, the Great (926–973), the great-grandson of Widukind, was chosen by his father with the unanimous support of the electors to reign as emperor. By now the election of king-emperors was the province of a committee, so to speak, of electors (*kurfürsten*), though in law it was supposed to be the 'privilege of every free-born man.'

There were seven electors by the middle of the thirteenth century: the archbishops of Mainz, Cologne and Trier, and the secular rulers of the Palatinate, Saxony and Brandenburg, and Bohemia. Others were added over time: Bavaria (1623), Hannover (1692), and Baden, Hesse-Kassel, Württemberg and Salzburg (1803) – not much of an honour in the latter case, as the Empire was dissolved three years later.

Otto the Great

Otto worked to establish a centralized monarchy in the tradition of Charles the Great. He squashed ducal particularism and internal rebellion – organized in part around Otto's younger brother, Henry, who later repented and was made Duke of Bavaria. He then redistributed the duchies among members of his own family, save for Franconia which was allowed to lapse altogether, a fact that greatly pleased the Saxons. Otto also extended the Christian Empire into pagan lands by subduing and converting pagans in Jutland, Schleswig and between the Elbe and the Oder rivers. In the east, marches and bishoprics were created largely by replacing Slav princes – often brutally – with Germans, while marrying their female relatives to German nobles. In historian Veit Valentin's words, 'many a Slavic princess became the wife of a gallant "Junker" – a young noble or younger son.' An ecclesiastical organization was set up, centred in Magdeburg, to oversee the work of bringing Slavs beyond the Elbe into the Church. Otto collaborated with the duke of Bohemia to create the bishopric of Prague as a centre for Christian missionary work throughout that portion of Slavic lands. Meanwhile, he took on the Magyars in Hungary, whom Henry I had defeated but not subdued. In 955 at the Lechfeld near Augsburg, Otto both defeated and subdued the Magyars with a great army representing all of the German tribes. The conversion of Hungary to Christianity followed, and in 1001, Stephan (969–1038) was crowned king of Hungary by Pope Sylvester II (940–1003).

And, there was the occasional confrontation with Arabs, an on again/off again relationship with Constantinople, wars involving the western Franks (now French, for all practical purposes), Italians, and ducal rebellions once again, as often as not led by his own sons. Otto determined that the dukes should have the role of privileged royal servants, as they had in Charles' day, and had himself crowned on the imperial throne in Aachen cathedral to emphasize the point. The dukes would have none of it, and their landed power was sufficient to limit the degree of their submission. The basic structure of medieval Germany was now established, and it was not going to go away: dukes, counts, bishops and abbots had extensive economic and social power based upon land ownership. That included the power to found new towns and cities as trade and commerce centres through which they could enhance their wealth – such as Freiburg-im-Breisgau by the Count of Zähringen in 1120, and Munich by Henry the Lion, duke of Saxony in 1158.

A HOLY ROMAN ALLY

Otto needed help, and, as had Charles, he found it in Rome where the idea of a strong secular authority to ensure the safety of the Church still flourished. The other side of the coin was that kings and princes increasingly relied upon clerics to perform secular duties. The archbishop of Mainz was Henry I's chancellor, for example. And, it was increasingly common that clerics chosen for secular work came from the ranks of the higher nobility. By the tenth century, more often than not bishops and archbishops, as well as popes, were both temporal and ecclesiastical lords. The papacy regarded Charles' successors as Defenders of the Faith; when Otto reached out to Rome, Rome reached back. From Otto's point of view, it was a good thing.

'OTTONIAN PRIVILEGE'

Otto crossed the Alps in 951 to received homage as King of the Lombards, a Carolingian tradition. In 960 Pope John XII promised him the imperial crown if he would guarantee papal security. Otto agreed. In 962 he entered Rome, sorted out anti-papal factions, married Adelheid, widow and heiress of a former Lombard ruler, declared himself King of Italy, and was crowned Holy Roman Emperor. The deal, the 'Ottonian Privilege,' was that in exchange for being recognized as the most powerful ruler in Europe, Otto would defend the faith and accept the principle of the Church holding symbolic power over the State. Thus was born the Holy Roman Empire of the German Nation (though that designation was used only beginning in the fifteenth century), an arrangement that survived – in the broadest sense of the term – despite tension and rivalry between popes and emperors, until 1806.

AFTER OTTO

Otto's successors were simply variations on a theme: Otto II (973–983) faced conflict with France, rebellions in Bavaria, uprisings by Wends and Danes, and war with the Arabs. He also improved relations with Bohemia, Poland, Hungary and Byzantium, in the latter instance by marrying Princess Theophano, who as regent for their son kept the realm from falling apart – no mean accomplishment in the context of the times. Otto III (983–1002) styled himself 'the servant of Christ,' and thought in Roman more than in German terms. He inscribed the imperial seal with *Renovatio Imperii Romanorum*; this made his German dukes resentful.

Ottonian Revival

The Carolingian renaissance 'atrophied,' as one historian phrased it, until Otto the Great revived and expanded it. Education was made a central function of imperial churches. Cathedral schools were founded, or expanded, in Cologne, Magdeburg, Würzburg, Hildesheim, Trier, Bremen, Mainz, Worms and Paderborn. Their object was to produce bishops and statesmen trained to serve and protect the state 'by their faith and their strength.' Monastic schools also flourished, including convent schools attended by girls preparing for religious life and girls of noble families who were not. Both monastic and cathedral schools emphasized learning and the arts, and with such success apparently that bishops and 'men of state' often became patrons of the arts.

WRITINGS

Textbooks and theological treatises from Charles' time were considered adequate for the needs of the day. Liturgical writing did change, however. Sacramentaries, gospel books and books designed for bishops, were more detailed regarding rites, services and appropriate prayers, and were illuminated and ornamented, sometimes with jewelled bindings. Book illumination expanded throughout the Ottonian epoch, not least because Otto II had the document confirming his wedding gift to Princess Theophano lavishly decorated in the Byzantine fashion in order to impress her. The Byzantine style thereafter was a major influence in Ottonian visual expression. Theophano encouraged both Otto II and Otto III to supported the arts and learning.

History, or rather chronicle, writing also reemerged. The Ottonians were proud of what they had accomplished for both God and man. Examples included Adalbert of St Maximin's *Continuatio Reginonis,* which took up where Abbot Regino of Prüm's *Chronicle* left off, but in a more hagiographic vein; Widukind of Corvey's *History of the Saxons* explained that Otto was Great because of his Saxon origins; Hrotswitha of Gandersheim's *The Deeds of Otto* tied Otto's imperial image to that of the Roman Caesars; and Wipo the chaplain wrote monastic histories under the general heading *Gesta Chuonradi.*

Church, Empire and Principalities

The eleventh century was a time of troubled relations between Rome and the German emperors, and between the emperors and the territorial princes. Whatever began well seemed to reverse itself soon after. It was rather like a journey on a see-saw.

HENRY II

Henry II (973–1024), whose motto was *Renovatio regni Francorum,* saw his primary responsibility as preserving the Empire from exterior dangers; not that he was uniformly successful, losing Bohemia to the Poles, and the Schleswig March to the Danes. Henry maintained close and devout relations with the papacy, and Pope Benedict VIII (?–1024) consecrated his new Bamberg cathedral in 1020. Bamberg soon emerged as a centre for connecting the Church and the secular Empire. Its cathedral school educated the clergy in the ways of imperial administration, while the city became a Bavarian cultural and spiritual centre. The papacy approved Henry's support of Cluniac reforms, the intent of which was to purify, elevate and empower Church and clergy. This included imposing clerical celibacy, which now became imperial law for the first time – a law, be it noted, that did not go down well with rank and file clerics.

CONRAD II

Conrad II (990–1039) reduced the papacy to the level of a minor Italian principality, treated the clergy as state officials, and installed Germans in such Italian religious offices as the abbacy of Monte Casino. He recognized Danish suzerainty over Schleswig (which lasted until 1864), and ceded territories to Hungary while regaining overlordship of Poland. And he gained the backing of small barons and burghers for imperial centrism at the expense of ducal particularism, by recognizing their social and class rights; this also was good for the economy. Of course, by demeaning the papacy, Conrad erased spiritual justification for the Empire and thereby its very reason for being; and he created a situation in Rome where war between popes and anti-popes (rival claimants to the papal throne) and the buying and selling of the sacred office became commonplace.

HENRY III

No matter. Henry III (1017–1056) restored papal honour, ousted several anti-popes and assured that the election of popes would adhere (more or less) to reputable standards. In this context Leo IX (1002–1054), a German bishop and Henry's cousin, was elected in 1048. Rome's break in 1054 with the Eastern Church, which had adopted the Caesaropapism (secular rulers exercising authority over ecclesiastical matters) that reformers in the Roman Church opposed, also came during Henry's reign. As to territorial issues, he forced Bohemia and Hungary into the Empire once and for all, strengthened ties with Poland, and established the river Leitha as the boundary between Hungary and Austria (which survived until 1919). Meanwhile, Henry maintained contact with his subjects by travelling constantly throughout the Empire. Actually, this was customary for king-emperors, which may explain why for centuries there was neither a German capital nor an official imperial residence.

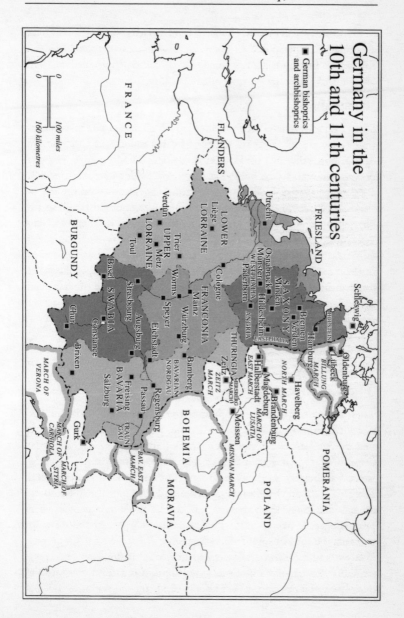

Germany in the
10th and 11th centuries

■ German bishoprics
and archbishoprics

0 ___ 100 miles
0 ___ 160 kilometres

FRANCE

FLANDERS

BURGUNDY

LOWER
LORRAINE

Liège

UPPER
LORRAINE

Verdun
Metz
Trier
Toul

Basel

SWABIA

Strasbourg

Chur

Brixen

Constance

Augsburg

Eichstätt

BAVARIA

Freising

Salzburg

Passau

Regensburg

Gurk

MARCH
OF
VERONA

MARCH OF
CARNIOLA

MARCH OF
STYRIA

BAV. EAST
MARCH

TRAUN
GAU

BAVARIAN
NORDGAU

Bamberg

Worms

Mainz

Speyer

Würzburg

FRANCONIA

Cologne

Utrecht

FRIESLAND

WESTPHALIA

Münster
Osnabrück
Minden

Paderborn

Hildesheim

SAXONY

ANGRIA

EASTPHALIA

THURINGIA

Halberstadt

Zeitz

MERSEBURG
(MARCH)

EAST MARCH

Meissen

MISNIAN MARCH

MARCH OF
LUSATIA

Magdeburg

NORTH MARCH

Brandenburg

Havelberg

Verden

Bremen

Hamburg

HOLSTEIN

Schleswig

BILLUNG
MARCH

Oldenburg

Lübeck

POMERANIA

POLAND

BOHEMIA

MORAVIA

Of course, particularism continued and in fact prospered in his reign at Imperial expense. The dukes of Bavaria, Saxony and Lorraine strained constantly at the imperial leash, and when Henry died in 1056, Swabia and Carinthia were in open rebellion.

HENRY IV

So too under Henry IV (1050–1106). Elected as a child, he was controlled first by his mother, and then by the Bishop of Cologne and Archbishop Adelbert of Hamburg-Bremen, all the while Imperial power being eroded by nobles seizing crown lands and crown rights. In 1066 at age fifteen, Henry took charge and sought to 'stop the rot' by establishing a royal demesne in the Harz southeast of Goslar – a sort of 'Ile de France' for German kings, as historian Martin Kitchen phrased it – surrounded by castles manned by Swabians. Thuringian and Saxon nobles protested this as tyranny, and agreed to join Henry in war against the Poles only if he would tear down the castles. The Emperor refused, took on the Saxons in war, and won; but it was clear all the same that particularist opposition was not going away. Indeed, civil war was common in Henry's reign, which resulted in the nobles building castles and taking away peasant rights, failed peasant revolts, and a feudal system more firmly based than ever before.

The Investiture Controversy

Then Henry fell out with Pope Gregory VII (1020?–1085). In 1075 Gregory summoned the Synod of Rome, which issued decrees against simony (the sale of ecclesiastical offices), clerical marriage, and lay investiture (secular authority investing clerics with symbols of ecclesiastical authority). These degrees were endorsed in Gregory's *Dictatus Papae*. To some the decrees purified and elevated the Church; to others, including Henry, they simply were a papal 'power grab.' The princes agreed, but also saw *Dictatus Papae* as opening the door for enhancing their power at Imperial expense.

It worked this way. *Dictatus Papae* asserted that the 'holy' pope was the Universal Church who alone could appoint and dismiss bishops and issue laws. Fair enough; but it also asserted, on the presumption that secular power derived from Satan while that of the pope originated with God, that all secular rulers, including emperors, were subject to the pope and that he had the power to dethrone them and release their subjects from imperial allegiance. Gregory began by forbidding Henry to fill bishoprics at his own discretion, and the war was on. Henry repudiated this order and all other papal claims to absolute power, and in 1076 when Gregory threatened to depose and excommunicate him, German bishops came to Henry's support and declared the pope simply 'Hildebrand, no pope, but a false monk.' The emperor then launched a propaganda campaign by calling upon Gregory to 'come down, come down, thou whom all ages will condemn!' The pope responded by excommunicating him and suspending every German or any other bishop who had supported Henry's defiance. This gave the princes an opening, for excommunication not only denied Henry communion but secular power as well, and they threatened to take away his crown if the excommunication was not rescinded. The princes invited Gregory to Germany to adjudicate their differences with the king. Henry was in a pickle. He had to make up with Gregory or lose his throne.

CANOSSA

Gregory set out for Germany to meet with the princes in 1077. Henry 'cut him off at the pass,' so to speak, forcing Gregory to seek refuge in Margravine Mathilda's castle at Canossa in the Italian Alps. When Henry was refused an audience, he stood barefoot in snow in the courtyard, wearing a hair shirt – the symbol of penitence – and waited. After three days, Gregory relented. Henry came before him, and all was forgiven – at least on the surface. It is said that while pretending to be grateful to the pope, Henry fumed internally. Interestingly, Gregory was persuaded to forgive the king-emperor by Abbot Hugh of Cluny, who represented the reform movement that had led to the pope's exalted view of his power in the first place.

The princes were not so forgiving. In March they elected Duke Rudolf of Swabia to replace Henry. Pope Gregory backed Rudolf and excommunicated Henry a second time. It was a lost cause, however, for Rudolf died in 1080, and by 1084 Gregory was discredited for such blatant political manoeuvring as allying himself with 'plundering

Norman hordes,' now a presence in Sicily, and even with Saracens. Meanwhile, Henry reasserted his primacy in Germany, despite dissident nobles sometimes backed by the Emperor's own sons, one of whom actually took him prisoner for a time. Still, Henry had popular support in Germany for trying to end civil unrest and further the economic interests of knights and burghers. He even avenged Jews victimized by pogroms in 1096, and supported others, who had been forcibly baptized, to return to their Judaic faith.

The Struggle for Empire

Henry V (1081–1125) worked with Pope Calixtus II (1060?–1124) to resolve the investiture controversy: they agreed that monarchs could give bishops a sceptre symbolizing their worldly powers, but that religious symbols, the ring and crozier, could be bestowed only by clerics. Henry, the last in the Salian dynasty, died in 1125 without issue. The result was controversy over the succession that lasted thirteen years. First, the Assembly first chose Lothar of Saxony (1075–1137), whose daughter was married to the duke of Bavaria, over Henry's nephew, Frederick of Swabia, and Margrave Leopold of Austria. Then Frederick, a Hohenstaufen (named after the family castle at Staufen), refused to give up royal estates inherited from his uncle; in 1127, Lothar attempted to take them by force. The Swabians then elected another Hohenstaufen, Conrad (1093?–1152), as anti-king. This began a struggle that went on for a century, between Bavarian Welfs and Hohenstaufen Waiblings – known in Italy as Guelfs and Ghibellines – for control of the imperial throne. Conrad made war successfully against the Welfs and upon the death of Lothar in 1138, was recognized by the electors as Emperor Conrad III. He died without having been actually crowned, the first German king to miss an imperial coronation since 962.

The Crusades

The Saracens were driven out of Sicily in the eleventh century; why not out of Spain as well, and even Palestine? Moreover, popes might prevail in their on-going power struggle with emperors if attention was redirected to a Holy War against Islam. In 1095 Pope Urban II (1042–

1099) declared a Christian Crusade to Palestine. Such religious purists as Peter the Hermit and Abbot Bernard of Clairvaux 'spread the word,' and beleaguered clerics and secular princes 'took the Cross' as a way of enhancing their moral stature. The latter also looted Muslim and Byzantine Empire lands as a way to fill strained coffers. Conrad III was the first emperor to go on Crusade in 1147, accompanied by his nephew and successor, Frederick I (1123?–1190), known as 'Barbarossa' because of his red beard. Frederick launched the Third Crusade in 1189 against Salah-al-Din, perhaps the most significant Sultan in Muslim history before Suleiman; it continued under his son, Frederick of Swabia. Emperor Frederick II (1194–1250) took the Cross in 1228 and after negotiations with the Sultan, emerged as king of Jerusalem.

TEUTONIC KNIGHTS

The Crusades produced at least one development of great consequence for Germany's future, the Teutonic Knights. Founded in 1190 at the siege of Acre, the order was to care for the poor, wounded and sick, and do battle against heathens: Saracens in Palestine and later pagans in eastern Europe. Members were German knights, priests and lay brothers, who took an oath of celibacy, poverty – their weapons belonged to the order not to themselves as individuals – and above all, obedience. In 1230, with the permission of Frederick II, they went north under the leadership of Grand Master Hermann von Salza (1170–1239), to do battle against the pagan Prusi east of the Vistula. This launched the 'crusade' that led to founding Prussia, the ruling Junker aristocracy of which included many descendants of Teutonic knights. Their black cross on a white mantle eventually became the Prussian flag.

'Barbarossa'

Frederick 'Barbarossa' was elected German king in 1152, and crowned in Rome as emperor in 1155. His tasks were to shore up a power base in disarray owing to papal schisms, rebellious Italians, and dissident German princes, and protect the papacy from Sicilian Normans, rebellious Romans and ambitious Byzantine emperors. His coronation in Rome was marked by popular unrest in the city. Barbarossa never did solve the Italian problem: disputes over papal succession, mixed success in wars fought in Italy, and rising opposition in England and France to a 'Holy Roman Empire' ruling Christendom. Moreover, Henry the Lion, duke of Saxony (1124–1195), his cousin and principal Welf rival, refused to provide aid in Italy when requested. Barbarossa finally had to admit that he would never realize his dream of resurrecting the Empire of Otto the Great.

HENRY THE LION

He was more successful in Germany, but at a price. While Barbarossa concentrated on Italy, Henry the Lion expanded his power in Germany, including colonizing and Christianizing Mecklenburg. The North German princes complained to the emperor that Henry was a threat. Barbarossa responded by ordering him to appear before him at court. He refused, was declared outlaw, and fled to England. The princes issued the Gelnhausen decree in 1180 which subdivided and redistributed Henry's vast estates among such as the archbishop of Cologne (Westphalia), Bernard of Anhalt (Lower Saxony), and the Wittlesbachs (Bavaria). The decree also laid the foundations for the kingdom of Hannover and the duchy of Brunswick. The Welfs retained only their estates around Brunswick and Lüneburg. Gelnhausen was a mixed blessing for Barbarossa. It gave him needed allies, but also produced a plethora of small self-governing states between the Rhine and the Weser. This was the beginning of the *Kleinstaaterei* (the particularist principalities asserting their independence). Moreover, Henry the Lion was not finished; after Barbarossa's death, he returned from England and forced a compromise peace with Barbarossa's successor, Henry VI (1165–1197).

Meanwhile, Barbarossa launched the Third Crusade in 1189; it ended for him in 1190 when he drowned while bathing in the river Saleph in Asia Minor. The result was the Kyffhäuser legend, originally associated with Frederick II (1194–1250) but transferred to Barbarossa in the sixteenth century. It held that he was asleep in Kyffhäuserberg in Thuringia, and would awaken one day to lead the German people to unity and glory – ironically, the legend referred to this unity as the 'Third Empire.'

Chivalry

The twelfth through the fourteenth centuries was the 'Age of Chivalry' in Germany as elsewhere, which turned around knights – trained professional soldiers: 'a man was not born a knight, he became one,' Robert-Hermann Tenbrock noted – to whom the Crusades had given an exalted social and religious significance. A man 'called' to the order was special. He knelt in prayer before the altar for an entire night, attended Mass in the morning, received communion, and swore loyalty to the 'virtues of his calling,' which were to be 'magnanimous, helpful, courteous, truthful, loyal, and brave; to aid the Church; to protect and defend widows, orphans, pilgrims, and the poor and oppressed; to obey the Roman emperor in all temporal matters; and to keep himself untainted in thoughts, words, and deed.' Sword, shield and spurs were then handed to him, the 'accolade' (*Ritterschlag*) – three taps on neck and shoulder – was delivered by a person of authority and he was knighted; or, put another way, became grist for the mill of medieval romantic and heroic literature. The former included the *Minnesäng* (love song) poetry by the legendary Walther von der Vogelweide, which extolled the homage knights paid to fair maidens. The latter included such works as *Parsival* and *Tristan,* which were the bases for two of Richard Wagner's most famous operas.

From Hohenstaufen to Habsburg

After Barbarossa came internecine strife over the Imperial throne. His successor, Henry VI, left it to his son Frederick. He was only four years old, however, and a Welf–Hohenstaufen quarrel began over whether he should be replaced by Henry the Lion's son, Otto of Brunswick, or Henry VI's brother, Philip of Swabia. The issue was resolved in 1208 when Philip was murdered, and Otto enthroned in 1209 as Otto IV (1175–1212). However, as Otto made clear his intention to rule over both State and Church, Pope Innocent III (1160?–1216) excommunicated him and the Hohenstaufens proclaimed Frederick. They launched, and won, a war against Otto with Philip II of France as ally. Frederick was crowned at Aachen in 1218.

FREDERICK II

The new emperor was shrewd, cunning, sceptical, cynical and ambitious, and lived mostly in Sicily. He was a patron of the arts and sciences, an intellectual – his *De arte venandi cum avibus* (*The Art of Hunting with Birds*) was 'the definitive work on ornithology for several centuries' – and a connoisseur of the exotic. When Frederick travelled to Germany in 1235 to deal with his rebellious son, Henry, he took along a 'retinue of Saracens and Ethiopians along with a menagerie of leopards, apes, and camels.' He also went to Vienna to deal with Henry's ally, Duke Frederick the Pugnacious of Austria (1210?–1246), after which he declared Vienna an imperial city. He then returned to Sicily, and the Pugnacious came back to Vienna, which, with him in control, was *not* an imperial city. An omen for the future, when the Habsburgs took the imperial crown and made Vienna the centre of the Holy Roman Empire of the German Nation? Perhaps.

Meanwhile, Frederick II saw himself as Italian – his mother, Constance, loathed the Germans – and put much time and effort into improving administration and economy in his Sicilian and southern Italian lands. He spent less than eight of his years on the throne in Germany, which fact diminished the imperial centrism that he espoused. Indeed, to maintain imperial control in Germany he had to increase the power of German nobles, which was the essence of *Constitutio in Favorem Principum* (Constitution in Favour of the Princes) granted in 1231–32. Kurt Reinhardt has argued that it established 'a legal basis for the future particularistic dismemberment of the Empire.'

Then there was doing battle with the papacy. In 1227, Frederick promised to go on Crusade and assembled his forces in Brindisi on the east Italian coast. An outbreak of plague forced postponement of their departure for Palestine; however, Pope Gregory IX (1145–1241) concluded that a plot to take control of Italy was the real reason, and excommunicated the Emperor. The following year Frederick did launch his crusade, did a deal with the Sultan of Cairo, and got himself crowned king of Jerusalem. Gregory was not pleased by all of this, but 'forgave' and reinstated Frederick – and then excommunicated him a second time in 1239. So continued the well-established tradition of contesting whether pope or emperor reigned supreme, which produced one of the great propaganda wars of the Middle Ages: the pope denounced 'Frederick, the so-called Emperor' as 'the Antichrist' and accused him of calling both Moses and Jesus Christ 'swindlers'; Frederick called Gregory 'the Pharisee occupying the chair of perverted dogma'; and so on. Frederick's war with the papacy continued under Innocent IV (?–1254), and had not been resolved when the emperor died in 1250.

'The Terrible Time Without an Emperor'

Eighteenth-century poet Friedrich Schiller created this dramatic phrase – in German *'die Kaiserlose, die schreckliche Zeit'* – to describe the 'interregnum' from 1254 to 1273. William of Holland claimed the throne after Conrad IV (1228–1256), supported by the seventy towns of the League of the Rhine stretching from Lübeck to Zürich. He was killed in battle in 1256 and the electoral princes split between Richard of Cornwall, son of King John of England, and King Alfonso of Castille – not Germans, but related to Germans. The issue was resolved by default. Alfonso had bribed the electors to vote for him, but his own nobles were so opposed that he dared not leave Castille to claim the throne. Consequently, Richard was elected in 1257; however, in 1261 he went to England to help Henry III put down a rebellion of English barons, and never returned to Germany, and never was crowned. This was indeed a 'time without an emperor,' and it marked the end of the Hohenstaufen dynasty and the first appearance of the Habsburgs. They would be the last imperial dynasty.

RUDOLF VON HABSBURG

Rudolf I (1218–1291) took the throne in 1273; it solved nothing, for though he was recognized by the pope, he was never crowned emperor. Rebellious princes opposed him throughout his reign, which probably explains why he gave up on the Italian interests that had so obsessed the Hohenstaufens. First it was King Ottokar of Bohemia (1230–1278), in whose honour Königsberg (Mount Royal) was named by the Teutonic Knights in gratitude for his assistance in their war with the Prusi. Rudolf faced him with the backing of Bavaria, Saxony and Hungary, whose rulers were married to his daughters. Ottokar was defeated and killed, and his successor married still another of Rudolf's daughters. Rudolf agreed on the condition that Bohemia return lands taken from Austria in 1250. Martin Kitchen saw this as 'the beginning of the Habsburg Empire.' Then there was Burgundy, whose prince pledged allegiance only when confronted with an imperial army, and Thuringia, brought under control in 1289, just two years before Rudolf's death.

Society, Religion and Culture

Happily, there was more to medieval Germany than the endless struggle over who was, or was not, emperor.

CITIES AND TRADE

The money economy that began in Italy spread to Germany. Trade expanded and some two thousands new towns and cities emerged. Of course, many were 'new' only in the sense of breaking away from feudal overlords to become largely independent trading centres. These included Cologne, which began as a Roman fort and became self-governing in 1288; Vienna, also of ancient origins; and Nuremberg (Nürnberg), Munich, Augsburg, Strasbourg, Mainz, Hamburg, Bremen, Lübeck and Danzig. Money lending – usury – was an essential stimulant for economic growth. Usury was a no-no for Christians in the Middle Ages; they could borrow, but not lend. Lending was left to the Jews, who gained a negative reputation as usurers, for which they were often persecuted. This stigma continued long after money lending had become a part of the Christian economy as well.

These cities were powerful, but hardly works of art. Entry was through carefully guarded gates in walls with watch towers, sometimes over a moat. Streets were narrow, frequently unpaved, and without a drainage system. The houses, including those of wealthy merchants, were crammed tightly together. The only significant open space was the market square where was found the church, town hall (*Rathaus*) and merchant's hall (*Kaufhaus*). These buildings were done on a grand scale in wealthy cities such as Hildesheim, Hannover, Regensburg and Überlingen. The City Council (*Stadtrat*) ran city government, and usually was composed of wealthy merchants and representatives of the merchant and craft guilds, which controlled buying, selling and the training of craftsmen. The Mainz council, for example, was entirely in the hands of the guilds by 1444.

ART AND ARCHITECTURE

Gothic, a style Germany adopted from France, replaced Romanesque in the thirteenth and fourteenth centuries. It was manifested in palaces, but most obviously in churches and cathedrals. Gothic was characterized by height: tall towers and spires were made possible by the pointed as opposed to round arch, and the flying buttress. Kurt Reinhardt described the double-aisled choir with small chapels along the ambulatory in Gothic churches as indicating 'a growing desire for private devotions and a more personal relationship to the Deity.' The nave was divided into oblong rather than square bays, there was a greater profusion of ever larger stained-glass windows with religious themes, the

The cathedral in Cologne

'rose window' being a particular favourite, and triple doors in church facades were now increasingly elaborate with statuary and other carvings. Plant and animal motifs in ornamentation, particularly on the spires, were commonplace: violets, clover, strawberry, geranium, thistle, maple, hops, and much else. Gargoyles in great profusion also were a feature of Gothic church building.

RELIGION

In medieval Germany theology was 'enriched and coloured' by popular imagination. Devotional relics were customary, and whether they were genuine or not was immaterial, since they were assumed to be. Relics of saints were very popular, such as locks of hair and pieces of garment from the remains of St Elizabeth of Thuringia following her death in 1231, and the bones of the Three Wise Men of the East (*die heiligen drei Könige*) transferred by Frederick Barbarossa from Milan in 1164. Cologne cathedral, the leading 'shrine of relics,' housed these bones. Mendicant orders, Franciscans and Dominicans, established priories and abbeys in such German towns as Augsburg, Regensburg, Mainz and Worms; St Dominic himself was succeeded as general of the Dominican Order by Jordanus of Saxony in 1222. Of course, heresy of one sort or another was present also. Albigensians and Waldensians spread to Germany, inspiring inquisitions to root them out. In 1232, Frederick II decreed that heretics should either have their tongues cut out or be burned at the stake. Meanwhile, marriage performed by priests in churches was regarded as sacred; in practice it often was not. Adultery was commonplace among both sexes, abortions were frequent, and crippled or malformed infants often were simply killed.

Which is not to say that religious superstitions, witch hunts and the abuse of marriage vows indicated an absence of learning in Germany. St Albert the Great of Swabia (1206–1280) was one of Europe's greatest medieval scholars. He taught in Hildesheim, Freiburg, Regensburg, Strasbourg, Cologne and Paris, was a Provincial for the Dominicans, and bishop of Regensburg after 1260. St Albert used Aristotelian logic in exploring everything from Judaic, Arabic and Greek literature, to gardening and cattle breeding.

WOMEN

Medieval society in Germany as elsewhere was male-dominated. Christian philosophers accepted and encouraged male supremacy, even though Christian dogma recognized women as the equal of men. In practice, a woman was the weaker sex who, in the words of Thomas Aquinas, 'exists for the sake of man . . . ; she is free, and yet she is not a full-fledged citizen. . . .' This applied equally to women of the upper and lower classes. But what happened when a woman of noble birth was not only talented but strong willed and assertive? Eleanor of Aquitaine comes to mind, along with Marie de France, Héloïse, and Catherine of Siena; and above all, Hildegard von Bingen (1098–1179).

HILDEGARD VON BINGEN

This daughter of Hildebert of Gut Bermersheim, a German noble from Rhinehessen, ascended to remarkable heights in spiritual, intellectual and artistic productivity. She was trained and nurtured by Jutta von Spanheim, whom she succeeded as abbess of Disibodenberg in 1141. In 1150, in defiance of the abbot, Hildegarde founded her own convent near Bingen (hence her last name) on the Rupertsberg, the physical construction of which she oversaw personally. The archbishop of Mainz dedicated the cloister church in 1152.

Hildegard achieved fame throughout Europe as a mystic, naturalist, musician and composer, apothecary, poet, politician and diplomat. She became known as the 'Sybil of the Rhine,' who 'offered advice on all manner of topics from herbal medicine to heresy.' Over a long career, Hildegard corresponded with such as Bernard of Clairvaux and Emperor Frederick Barbarossa, and various kings, popes and archbishops. Her written work was impressive: three illustrated books of visions including *Scivias* (*Know the Ways*), in which she describes her vision of Pentecostal flames descending from heaven and surrounding her on the occasion of her consecration as abbess – after hearing of this, Pope Eugenius III (?–1153) recognized her as 'a true visionary and prophet'; thirteen works on theology, medicine and the physical sciences, many stories of saints' lives; and almost eighty vocal music compositions and poetic works, including the musical morality drama, *Ordo Virtutum*.

Hildegard's music is like the woman herself: powerful and conceptually unified, yet claiming to speak the truth as God revealed it. 'The words I speak come from no human mouth,' she wrote; 'I saw and heard them in visions sent to me ... God moves where He wills, and not to the glory of earthly man. I am ever filled with fear and trembling. I have no confidence in my own capacities. . . .' Martin Kitchen concluded that Hildegard 'provides a striking example of the extent to which women could pursue successful careers in the Middle Ages.' Of course, she was noble, and shared the social prejudices of her class and culture. When asked why she admitted only aristocrats into her convent, she replied: 'Who would keep all his animals in one barn – ox, donkey, sheep, and goats?'

CHAPTER THREE

Princes, Cities and Emperors,
1300–1519

The German Middle Ages ended and the Renaissance began in the fourteenth and fifteenth centuries. Urban and princely power expanded, emperors often had their backs to the wall, and everyone dealt with plague and ecclesiastical corruption. It was, as Charles Dickens might have said, 'the best of times and the worst of times.'

Burg and Bürgertum

Cities expanded their power and presence, sometimes at the expense of princes. It was a matter of money; the freedom to make it and the right to keep it. By the fifteenth century merchants and bankers had surpassed territorial princes in wealth, and cities had achieved an unprecedented degree of independence.

URBAN LEAGUES

The process began in the Middle Ages. As city dwellers grew in power and independence, they sought to control the surrounding countryside, eyeing the agrarian nobility with animosity and even hatred. They acquired monopolies in these areas, and demanded freedom from paying tolls imposed by the princes. Cities organized themselves into leagues, defined by Kurt Reinhardt as 'co-operative associations for the protection of mutual commercial interests.' These included: the Rhenish League (1254–55) with such cities as Speyer, Worms, Cologne, Mainz, Basel and Strasbourg; the Swabian League (1331) stretching into Switzerland, which included some forty towns and cities by 1385; and the Hanseatic League, begun in 1241 with an alliance between Hamburg and Lübeck and by 1350, included 150 cities stretching from Norfolk in England to Novgorod in Russia. These leagues sometimes made war successfully against territorial princes; however, princely power was expanding relative to the empire, and emperors did not always side with the cities against the princes. Urban league political influence waned even as urban wealth expanded.

HANSEATIC LEAGUE

Save for the Hansa. Hanseatic League power and influence waxed even as that of the others waned. It played a major role in German expansion into, and colonization of, territories east of Brandenburg. Hansa merchants traded mainly in cod and herring, but also in fur, salt, timber, honey, grain, minerals and amber up and down the coasts of the North and Baltic Seas and the rivers Rhine, Weser, Elbe, Oder, Vistula and Nieman. Legal documents from Hansa cities often contained illustrations featuring merchants, sailors and ships. In the end, it was not the princes, but competition with Scandinavian traders and refusal to cooperate with Scandinavian trade laws that brought the Hansa down. Meanwhile, trade fairs were an important feature of the Hansa and other trade cities throughout Germany, and remain so today. Germany has the largest trade fairs held anywhere in Europe, especially in such cities as Frankfurt-am-Main.

THE FUGGERS

Frankfurt, Nuremberg and Augsburg were central to expanding urban independence. Hans Fugger of Augsburg (1345?–1408) established a weaving empire and passed it on to his descendants, one of whom, Jacob (1459–1525), expanded into trade in minerals and acquired a monopoly of mining rights in Hungary. He became banker to Emperor Frederick III (1415–1493), who raised him to noble status. Jacob's brothers married into the nobility, and the family was commissioned to provide all of the cloth for imperial uniforms. The Fuggers became the principal financiers and suppliers of Habsburg political and military ambitions, which, needless to say, resulted in a fair profit. They emerged as the richest, most important and innovative banking, mercantile, and manufacturing family in Germany. They published *das*

Fugger Rundschreiben (The Fugger Newsletter), and built the *Fuggerei* to house workers, an estate consisting of fifty-four houses divided into two residences and arranged in six streets, each renting for one florin a year. Their 'Golden Counting House' became the symbol of banking wealth. It was the 'marvel of Augsburg,' and Jacob Fugger's office was said to be even more lavish than the imperial throne room.

Urban Culture

Increased urban wealth and a new-found burgher's pride of place contributed to a lavish and self-indulgent urban culture with characteristics that intellectuals in later times would dismiss sneeringly as 'bourgeois.'

FASHION AND SEX

Fashion was excessively lavish, despite efforts to curtail it, as when in 1445, Regensburg issued an ordinance limiting a woman's wardrobe to eighteen dresses and coats. Both men and women went to extremes of long, curled hair, bared necks and shoulders, draped themselves in jewellery, and wore shoes with pointed toes so long they sometimes had to be tied to the knees with chainlets. Again Regensburg: a 1485 ordinance limited shoe points to two inches.

Sexual freedom expanded as well. Neither law nor opinion opposed adultery and prostitution as severely as it once had, indeed prostitution was 'legalized,' so to speak, and illegitimate children often shared family rights of inheritance. Of course, sin had been around a long time, and by the fourteenth century included public bath houses – there were four in Mainz alone – where men and women (including clergy) gossiped, ate, drank, listened to music, and then as Martin Kitchen phrased it, 'retired to neighbouring bed chambers for more intimate delights.'

DINING AND DRINKING

Greater wealth meant more servants, among whose tasks was to cater to the indulgent eating habits of their masters. The first German cookbooks date from the fifteenth century. Bishop Johann II of Speyer's ordination in 1461 was followed by a banquet of mutton and chicken in almond milk, fried baby pigs, geese, carp and pike with baked dumplings, venison in black pepper sauce, rice with sugar and baked trout, gingered all over, sugar cakes, fried geese filled with eggs, carp and pike in gravy and berry jam, and baked pastry with red and white wine. Wine and beer were the most popular drinks, as they had been since ancient times; only now they were a major part of expanding trade. The best beers came from such Hansa cities as Erfurt, Naumburg, Einbeck, Goslar and Magdeburg, while the best wines were produced along the Rhine, Moselle and Neckar rivers. Austria and Hungary also produced wines traded and consumed in Germany.

FESTIVALS

Urban holidays were celebrated more expansively than ever before. The twelve nights of Christmas (*Weihnacht*) included carol singing from house to house, and there were New Year revelries, the feast of epiphany, Easter, and, of course, *Saturnalia* on the eve of Lent, when 'old pagan instincts would come to life.'

FOLK TRADITIONS

When the *Minnesänger* tradition, a product of the Age of Chivalry, reached urban Germany it turned into the *Meistersinger* tradition, a stultified *bürgertum* version of the *Minnesänger*. *Meistersingers* trained in guild-controlled schools where, as Kurt Reinhardt put it, the 'simpler and sober tastes of the burgher class' and the application of 'the strict rules and statutes of the guild system' cut 'the wings of poetic imagination and stifl[ed] creative genius.' This included Nuremberg shoemaker-poet Hans Sachs (1494–1576), who 'hardly ever succeeded in transcending the unnatural limitations imposed on his art by the social prejudices and artistic misconceptions of his age.' Sachs produced 6,200 poems and songs in his life, and was an advocate of Martin Luther and the Reformation.

PUBLIC EDUCATION

Cathedral and monastery schools continued to flourish, but schools founded and run by a schoolmaster (usually a layman with university education) appointed by the city councils, now flourished as well. These schools were for both rich and poor, though obviously the rich fared better. Private schools – as opposed to ecclesiastical or council schools – for boys and girls first appeared in the mid-fourteenth century, and coeducational schools were not uncommon in the fifteenth century. The curriculum included writing, reading, rudimentary science, religion, Latin and liturgical singing. Discipline was harsh.

Politics as Usual

Meanwhile, the empire experienced post-Interregnum rivalries for the throne, conflicts with the papacy, the expanding power of territorial princes, and a French presence that created occasional difficulties. It began with Albrecht I (1250–1308). Elected in 1291, he secured the throne only in 1298 when his rival, Adolf of Nassau, was killed in battle. He then made an alliance with Philip IV of France, which sparked a rebellion among the Rhenish electors, and fell out with Pope Boniface VIII (1235–1303) over returning Tuscany to imperial control. They made amends only after Boniface proclaimed that Philip was subject to the emperor as well as to the pope. Not that it mattered; Philip rejected the idea, took Boniface prisoner, and treated him so badly that he died.

THE 'BABYLONIAN CAPTIVITY OF THE PAPACY'

Clement V (1264–1314) succeeded Boniface, but was under French control virtually from the start. In 1309 the papal seat was removed to Avignon in the south of France, where it remained until 1417. This was the 'Babylonian Captivity of the Papacy,' and it contributed to significant changes in the empire and in Germany.

FRENCH EXPANSION

For one thing, French monarchs were emboldened to push into German territories along the Franco-Imperial frontier from the North Sea to the Mediterranean; a move that encouraged French expansionism in centuries to come. Some German princes became subject to France; France allied with cities against princes and with princes against cities; and the captive papacy established pro-French prelates in German Sees. Philip IV and his successors also claimed that France should have the Imperial throne because Charles the Great really was 'Charlemagne,' not 'Karl der Grosse.'

Meanwhile, the Habsburgs pushed for a hereditary Imperial monarchy, and offered territorial concessions at the expense of German princes in exchange for French support. Electors both secular and ecclesiastical saw this as undermining territorial rights, and opposed French 'infiltration.' In the process, they strengthened the degree of their independence relative to the empire. Territorial particularism was reaffirmed in Germany, as opposed to the national outlook then taking root in France.

IMPERIAL DECLINE

With the papacy in Avignon, emperors were inclined to act on their own initiative regarding imperial matters; such as Henry VII (1275–1313) planning to restore imperial power in Italy on the Hohenstaufen model despite the objection of the papacy. Italian poet Dante Alighieri liked the idea as did the pro-empire Ghibellines, who invited Henry to Rome for his coronation; the anti-empire Guelfs opposed it. For two years Henry was caught in the middle of an Italian civil war. His coronation in 1312 was hardly a stellar event. Henry wanted the coronation at Saint Peter's, but the Guelfs would not hear of it, and he had to settle for the Basilica of John Lateran. The Guelfs then disrupted the celebration by firing arrows at the guests.

Henry was succeeded by Frederick of Austria (1286–1330) and Louis of Bavaria (1314–1347) who, after several years of conflict, shared the Imperial throne until Frederick died in 1330. Louis then was crowned Louis IV in Rome by an excommunicated bishop, rather than by Pope John XXII (1249–1334), with whom he had quarrelled – and been excommunicated by – over Annates, the pope taking a new bishop's first year income. Louis then fell out with the princes when he claimed, as a Wittelsbach, rights to the Brandenburg March and the Tyrol; in response the princes elected and crowned a rival emperor, and held Diets in Rhens (1338) and Frankfurt (1344) where it was established that princes, not emperors, looked after German interests. 'Diets' originally were assemblies of landholders and burghers summoned by local rulers to discuss economic issues; under the Empire they represented Imperial cities, territorial and ecclesiastical princes, including the electors after 1489, who met when summoned to deal with a wide range of matters, including war and peace. As indicated at Rhens and Frankfurt, Diets never were an extension of centralized Imperial power so much as a form of opposition to it.

Charles IV

Charles of Bohemia, opposed unsuccessfully by Günther of Schwarzburg, took the Imperial throne in 1347. He reigned without papal coronation, recognized the claims of the German princes, and focused on restoring a sense of German unity. Under Charles IV (1316–1378) the Empire became truly German, which it would remain even though from a papal point of view Rome still was the Imperial core.

RISE OF BOHEMIA

Charles was born in Bohemia, but grew up and was educated in Paris. Baptized Wenceslaus, he chose Charles as his Imperial name in honour of the king of France. Nevertheless, Bohemia was his first love, especially the city of Prague, where he built the Hradschin, the Neustadt, the Charles Bridge and Charles University (University of Prague), the first university in German-speaking lands. Under Charles IV, Bohemia effectively became the centre of the Empire, a fact resented both by rival royal houses and Rhenish electors at the opposite end of the Empire. The result was an 'epoch-making Imperial law' issued over the Imperial seal after the Diet of Nuremberg in 1356, to the contents of which the princes hardly could object.

THE GOLDEN BULL

Martin Kitchen depicted the Golden Bull, issued after the Diet of Nuremberg in 1356, as 'the nearest medieval Germany came to a constitution.' It strengthen the Imperial Diet, enhanced the prestige and powers of the electors (with an eye toward making them less contentious in relation to the emperor), and established clear procedures – including the hereditary principle – for Imperial election. The electoral seat was established at St Bartholomew's Church in Frankfurt, with Aachen the site of coronations. It also established seven electors, the archbishops of Mainz, Trier and Cologne, the king of Bohemia, the count palatine of the Rhine, the duke of Saxony, and the margrave of Brandenburg. They were summoned by the archbishop of Mainz who presided, cast the first vote, and counted the others. A simple majority was sufficient for election, and an elector could vote for himself. The pope was denied a voice in approving or disapproving the outcome.

The Golden Bull gave the princes dominant power within a 'federated' Imperial Germany. The electors' positions were made hereditary with full sovereign power within their territories. Appeals to the emperor against judgments in their courts were banned, and their rights over coinage and monopoly of gold and silver were confirmed. Cities lost power in consequence. Guilds were dissolved, city leagues forbidden and countrymen without permanent residence within city walls denied the protection of city law. It affirmed, in Charles' words, that the princes were 'a part of our body, the solid foundations and the immovable pillars of the empire.'

THE BLACK DEATH

Was it the visitation of natural disasters on Germany that encouraged Charles IV to assent to such an expansion of princely power? Perhaps, because these disasters had the unsettling affect across Germany of making towns richer and lesser nobles more dependent on powerful princes – and inspiring religious fanatics, to whom people flocked in droves. Fourteenth-century Germany resembled a scene from the Old Testament: in 1315 a famine began that lasted three years; in 1335 locusts wiped out much of southern Germany's agricultural production; and 1349 brought the Black Death. This plague was carried by fleas in the fur of rats on merchant ships engaged in trade between Europe and Asia. No one had a clue what it was or how to deal with it, including physicians, who largely applied leeches as a cure or resorted to astrology in search of cures. And travelling con artists sought out the gullible. 'Give me your *pfennigs* and I'll give you a cure,' one might have heard. None of this had the slightest effect. Death was everywhere: a hundred people a day died in Cologne and Mainz, for example, and the Grim Reaper became a dominant theme in preaching, teaching, and the arts. In all, Germany lost perhaps a third of its total population to the Black Death.

What – or who – was to blame? Many believed that it was God's Judgment on a 'faithless generation'; many others blamed it on the Jews. For example, the locust infestation was God punishing the Jews for 'desecrating the Host,' and the Black Death was caused by Jews poisoning the wells. Dominican Heinrich von Herford did *not* believe Jews caused the Plague, and expressed horror when in retribution Jews were killed 'in the most horrible and inhumane manner, by iron and fire'; 560 in Nuremberg alone in 1349. Of course, punishment for any transgression against the teaching of the Church was horrific in the Middle Ages, and not only in Germany: '[a]dultresses were buried alive, traitors quartered, blasphemers had their tongues ripped out, and murderers were skinned alive.'

But what if all the Jews were slaughtered (for their property as likely as for causing the Plague) and there was no one else to blame, and the Plague still did not go away? Then every true believer had to share the blame and be punished. Processions of flagellants, stripped to the waist and loudly confessing their sins and praying while others flogged them, was a widespread response to the Black Death. The Church disapproved, of course, because such practices put the initiative for forgiveness of sin in hands other than those of the clergy.

Other Troubles

The Black Death passed in 1350, and the Golden Bull was in place a decade later; but German and Imperial troubles did not end. While southern German towns revolted against the nobility, Prague rioted against Charles IV's successor, Wenceslaus (1361–1419). In 1400, the Rhenish electors deposed Wenceslaus in favour of Elector Rupert of the Palatine (1352–1410). Wenceslaus did not contest the decision. Rupert was no prize, but he did try to end the schism between Rome and Avignon, and founded Heidelberg University to provide support for the Roman papacy and a haven for scholars who had fallen out with its Avignon rival. He died in 1410 and it got a little bit crazy. Both his cousin Jobst, and his brother Sigismund, king of Hungary (1361–1437), claimed the crown, while deposed Wenceslaus was still alive and king of Bohemia; which meant that technically, there were three emperors, just at this precise moment there were three popes, owing to the Great Schism that came out of the 1409 Council of Pisa. Sigismund won the day and emerged as the defender of Christianity against a rising tide of Turkish aggression in southeastern Europe. Thus was laid an important foundation: by the early nineteenth century, their history as defenders of Church and Europe against the Turks was the only platform left upon which the Habsburgs could rest their claim to supremacy within Germany.

Empire in Transition

Frederick III (1415–1493), a Habsburg, was unanimously elected emperor in 1439, the last to be crowned in Rome, in 1452. He reigned for fifty-three years, a staunch supporter of the papacy against the rising tide of Church reformers.

FREDERICK III

In 1453 Constantinople fell to the Turks, ending once and for all the Eastern Roman Empire. Frederick declined to come to Constantinople's aid. On the other hand, he did fight, successfully, against the Dutch, French and Burgundians. The Burgundian war produced two significant developments. First, Burgundy invaded Germany with a 'host of armoured knights' who were defeated by Swiss infantry armed with lances – proving, in Martin Kitchen's phrase, that 'the knight-in-arms was now a romantic anachronism,' a point Henry V of England had already made in 1415 at Agincourt. Second, Frederick's army, drawn from across the empire, exemplified German princes rallying to the defence of the empire – or, in Kitchen's view, to the defence of the nation: 'The German princes made common cause against a brutal invader, and the concept of nation, first used to classify students at the universities, then more broadly by the Church councils, was now used in its modern sense.' On the downside, Frederick did not deal successfully with rebellious estates in Prussia backed by the king of Poland, or others in Bohemia and Hungary, where Frederick's ward, Ladislaus Posthumous, was heir to both thrones. In 1458 the Hungarians proclaimed Matthias Corvinus (1443–1490) king while the Bohemians gave their throne to George von Podiebrad (1420–1471). He advocated receiving the Eucharist in both forms (Bread and Wine), which got him in trouble with Pope Pius II (1458–1464). He also called for reform of the empire and a crusade against the Turks, but with little success in either.

After Podiebrad died, Matthias Corvinus seized Moravia, Silesia and Lusatia from his successor, and Bosnia, Wallachia and Moldavia from the Turks. He then declared war on Frederick and took Vienna. The emperor retired to Graz from where, metaphorically speaking, he stared helplessly at his occupied city. The bright side was that Matthias had no heirs and had signed an agreement in 1463 that if should the house of Corvinus die out, the Habsburgs would inherit Corvinus lands. That came to pass in 1526 when King Louis of Bohemia and Hungary, who had not produced an heir, was killed in battle; Hungary, Bohemia and Austria became Habsburg possessions, and remained so until 1919.

'Habsburgs Forever'

So too the Holy Roman Empire of the German Nation. After the election of Frederick III, the empire, with its centre now in Vienna, belonged to the Habsburgs. No other German house would ever again rule over it.

MAXIMILIAN I

In 1493, Frederick was succeeded by his son Maximilian (1459–1519). A brilliant, charming, vibrant personality who loved hunting, jousting, literature and the arts (the doting patron of Albrecht Dürer, perhaps Germany's greatest Renaissance artist), he embodied the ideal of knighthood in the Age of Chivalry. Maximilian also was devoted to military science and developed new kinds of artillery and transport wagons. Inspired by the model of the Swiss mercenaries (*Landsknechte*), he also began replacing mounted knights with well-regimented infantry. This did not guarantee success in war, however.

Maximilian was active in imperial military and political affairs – which is to say family affairs – long before he ascended the throne. Upon the death of Charles the Bold in 1477, Frederick III enfeoffed (invested as ruler) Maximilian with Burgundy, against the protests of France, and in 1490 took Tyrol from his cousin Sigismund. He then defeated the Hungarians, and was made king of Hungary by the Treaty of Pressburg which followed. Maximilian was less successful against France and the Netherlands, being taken prisoner on one occasion by the Dutch. Frederick had to intervene, forcing the Treaty of Senlis in 1493, which freed his son, secured his position in Burgundy, and made him duke of Artois and Flanders. Frederick then died and Maximilian became emperor. In 1494 he married the daughter of the duke of Milan and made an alliance with Pope Alexander VI (1431–1503), Spain and Venice against French incursions into northern Italy. It achieved little. On the other hand, Maximilian's fund raising efforts in 1495 aimed at German princes, inspired startling changes in relations between empire and principalities – at least in theory. Practice was something else.

MONEY

In 1495 a Diet at Worms agreed to a 'modest grant' for Maximilian's Italian expedition in exchange for the emperor proclaiming an 'Eternal Peace' within the empire, outlawing feuds and settling all disputes before an imperial court (*Reichskammergericht*). How the court would actually function, or imperial taxes (*gemeiner Pfennig*) be collected, was not clear, and many princes opposed the reforms. Maximilian again applied for money to go to Rome for his coronation – which he could not do in any case, because the French were in control of northern Italy. On this occasion, he agreed to a Reich government (*Reich-regiment*) made up of lay and clerical princes and burghers, which would guarantee the peace and oversee imperial administration, and without the consent of which he could do nothing. He was 'theoretically rendered powerless.' But only theoretically; such restriction was too much for Maximilian, and he refused to recognize the powers of this 'government.' In any case, the money promised was never delivered, and the *Reichregiment* proved so ineffectual that it was abandoned altogether in 1502. On the other hand, local district organizations (*Reichskreise*) created to keep the peace and intermediate between king and princes, did survive. Maximilian finally was crowned emperor at Trent in 1508, fifteen years after his succession as German king. He was the last to experience such a time lag. All of his successors received royal and imperial crowns simultaneously.

THE SPANISH CONNECTION

Though not a great success on the imperial throne, Maximilian did lay the foundation for the empire of his grandson, Charles V (1500–1558). This through the fortuitous marriage of his daughter, Margaret, to Prince Juan, son of King Ferdinand of Aragon and Queen Isabella of Castille. Charles' empire would stretch from Madrid to Vienna and beyond, and would include Burgundy, the Netherlands, the kingdom of Naples, and the Spanish empire in the New World, then just beginning to take shape. When Charles ascended the imperial throne in 1519, as Martin Kitchen phrased it, 'his grandfather's dream of a universal empire seemed finally to have been realized.'

Switzerland

In 1499, Maximilian made the Treaty of Basel, which recognized the independence of the Swiss cantons – and the fact that the Swiss had defeated his armies a number of times. What exactly was this mountainous region so historically intertwined with Germany?

HELVETII

The Helvetii were Switzerland's earliest historically recorded inhabitants, conquered by the Romans in 58 BC, by the Alemanni and Burgundians in the fifth century AD, and by the Franks in the sixth century. The land was divided between Swabia and Burgundy in the ninth century, and the Holy Roman Empire took it over in 1033. Various German feudal houses, notably the Zähringen, ruled parts of the territory until supplanted by the houses of Habsburg and Savoy in the thirteenth century. German emperors and princes respected privileges held by the mountainous regions of Uri, Unterwalden and Schwyz, the latter being the name from which 'Switzerland' derives; or did so until the Habsburgs appeared on the scene. War followed between the Habsburgs and the formidable Swiss League, formed in 1291 and led and organized, according to legend, by Wilhelm Tell. The League won victories at Morgarten (1315), Sempach (1386) and Näfels (1388). This enabled Switzerland to take over Lucerne, Zürich, Zug, Glarus, Bern, and in the fifteenth century, Aargau, Thurgau and the valleys of Ticino. By 1513 the number of cantons had risen to thirteen.

Then a French army defeated the League at Marignano in 1514, after which Switzerland embraced the policy of neutrality in European affairs, recognized by its neighbours, that persists to the present day. Moreover, popes employed Swiss Guards to patrol the Vatican, which they still do, wearing sixteenth-century uniforms.

WILHELM TELL

There is no historical evidence that this hero who resisted Habsburg tyranny actually existed, or that the apple legend had any basis. But never mind; in 1805 Friedrich Schiller wrote the dramatically romantic play in which Tell confronts Hermann Gessler, Imperial Governor of Schwyz and Uri, who forces him to shoot an apple from the head of his son with an arrow – which he does successfully, of course. In the 1830s, Giacomo Rossini set the play to music in opera form, including the famous William Tell Overture, which became the theme music for the 1950s American radio series 'The Lone Ranger.' In 1923 German actor Konrad Veidt played Gessler in a film version of the legend.

German Arts and Sciences into the Sixteenth Century

German artists, composers, craftsmen and creative minds benefited from the spread of the Renaissance from Italy northward, beginning in the fifteenth century. It was a time of cultural revolution.

MUSIC AND MUSICIANS

Not everything changed, of course. Folk music, 'the expression of the communal experiences of an entire people,' continued to be a staple of German culture, changing little in either form or style. Subjects for songs included hunting, soldiering, religion, work, nature, and even student life, varying in context from the lighthearted to the tragic. One change of note did occur in singing when French chanson style arrived in the late fourteenth century. This was voice accompanied by instruments, with numerous rhythmic and melodic variations, including counterpoint. Austrian Oswald von Wolkenstein (1377–1455) was a notable adapter of chanson style to German folk music.

The arrival of the organ in the fifteenth century also was a significant change, as organists began composing variations on church music that traditionally was *a capella*. Conrad Paumann (1410?–1473), organist for the duke of Bavaria and others, wrote organ arrangements for Gregorian Chants and secular melodies. So too Paul Hofhaimer (1459–1537), court organist to Archduke Sigismund at Innsbruck. His liturgical *Salve Regina* is a classic example.

And that was pretty much it. There were no German rivals to Flemish composers Johannes Ockeghem and Josquin des Prez. Great German composers appeared only in the seventeenth century, beginning with Dresden *Kapellmeister* and choral composer, Heinrich Schütz.

CRAFTSMEN

The Renaissance was manifest first on a large scale among the goldsmiths, metalworkers, and carpenters who flourished in Augsburg, Nuremberg, Cologne, Vienna, Prague and Ulm, among other cities. Their work was prized throughout Europe, and they attracted wealthy burghers as patrons. This may explain what Kurt Reinhardt depicted as the fifteenth-century shift in architecture and decorative sculpture 'from high Gothic solemnity and sublimity to the descriptive, intimate and psychological, which reflect a vibrant city life.' Meanwhile, German book illuminators and miniature painters were learning their skills from Burgundian schools.

ARTISTS

German painters followed Netherlands masters, who had learned their art from Italians. Cologne led the way in the early fifteenth century, until Ulm, Augsburg and Nuremberg took the lead a half century later. Artists there did less religious and more secular, and sometimes mythological, work than was characteristic in Cologne; for example Lucas Cranach the Elder's *Cupid Complaining to Venus* and *The Close of the Silver Age*. Meanwhile, Hans Holbein the Elder, Lukas Moser, Konrad Witz and Martin Schongauer contributed to the education of a younger generation of artists, including Holbein's son, Hans Holbein the Younger.

Matthias Grünewald (1470–1528), Albrecht Dürer (1471–1528) and Hans Holbein the Younger (1497–1543) are the best examples of German painting progressing from Medieval to Renaissance. Grünewald, from Würzburg, was, among other things, court artist to

After Dürer – 'The Knight, Death and the Devil'

Albert of Brandenburg. Albert was a humanist; his court painter was not. Grünewald's most famous work, the nine-panel Isenheim Altar-piece, is Renaissance in its realistic representation of human forms, but Medieval in its depiction of the gloom and suffering of Christians associated with the torture and death of Christ on the Cross. Dürer, from Nuremberg, was Grünewald's contemporary, and was more Renaissance but not entirely separate from the Medieval. He worked in drawing, oil, watercolour, woodcut and engraving. The last is well represented by *The Knight, Death and the Devil* in which a courageous knight faces emissaries of evil who seek to detract him from his path to do good works. The work suggests Medieval concepts of good versus evil – and employs Medieval symbols – but also spiritual and secular conflicts and complexities characteristic of the century leading to the Reformation. Like Grünewald, Dürer combines realistic human figures, religious subjects and landscapes (Renaissance), with apocalyptic visions (Medieval). Holbein the Younger was the most Renaissance of the three for his portraiture, a Renaissance main-stream genre. He did religious paintings and illustrated Desiderus Erasmus' Humanist satire *In Praise of Folly*, and Martin Luther's Ger-man translation of the bible, among other books; but his fame rested upon the work done in his position as court painter to Henry VIII of England. There he did portraits of such as Sir Thomas More, Sir Richard Southwell, Sir Brian Tuke, William Warham and, of course, Henry VIII himself.

PHILOSOPHY, SCIENCE AND EDUCATION

Germans also excelled in Renaissance philosophical and scientific thinking. Nicholas of Cusa (1401–1464), a university-educated cleric, served the papacy as a legal representative and favoured Church reform, and expressed views on the nature of God that may or may not have been influenced by the fourteenth-century mystic Meister Eckhart. Cuso speculated that 'God is possible, therefore actual,' a view almost as pantheistic as that of Enlightenment period Deists. He also advanced astronomical calculations which concluded that the earth was not the centre of the universe. Nicholas Copernicus (1473–1543), reckoned to be the 'father of modern astronomy,' drew the same conclusions but on his own as he was not familiar with Cuso's writings. Copernicus, a cathedral canon in Thorn, East Prussia then under Polish jurisdiction, discounted the earth as the centre of the universe (he believed that it was the sun), and argued that the earth rotated every twenty-four hours on its own axis. This did not square with Church doctrines, so he made the official Church censorship list, the *Index of Prohibited Books*. Johannes Kepler (1571–1630), a Protestant from Swabia, professor of mathematics at Graz, and assistant to astronomer Tycho Brahe (1546–1601) in Prague, followed in Copernicus' footsteps on matters astronomical. He too was targeted by theological bigotry, including Protestant objections when he advocated acceptance of the new calendar Pope Gregory XIII (1502–1585) had mandated in 1582. Protestant Germany proscribed the Gregorian calendar until 1700.

Other sciences, including medicine, also entered a Renaissance era of progress. Saxon Georg Bauer, known as Georgius Agricola (1494–1555), founded geology as a scientific discipline. He practised medicine, but was more interested in the science of rocks and minerals, about which he wrote in *De Natura Fossilium* and his most important work, *De Re Metallica*. Württemburger Theophrastus Paracelsus (1493–1541), on the other hand, made the progress of medicine his life's work, aiming at finding a specific remedy for every known disease. He broke new ground in therapeutics, and pioneered the evolution of scientific chemistry, including being the first to use mercury as a cure for syphilis. Unfortunately, he kept no tight control over the manuscripts of his medical writings, and it has been difficult to determine what he did, and what he did not, actually formulate.

German Humanism

Humanism, which emphasized the human element in classical learning and literature, also came into Germany from Italy in the fifteenth century. Many ecclesiastics opposed Humanism, but Emperor Charles IV, later described as 'the father of German humanism,' embraced and patronized it. So too did princely courts at Württemberg, Saxony, Brandenburg and the Palatinate, and such ecclesiastic rulers as Archbishop Albrecht of Mainz and Bishop Johann von Dalberg of Worms.

UNIVERSITIES

German universities, important venues for the study of the classics of antiquity in Latin and Greek, contributed significantly to Humanism. The university concept began effectively in the twelfth century in England and France, where many German scholars studied, and spread to German lands in the fourteenth. Charles University in Prague (1348) was the first in the empire, followed by Vienna (1365), Heidelberg (1385), Cologne (1388), Erfurt (1392), Würzburg (1402), Leipzig (1409), Rostock (1419), Greifswald (1456), Freiburg (1457), Trier (1473), Mainz and Tübingen (1477), and Wittenberg (1502). Students lived in halls or colleges, and over time more and more of them belonged to guilds. The length of time a student matriculated depended upon the rules of a given university, and, of course, the student's capabilities and commitment. Degrees were awarded upon the passing of examinations. Curricula and methods of study and teaching differed, but all universities included faculties of law, arts, theology and, in due course, the sciences. By the fifteenth century they were inspiring Humanist reformers by teaching the classics with a critical eye turned toward Church traditions. Indeed, by the end of the century, the universities at Heidelberg, Vienna, Prague and Erfurt were strong Humanist centres, as were the cities of Augsburg and Nuremberg.

Did the concept of 'nation' begin at the universities? Perhaps. German students at Bologna were designated the 'German Nation,' English students at Paris the 'English Nation,' and so on. Moreover divisive ethnic rivalry appeared at Charles University in 1409 when Hieronymus of Prague spoke of 'the most holy Bohemian nation,' and King Wenceslaus gave Bohemians the majority vote in the Charles University council. German scholars protested by going to Meissen, where the margrave built Leipzig University for them. And, it has been argued that the last two movements of Bedřich Smetana's *Má Vlast* (My Country) pay tribute to the 'patriotic' heroism of the Hussites, followers of Charles University professor Jan Hus, martyred in 1415 for protesting against corrupt popes.

German Humanists and the Church

The 'religious and moral earnestness' of the Germans made German Humanism more practical, educational and moral than its intellectual and philologically focused Italian counterpart. It is hardly surprising that German Humanists were among the strongest critics of papal abuses and ecclesiastical narrow-mindedness.

'LETTERS OF OBSCURE MEN'

Johann Reuchlin's interest in the study of ancient documents, which many Churchman opposed, led to the publication in 1515 and 1519 of *Epistolae Obscurorum Virorum* (Letters of Obscure Men), a propaganda barrage created by Humanist radical Ulrich von Hutten (1488–1523) and others. The letters purported to be written by anti-Humanist theologians with names such as 'Goatmilker,' 'Baldpate,' 'Dung-spreader,' and 'Hermann Sheeps-mouth.' They mixed Latin and German with barbarous ineptitude, and exhibited a remarkable combination of vanity, stupidity, ignorance and obscenity, such as that Julius Caesar did not actually write Latin histories because his military exploits left him no time to learn the language. The idea was to make fools of anti-Humanist Churchmen. It worked.

ULRICH VON HUTTEN

Hutten was among the most colourful German Humanists, part of a group who called themselves 'the poets.' A Franconian noble whose family had sunk to the level of 'robber-knights,' he was sent to the monastery at Fulda. This was not his cup of tea, however, and he ran away to become a Humanist. In Kurt Reinhardt's words, as a Humanist Hutten was 'a fiery German nationalist who was untiring in his efforts to arouse Germany to wage a life-and-death struggle against the power of the Roman Catholic Church and all "ultramontane" influence in the north.' He was admired by Emperor Maximilian I, but rejected by Martin Luther, who found appalling his call-to-arms anti-Rome rhetoric: 'They have sucked our blood, they have gnawed our flesh, they are coming to our marrow; they will break and crush our every bone! Will the Germans never take to arms, will they never rush in with fire and sword?'

Hutten lived recklessly, and wastefully, and was only thirty-five when he died of the 'French disease,' as syphilis was then known.

DESIDERUS ERASMUS

Far more notable and admirable to German Humanists was Desiderus Erasmus (1466–1536). Born near Rotterdam, the illegitimate son of a priest, his origins were an appropriate commentary on ecclesiastical laxity. Like Hutten, Erasmus was forced into a monastery as a youth; only he did not run away. Rather, he devoured the classics and the writings of many Church leaders. He went on to the University of Paris where he obtained a bachelor of divinity degree, and experienced what he regarded as the poverty of Scholasticism. Thereafter Erasmus took the direction of witty, urbane and intellectually challenging writing that earned him the title 'prince of Christian Humanism.' He was a close friend of Sir Thomas More, the English Humanist and later Catholic martyr at the hands of Henry VIII. His best-known work was

Desiderus Erasmus: 'The prince of Christian Humanism'

The Praise of Folly, which condemned ignorance and superstitious among ordinary people, and pedantic dogmatism among traditional ecclesiastics and other scholars. Humanist critique of the Church underlies all of his writings, such as *Handbook of the Christian Knight*, *Institution of Christian Principles,* a guideline for how a Christian prince should govern, *Complaint of Peace* and *Colloquies*. Erasmus also wrote satire critical of the papacy.

It has been suggested that German Humanism opened the door to a German national Church (not unlike that emerging in France at this time), which was favoured by territorial princes and urban guilds chafing at the privileges invested in Church property, including freedom from taxation. In Veit Valentin's words: 'The irritation every good German felt regarding the Roman church was sharpened by a deep sense of disappointment.' Moreover, in these centuries literacy was increasing and an ever larger number of people wanted to think, learn and express their own ideas. No wonder the Protestant Reformation was just around the corner.

CHAPTER FOUR

Reformation and Counter-Reformation, 1519–1648

The Reformation was, for all practical purposes, a revolution. It divided Germany between Protestant and Catholic and changed for all time the relationship of the German princes with the Holy Roman Empire of the German Nation.

Papal Troubles

Papal corruption was commonplace by the end of the Middle Ages, paralleled by popes behaving like princes. The latter increased tension between secular and ecclesiastical rulers. By the fifteenth century, popes seemed to care more about accumulating wealth for war and pleasure than the 'care of souls'. Wealth was amassed through 'Annates,' taking a new bishop's first year income, 'Reservation,' not filling a vacant bishopric for an extended period during which time the pope appropriated diocesan income, and 'Indulgences,' remitting sins in advance through the payment of a fee, a practice began by Boniface VIII for the benefit of soldiers on Crusade who might be slain in battle and not receive last rites. By Martin Luther's time it had spread to include everyone, and was as common as going to confession. In the fifteenth century, demand for Church Reform was on the rise.

ANTI-PAPAL COUNCILS

A Church Council deposed Gregory XII (1327–1415) in 1415. Subsequent councils set out to 'clean up the papacy' and limit papal power. In 1438 the Council of Bourges ruled that 'a Church Council is superior to a pope,' revoked certain papal taxes, and decreed the

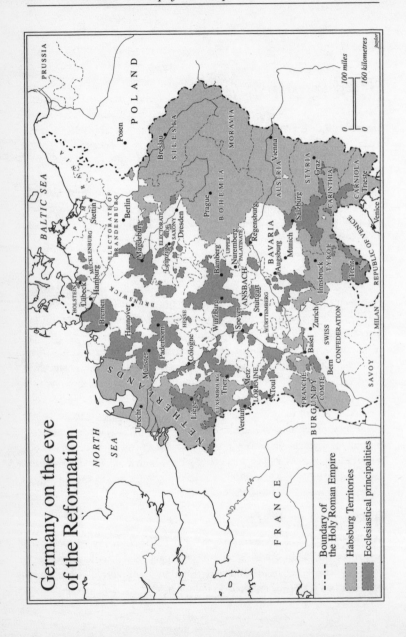

Germany on the eve
of the Reformation

PRUSSIA

POLAND

BALTIC SEA

Posen

Stettin

Berlin

ELECTORATE OF BRANDENBURG

MECKLENBURG

Hamburg

Lübeck

HOLSTEIN

Bremen

BRUNSWICK

Hannover

Magdeburg

Leipzig

Dresden

ELECTORATE OF SAXONY

Breslau

SILESIA

MORAVIA

BOHEMIA

Prague

Regensburg

Vienna

AUSTRIA

STYRIA

Graz

Salzburg

CARINTHIA

CARNIOLA

Trieste

Venice

REPUBLIC OF VENICE

Bamberg

Nuremberg

UPPER PALATINATE

BAVARIA

Munich

Augsburg

Innsbruck

TYROL

Trent

ANSBACH

Würzburg

Speyer

Stuttgart

WÜRTEMBERG

Basel

Zurich

SWISS
CONFEDERATION

Bern

MILAN

SAVOY

Paderborn

HESSE

Münster

Cologne

Trier

LUXEMBOURG

Liège

NETHERLANDS

Utrecht

NORTH
SEA

Metz

LORRAINE

Toul

Verdun

FRANCHE-
COMTÉ

BURGUNDY

FRANCE

Taylor

100 miles

160 kilometres

0

Boundary of
the Holy Roman Empire

Habsburg Territories

Ecclesiastical principalities

Church in France to be subordinate to the monarch rather than the pope. In 1516, the Council at Bologna re-established papal *honour*, but decreed that selection of bishops and abbots should be in the hands of secular rulers. The impact of all this on the papacy was negligible, at least in appearance. Innocent VIII (1432–1492) gave banquets with female guests, and behaved in a manner suggesting ancient rather than Christian Rome. Alexander VI fathered children (notably Césare and Lucretia Borgia), and upon being elected, is supposed to have remarked: 'Now that we have the papacy, let us make the most of it.' Julius II (1443–1513), known as the 'warrior pope,' spent as much time at war with various princes as he did with Michelangelo and the Sistine Chapel project, or fulfilling ecclesiastical duties; and Leo X (1475–1521), a Medici, was a patron of the arts and an avid hunter.

PAPAL CRITICS

In 1412, Jan Hus was so offended by papal corruption that he proclaimed Jesus Christ and not the pope, to be the head of the Church. Hus was tried for heresy, condemned, burnt at the stake and made into a martyr. Hussite rebels rose against the Church, but did harm to the Hus perspective by behaving with extreme brutality. In 1440 Italian scholar Lorenzo Valla claimed that the Donation of Constantine – the document in which Emperor Constantine supposedly gave Rome to the papacy – was a forgery perpetrated by the Vatican. And ca. 1510, Desiderius Erasmus wrote a biting satire in which Pope Julius dies and demands entry at the Heavenly gates. Saint Peter inquires if he is 'Pontiff Maximus' or 'Pestis Maxima' (extreme plague), and, after an exchange with Julius, concludes that he is indeed the latter, 'that most pestilential heathen Julius returned from hell to make sport of me.'

The Printing Press

Propaganda was a central feature of Reformation and Counter-Reformation, both of which needed access to a 'mass' audience. It was enabled by the moveable metal type press, not invented but rather perfected by Johannes Gutenberg (1400–1468).

JOHANNES GUTENBERG

Gutenberg established a successful printing business in Mainz based upon his invention of moveable metal type. The printer engraved typefaces on steel dies from which negative forms were made by pushing them into a softer metal. They were stored in a case from which the printer would slot them into a composing stick, then transfer them to the chase (printing frame) containing one page of print, making printing more efficient and faster. And there was a market for Gutenberg's press because it coincided with a general increase in literacy. Some 1,100 print shops across Europe produced some five million volumes of *incunabula* (books printed before 1500) using his technology; 27,000 titles in all, including the writings of Humanists and papal critics. In the sixteenth century his press would be employed to produce Reformation and Counter-Reformation essays, handbills and satirical cartoons.

Martin Luther

He was the architect of the Reformation, but by chance more than intent as he wanted the Church to be as it had been before (the

Martin Luther at the age of thirty-seven

apostate' Gregory VII 'corrupted the doctrines and practices of the true Church' with his *Dictatus Papae* of 1075.

LUTHER BEFORE THE REFORMATION

Martin Luther (1483–1546) was born in Eisleben near Halle in Saxony. Of peasant stock, the family rose in society when his father, Hans Luther, married into a well-to-do burgher family and started a copper smelting business. At age fourteen, Luther entered the school of the 'Brethren of the Common Life' in Magdeburg, where Thomas à Kempis and Nicholas of Cusa had studied, and the following year, moved to the Latin school at Eisenach in Thuringia. Both schools emphasized humility and compassion for the poor and forgotten, by requiring students to earn their keep by singing and begging in the streets. In Eisenach Luther found a home with Kuntz and Ursula Cotta, who were as warm and caring as his own disciplinarian parents had been strict and unyielding.

Hans Luther wanted his son to move still further up the social ladder and in 1501 entered him at Erfurt University to study law. Erfurt, sometimes referred to as the 'new Prague,' was a leading centre for German Humanists. Luther was much impressed by their brilliance, style and linguistic mastery, but not by 'the pagan aspects' of their writing. This likely was because at Erfurt he discovered and became engrossed in the Bible, which he saw in its complete form for the first time in the university library.

ST ANNE

The study of law did not engage Luther; moreover, he was inclined towards a negative view of life generally, and feelings of melancholy and despair when it came to religion. Then one day in 1505, as he returned to Erfurt from visiting his parents, he was thrown to the ground by a bolt of lightning. Terrified, he called out to the patron saint of miners: 'Saint Anne! Spare me and I will become a monk!' And he did. Over his father's objections, he entered the Augustinian cloister at Erfurt, was made subdeacon and then deacon in 1506, and ordained in 1507. When he celebrated his first Mass, he was 'so overcome with the tremendous majesty of the Almighty that the assisting priest had to restrain him from running away.'

WITTENBERG

In 1508 Luther continued his studies and taught philosophy at the University of Wittenberg, recently founded by Elector Frederick the Wise of Saxony (1463–1525). He lectured on St Augustine whom he admired, Aristotle whom he did not, and the nature of Christian Salvation, about which he was having doubts. In Church doctrine salvation resulted from Good Works: penance, veneration of saints, sacraments and Mass, pilgrimages, fasting and performing rituals. It was not adequate for Luther. 'My heart trembled when I thought of God's grace,' he wrote, and, what might be termed the St Anne paradigm: 'The name of Jesus frightened me, and when I looked at Him crucified, He appeared to me as a flash of lightning.' Then there was Paul's Epistle to the Romans, which Luther read as meaning that man would be 'justified by faith *alone*, through the merits of Christ being attributed to the sinner.' Salvation through faith, yes; through Good Works, no.

In 1510 Luther went to Rome and was appalled to find it not the Holy City so much as a centre of art, sophistication, taste and luxury where 'religious spirit was drowned in worldliness and moral corruption.' He prayed at the seven churches of the Via Dolorosa, knelt before the pope and begged reassurance that Church doctrine was true, and crawled on his knees up the steps of the Church of the Holy Virgin, at each moment asking himself whether he was closer to God than before. Clearly, he was not, and when he returned to Wittenberg, Luther began preaching for the Doctrine of Salvation through Faith, and against the Doctrine of Works and Church venality, above all the sale of Indulgences. These 'letters of safe conduct to salvation' were being hawked in Wittenberg by Dominican friar, Father Tetzel, in this language: 'No matter what sin one might have committed, with these confessional letters you will be able to obtain full indulgence for all penalties imposed upon you.' Luther found this outrageous.

THE NINETY-FIVE THESES

On 31 October 1517 Luther posted Ninety-Five Theses on the church door in Wittenberg, condemning Church abuses and dogmas which he disputed. They were a sensation, and were widely embraced because they voiced a widespread popular resentment against the 'overbearing manner' of the Church generally. Father Tetzel countered with published theses of his own, and the Reformation was on – though no one then was necessarily aware of the fact.

The Reformation

That included Luther, who defended his views before his order at Heidelberg in 1518, preached them before the Duke of Saxony in Dresden, and revised them as 'resolutions' dedicated to Pope Leo X. Luther asked Leo's advice regarding the resolutions, concluding: 'Most holy father! I prostrate myself at the feet of thy Holiness with all that I am and all that I have. Do what thou wilt, give life or death, call or revoke, approve or disapprove! In they voice I will recognize the voice of Christ, who dwelleth and speaketh in thee. If I have deserved death, I do not refuse to die.' Hardly a call to revolution.

DIET OF WORMS

But it led to revolution. Luther defended his views in a debate with Johannes Eck at the University of Ingolstadt, wrote *On the Freedom of a Christian,* and joined Philip Melanchthon in Wittenberg for a public burning of a papal bull of excommunication and pro-papacy theological writing. Throughout, he had the support of Elector Frederick the Wise of Saxony. Then in 1521 Luther was summoned by the new, and staunchly Roman Catholic, Emperor Charles V to the Diet of Worms, where he was called upon to recant. He would not, and drew the line in the sand with these words: 'I cannot submit my faith either to the Pope or to the Councils, because it is clear as day they have frequently erred and contradicted each other. . . . I cannot and will not retract.' The last line was altered in broadsheets circulated among the populace to read: 'Here I stand, I can do no other. So help me God, Amen.' It made more effective propaganda.

LUTHER OUTLAWED

Charles V then issued the Edict of Worms which declared Luther an outlaw (anyone could take a potshot at him and be rewarded for it), and ordered that all of his writings be burnt. Too late. As he returned home from Worms, Luther was taken 'prisoner' by bandits who carried him to Wartburg Castle. It had all been planned in advance by Frederick the Wise as an escape for Luther, and as an excuse for himself to claim that he was not protecting a heretic. Luther remained in the Wartburg for eleven months and began the writings that justified and detailed his reformed theology.

LUTHERANISM

Luther's object was replacing Works with Faith, which he regarded as the original basis for Christianity. 'Faith redeems, corrects, and preserves our consciences so that we know that righteousness does not consist in works, although works neither can nor ought to be wanting ... yet our righteousness is not in them, but in faith.' He wrote extensively and preached across Germany, protesting – hence the term 'Protestant' – against the 'Romanists' led by a wicked papacy that placed Works above Faith. Luther also defied Church tradition regarding a Latin-only Bible, and translated first the New and then the Old Testament into German – a work begun in Wartburg Castle. The Bible must be in the vernacular (*im Volksmund*), the language of the people. This resonated well among Germans, for by the time of his death a million copies had been sold. It is often said that by translating the Bible into German, Luther laid the foundations for a German national consciousness. Indeed he seemed to have a sense of Germanness himself. 'It is for you Germans that I seek salvation and sanctity,' he wrote. Of course, southern Germany remained Catholic, preferred Latin for religion, and came to view high German with its Saxon and Thuringian roots as a Protestant language. To this day, wrote Martin Kitchen, Germans in Catholic areas 'tend to speak in dialect rather than standard German.'

Meanwhile, in Wittenberg, Augustinians were leaving the order, students destroyed the altar at the Franciscan monastery, and Communion was celebrated in German and the laity received the cup as well as the bread. The first Protestant martyrs were burned in Brussels in 1523, and support for Luther's views on Church and Christianity spread across Germany, Holland, Scandinavia and into England.

Actually, English discontent with Rome was present in the fourteenth century when John Wycliffe, a role model for Jan Hus, began the Lollard movement. Now, Henry VIII defended Rome theologically (*In defensor Septem Sacramentorum*), but broke with the papacy over political matters and summoned a parliament in 1529 that proclaimed Henry Head of the Church in England in place of the pope. As Protestantism spread, because Luther symbolized the break with Rome, his advocates were being called in German, *evangelisch* and in English, 'Lutherans.'

THE SPREAD OF PROTESTANTISM

Other reformers emerged almost at the outset of the Reformation, with doctrines similar to Luther yet different. Ulrich Zwingli was 'Lutheran' only more militant; Conrad Grebel launched the Anabaptists, a radical, communal sect that took over Münster, where Dutch tailor Jan van Leyden announced the New Zion with himself as king; then came Menno Simon, who modified the Anabaptists into the Mennonites. The most important post-Luther reformer was John Calvin of Geneva (1509–1564), who in his *Institutes of the Christian Religion* argued that the saved were elected for salvation by God for having achieved goodness, and that all authority was based on the Bible, including that of the state; hence, he made Geneva a theocratic city-state. John Knox took Calvin's views to Scotland in the mid-sixteenth century, where they became the basis of Presbyterianism. Then there were Anglicans – not quite Protestant yet not quite Catholic – Congregationalists, Baptists, Brownists, Puritans (not a sect so much as an attitude) and many others ranging from moderate to extreme variations on the Lutheran theme. Extreme Protestant sects condemned Church music as sensual and therefore sinful, and opposed the artistic elaborations of the Roman Church. It was not uncommon for the interiors of churches taken over by Protestants to have their walls whitewashed to cover murals and other decorations. And, of course, altars were stripped of all iconic symbols including the Cross.

Lutherans, on the other hand, preserved old Church interiors, adding to them paintings and decoration indicative of their own catechism. The Church of the Blessed Virgin Mary in Wolfenbüttel, built in the early seventeenth century, was the first purely Lutheran example of ecclesiastical architecture, a combination of Gothic, Renaissance and Baroque. Lutherans also saw Church music as a gift from God that should be central to the service. Heinrich Schütz, appointed *kapellmeister* in Dresden by Elector Johann Georg of Saxony in 1619, was the first great Protestant German choral composer. And they stressed scholarship; Duke August the Younger of Brunswick-Wolfenbüttel founded a library which by 1666 contained more than 100,000 volumes.

Charles V

The Reformation changed the faith of north Europeans; and it produced civil war, anarchy and princely particularism to an unprecedented degree.

THE HOLY ROMAN EMPIRE AND REFORMATION

Charles V, Spanish rather than German (which the German princes did not let him forget), ascended the imperial throne in 1519, and was crowned emperor in 1530, the last to be so by a pope. His was the most extensive Holy Roman Empire ever, embracing Germany, Austria, Franche-Conté, Luxembourg, the Netherlands, Spanish possessions in the Americas, Spain itself, and Naples, Sicily and Sardinia. Ironically, it also was the weakest. Many princes embraced Protestantism and claimed greater independence, while the divide between Spanish and Austrian Habsburgs, which effectively split the empire in two, began in Charles' reign. His brother, Ferdinand (1503–1562), administered Austria and became king of Bohemia and Hungary as well in 1526. It was his job, with Charles' help on occasion, to stop the Turks under Suleiman the Magnificent advancing up the Danube and threatening the empire. Years of Habsburg–Turkish war – including a siege of Vienna in 1529 – ended in 1562 with the greater part of Hungary in Turkish hands. At the same time, Charles was at war with France, which, bordered on three sides by Habsburg territories, felt threatened and sought to push back this imperial frontier – sometimes with the aid of rebellious German princes.

Meanwhile, there was the Protestant Reformation. At the Diet of Worms, Charles placed himself firmly on the side of Rome; many of his German subjects put themselves on Martin Luther's side. It had been an embarrassment when, on Easter Sunday in 1527, rebellious and mostly Lutheran German imperial troops commanded by a French noble, the count of Bourbon, sacked Rome – even though the act did further Charles' interests in Italy. But only an embarrassment; the '*Sacco di Roma*' was small potatoes compared to what was going on at home.

The Reformation turns Violent

Within three years of its beginning, the Reformation became a cause for knights, peasants and princes to make war. Among Germans there was no compromise.

KNIGHTS' REBELLION

The princes rebelled against the emperor; then lesser nobles, such as Imperial Knights (*Reichsritter*), rebelled against the princes. The knights embraced the Reformation early on; ironic, since their titles came directly from the most Catholic emperor, but not surprising, since they blamed both ecclesiastical and secular princes for the erosion of their privileges and their reduced livelihood. Many reverted to mercenary soldiering or thievery in order to survive. Ulrich von Hutten, himself an imperial knight, 'claimed that life was so dangerous that he had to wear armour when hunting or fishing.' In 1522, a brotherhood of 600 Protestant Rhenish knights went to war under Franz von Sickingen, sworn to defend their new faith and their rights in newly forming princely states. However, they were outgunned (literally), out-manoeuvred and soon defeated. Sickingen, initially successful in Trier, was forced to retreat to his castle in Landstuhl, where he was killed in May 1523 and the castle razed to the ground. Yet despite defeat, Imperial Knights did not disappear; they reorganized on a local basis to defend their interests, and after 1540 allied themselves with the emperor against the princes – which demonstrates that their rebellion always was more social than religious – and many knights led imperial forces in the Thirty Years War. The alliance worked; by 1806 Germany could claim 1,700 Imperial Knights, many of whom had attained considerable wealth and influence.

PEASANTS' REBELLION

Martin Luther encouraged social reform on behalf of peasants and burghers. Recognizing the distress and misery of ordinary people, he wrote against the tyrannical nobles who 'drove and hunted men like wild beasts,' attacked usury for 'sucking out what little blood the poor have left,' and, of course, condemned selling Indulgences as the real 'bloodsucker' of the peasants. As Luther wrote, unrest generally was on the rise against territorial princes who, with increased independence from the empire, imposed more oppressive regimes upon the peasants over whom they ruled. These peasants also suffered from receiving set cash payment for labour rather than a share of the crop. That is, a field worker was paid, say, ten *pfennigs* the week with no additional benefit if productivity increased, which meant he had no protection against inflation. This increased the economic, social and political gap between peasants and landowners, and peasants across Germany who had escaped from serfdom into relative independence, faced being submerged again into serfdom. Luther appeared as their champion, a symbol for German peasants and lower orders in their struggle against oppressive masters. Many 'Lutheran' preachers led in advocating reform of manor laws; naturally, the Peasants Leagues (*Bundschuh*) expected Luther to be on their side.

THE BUNDSCHUH

Peasant suffering was on the rise, but the Peasants' War in Swabia and Franconia, pitting *Bundschuh* against landlords and princes, was more than the 'frustrated outburst of the desperately poor.' It was also a war in which well-off peasants fought to secure their political, social and religious rights. This is clear from the 1524 Twelve Articles, which laid out peasants' rights, including election of priests, keeping tithes within the parish, use of common lands and forests, hunting and fishing rights, and abolition of death duties owed by serfs to their lord. Open revolts began in 1525, some of which had the support of such as the duke of Württemberg and Tilman Riemenschneider, a former lord mayor of

Würzburg and a famous German sculptor. The peasants won an early round at Böblingen, after which the war intensified, with both sides committing atrocities. In the end the peasants were defeated by royal and imperial armies.

THOMAS MÜNTZER

Meanwhile, Anabaptist leader Thomas Müntzer of Münster (1488–1525) encouraged the peasants by preaching a radical restructuring of society to peasants, artisans, miners and the urban poor of Thuringia. All responded with enthusiasm. He spoke of a terrible bloodbath in which the elect of God would destroy the Turks and the unrighteous, and begin the 'triumphant thousand-year rule of Christ the saviour.' This was Münster as the New Zion. Müntzer led the rebels to disaster at Frankenhausen in May 1525, where 5,000 peasants were killed at a cost of exactly six royal soldiers. He was captured, tortured, and ultimately beheaded along with fifty-three followers. Hans Sachs, shoemaker, poet and *meistersinger* from Nuremberg, also was a peasant rebel leader; unlike Müntzer he survived the experience.

LUTHER REACTS

Martin Luther advocated peasants' rights, but was appalled by the rebellion and especially by Müntzer, his 'false brother.' He feared a 'Hussite' nightmare, and being in tune with the way things really operated – that is, that the German princes had the power and the common people had no chance of co-opting it – saw the princes as the only hope for the survival and flourishing of the Reformation. In 1525 Luther wrote *Against the Murderous, Thieving Hordes of Peasants* which called for the princes 'in God's name' to slaughter the rebels. 'Dear Sirs, whoever can should stab, smite and strangle.... The peasants have a bad conscience and an unjust cause and any peasant who dies thereby is lost, body and soul, and belongs to the devil for all eternity.' Later he expressed regret at being so extreme, but justified himself because Müntzer 'wanted to kill my Christ.'

Later German generations put a different spin on the Peasants' War. It was a ready-made inspiration for the *Sturm und Drang* movement of the late eighteenth century, the lead-in to German Romanticism.

Johann Wolfgang Goethe's play *Goetz von Berlichingen*, inspired by a nobleman of that name who collaborated with Sickingen, celebrated the heroism of a leader and spokesman for rebellious peasants. His final word in the play, uttered as he lay dying, is '*Freiheit!*' (Freedom).

THE SCHMALKALDIC LEAGUE

The real divide in Reformation Germany came with the Schmalkaldic War in 1546–47. Protestant princes grew steadily in number, and in 1530 Charles V summoned a Diet at Augsburg which issued a call for these 'heretics' to return to the fold. Philip Melanchthon countered with *Confessio Augustana* (the Augsburg Confession) which laid out Lutheran theology, and to which Martin Luther gave public support. The Catholics then reaffirmed the Edict of Worms in no uncertain terms, in the *Confutatio*. Protestant princes saw this as a threat, and in 1531, met at Schmalkalden in Thuringia where they formed a defence league.

At this moment, Charles was preoccupied with the Turkish danger and needed princely support. Therefore, he issued the Nuremberg Concession which established a truce regarding religious differences, in exchange for Protestant princes backing his war against the Turks. They did not dissolve the Schmalkaldic League, but rather used the truce to increase their strength and independence. In 1542, when Charles turned his attention to making Germany once again subordinate to both Church and empire – the beginning of his 'German decade' – the League was ready to do battle.

Only not on behalf of Duke Wilhelm V of Jülich-Cleves, a powerful state centred on Düsseldorf, north of Cologne, who in 1538 had taken the estates of Geldern. In 1543 Charles reclaimed the estates with the backing of the Diet of Regensburg. Wilhelm objected and war ensued; only the League stayed out of it. Wilhelm was defeated, lost much of his territory, and was forced to renounce his Protestant faith. Then in 1546, another Diet of Regensburg approved an army of 12,500 soldiers who took to the field against the Protestants. They were paid by Pope Paul III (1468–1549) and backed by the dukes of Bavaria and Saxony. The pope had encouraged compromise, but gave it up because the intransigence between German Protestants and Catholics was now extreme. The attitude was, as historian Norman Jones noted: '*Willst zu nicht mein bruder sein, schlage ich den schädel ein.*' (Be my brother or I'll smash your head.) The Schmalkaldic League War was underway.

It did not last long. Imperial forces were less than overwhelming, but in practice, as Martin Kitchen phrased it, 'the League proved to be a quarrelsome coalition unable to coordinate its strategy.' That inability brought the war to a quick end. Protestant Duke Maurice of Saxony (1521–1553), whom the emperor had 'bought,' led an imperial army into the lands of his cousin, Johann Frederick (1529–1595), who left the League army in order to defend them. He was defeated at Mühlberg and taken prisoner, along with Philip of Hessen (1509–1567), a principal League leader, who then rendered homage to the emperor in exchange for the promise of freedom. But Charles lied; both Johann and Philip were incarcerated in the Netherlands, and the war ended. Charles now sought to persuade the princes to accept a 'federated' empire with him as the central authority. However, the princes, incensed at the treatment Johann and Philip had received, refused on the grounds that such a system would involve 'bestial Spanish servitude.' Maurice of Saxony agreed, and intrigued to form an anti-Habsburg coalition of princes. This was his reasoning when he laid siege to Protestant Magdeburg in the emperor's name – or so he told the Lord Mayor. He joined the princes in signing the treaty of Chambord in 1552, wherein Henry II of France became 'protector' of German liberties in exchange for France receiving Cambrai, Metz, Toul and Verdun. The next year, Maurice was killed in battle by another prince whose aim, of course, was territorial aggrandizement.

It ended for Charles in 1555 at Augsburg. Unable to crush either Lutheranism or territoriality, he agreed to the principle of '*cuis regio, eius religio*' (whose the region, his the religion). The princes would pay imperial taxes, but they would determine whether their subjects would be Catholic or Lutheran; Calvinists were not included. With few exceptions, most princes did not force dissenting subjects to change their religion – at least not until the eighteenth century when, for example, 21,000 Protestants were expelled from Salzburg in 1731–32. The Holy Roman Empire was now the loose federation of quasi-independent principalities that it would remain until it disappeared altogether in 1806, despite Ferdinand II's (1578–1637) efforts to turn back the clock in the Thirty Years War. In 1556, disillusioned and gout-ridden, Charles abdicated the throne to his son, Philip II (1527–1598) – also Spanish far more than German – and retired to the monastery of San Jerónimode Yuste in Spain. He died there in 1558.

Counter-Reformation

The campaign to bring Protestants back to Rome was vigorously pursued across Europe, but with only nominal success; save in France where by the end of the sixteenth century large numbers of Huguenots (Calvinists) had been forced to leave. In France, the Counter-Reformation was an ideological war occasionally punctuated with acts of excessive violence, such as the St Bartholomew's Day Massacre in France in 1572; in Germany it was a war of control. Catholic princes enhanced their power in order to keep Protestant subjects in line; ditto for Protestant princes where Catholics were concerned. And it was all based upon the 'truth' of Church doctrine – and perhaps as well on the thinking of Thomas Erastus, a philosopher of 'national' religion who had argued that while doctrine was the responsibility of Church leaders, ecclesiastical organization was the Christian responsibility of secular rulers. That soon evolved into the view that a secular ruler could use religion as an arm of state power. Henry VIII of England found Erastianism appealing.

COUNCIL OF TRENT

The Council of Trent (1545–63) set the Counter-Reformation in motion with the *Tridentinum*, published in 1564. It confirmed Catholic doctrines such as redemption through grace transmitted through the seven sacraments, the Latin (vulgate) Bible as the true word of God, purgatory, the veneration of saints and holy relics, and repudiated all Protestant doctrines that differed from the Catholic. By 1570 Germany was divided between Catholics, Lutherans and a small group of Calvinists and Zwinglians; principalities and towns reflected these divisions, and the likes of Duke Albrecht V of Bavaria (1528–1579) worked to further both Catholic and Bavarian interests against those of Protestant regions. His successor joined a Spanish Habsburg effort in 1583–85 to oust Protestants from Cologne. Meanwhile, Ignatius Loyola, founder of the Society of Jesus (Jesuits), established the Collegium Germanicum in Rome to train German priests in 'strict Tridentinum orthodoxy.' They then set out for home to bring Protestants back into line.

PETER CANISIUS AND THE PRINCES

Between 1530 and 1570 it appeared that Protestantism was on the way to taking control of most of Germany. It did not happen. Peter Canisius (1521–1597), the first German Jesuit and often referred to as the 'Second Apostle of Germany' after St Boniface, was assigned by Loyola himself to work in southern Germany. Between ca. 1550 and his death in 1597, Canisius won over Catholic princes to his plan of Counter-Reformation, which focused on raising educational standards for Catholic youth, which then were far beneath those of Protestant schools. Over the years Canisius worked on educational reform in Vienna, Ingolstadt, Augsburg and Fribourg (Switzerland), and under commission from Emperor Ferdinand I (1503–1564) composed a new Catholic catechism in Latin and later in German. His labours resulted in a much improved educational system in Catholic regions, and that led to a strengthened Church in those areas. By 1700 Protestantism had been virtually eliminated in Bavaria as well as in western Germany. Of course, it helped that many Catholic princes took *cuius regio, eius religio* very seriously.

Princes also founded universities. In Catholic regions they mostly were under Jesuit influence: Dillingen (1549), Olmütz (1574), Würzburg (1582), Graz (1586), Paderborn (1615) and Salzburg (1623). These were State institutions where the professors were servants of the prince, and if the prince decided to switch from Catholic to Protestant, which occasionally happened, the faculty were required to follow his lead or be dismissed or even imprisoned. The same was true in the north and east, where Protestant princes, including Calvinists, predominated: Protestant Universities were started at Marburg (1527), Königsberg (1544), Jena (1558), Helmstedt (1574), Giessen (1607), Rintelen (1621) and Altdorf (1623). And in the Rhineland, where

Heidelberg University, which dated from 1385, was made Calvinist. Calvinism appealed to Elector Johann Sigismund of Hessen-Kassel and Brandenburg (?–1619), though his subjects generally stuck with Lutheranism.

Generally speaking, the Catholic Church in Germany as across Europe, responded to Protestantism by trying to 'clean up its act' and make the return to Rome a positive as well as necessary path to salvation. The Protestants strove to make their approach to Christianity clear and different from that of Rome. But they shared this with Catholics: harsh imposition of religious rules upon the faithful – as when John Calvin ordered Michael Servetus burned at the stake for refusing to drop Catholicism in favour of Calvinism.

WITCH HUNTING

A particularly ugly result of Reformation and Counter-Reformation was the increase in witch hunting. The Inquisition, introduced in the Middle Ages, took on heretics, Jews, anyone who disagreed with Church doctrine – Galileo, for example, faced an Inquisition Court in 1633 for refuting Aristotelian science which the Church had embraced – and witchcraft. In the sixteenth century, a 'climate of fear' developed on both sides of the Reformation, promoted by propaganda depicting Catholic clergy as devils, or Protestants as wicked defilers of true faith. Associating the other side with the practice of witchcraft was an easy step, and the persecution of witches became official policy for both Catholic and Protestant Churches. Those persecuted were usually, though not always, women, and as often as not, in connection with midwifery and the use of herbal medicines. Wrote Helen Ellerbe, 'churchmen portrayed the healing woman as the most evil of all witches.' Both Protestant and Catholic clergy took pride in waging war against witches: the bishop of Würzburg boasted of condemning to execution 1,900 witches over five years, while Lutheran prelate Benedict Carpzov claimed to have condemned 20,000 'devil worshipers.' Of course, there is no documentary evidence to support these numbers. Interestingly, men who engaged in black magic – fully as evil, one would think, as witchcraft – were not persecuted, as in Dr Georg Faust, the Swabian archsorcerer, physician and alchemist, who for centuries inspired plays and poetry by the likes of Marlowe, Lessing and Goethe.

The Thirty Years War

Then came the seventeenth century and the Thirty Years War (1618–1648), the culmination of the interaction of religion and politics that increasingly characterized the Reformation. It was a religious war that within a decade transmogrified into a struggle for political dominion; a war between Catholics and Protestants, though frequently Catholics and Protestants found themselves on the same side, between the empire and territorial princes, and between Habsburg and Bourbon, the latter the ruling house of France since Huguenot Henry IV had decided that 'Paris is worth a Mass.'

THE 'DEFENESTRATION OF PRAGUE'

In May 1618, Ferdinand nephew of Emperor Mathias (1557–1619) and king of Bohemia, sent a contingent of Jesuit priests to Prague to reason with a coterie of Calvinist Bohemian nobles who were in rebellion because Mathias had named Ferdinand king without consulting them, which was a violation of an ancient elective principle. The nobles threw two of the Jesuits from a window fifty feet up the side of the Hradzhin. Miraculously, they survived the fall and at once become the stuff of propaganda. Catholics claimed that angels appeared to bear them gently to earth; Protestants claimed that they landed in a dung heap. The nobles then took control of Prague, proclaimed the restitution of ancient Bohemian privileges, repudiated Habsburg rule and with it, Catholicism. Protestant princes across Germany, all anxious to depose the Habsburgs from the imperial throne, backed them.

The possibilities were there. Mathias died in 1619. Ferdinand was the heir-apparent, but of the seven Electors three were Catholic archbishops (Mainz, Trier, Cologne) while another three were Protestant princes (Saxony, Brandenburg, the Palatinate). Unfortunately, the seventh was Ferdinand himself as King of Bohemia. Despite pleas from the Protestants, even the three princes declined to vote against Ferdinand, and he was elected unanimously on 18 August 1619.

REBELLION

The Bohemian nobles responded by declaring Palatine prince and
Protestant Elector Frederick V (1596–1632), who had voted for Ferdinand, King of Bohemia. He accepted and the rebellion was underway. Unfortunately, Bohemia had no popular support among the
crowned heads of Europe, whereas Ferdinand II (1578–1637), as Holy
Roman Emperor, had support, including military, from Philip III of
Spain, Duke Maximilian of Bavaria, and the duke of Saxony, a Protestant. There was a price, of course; each demanded territorial concessions in return. The only battle of the Bohemian rebellion was at
Weissberg (White Mountain) in 1620, where the uprising was crushed
and Frederick V deposed. He was called contemptuously thereafter the
'*Winterkönig*' (king of one winter). He returned with his family to the
Rhineland. A note: his son Rupert joined the royal army of Charles I in
1640 to fight in the English Civil War. Not yet twenty-one, he proved
to be one of the king's most competent commanders.

THE MERCENARY WAR

The war might have ended at Weissberg, except that the armies in the
field were led by mercenaries such as Ernst von Mansfeld who were in
it for the money. Also, many German as well as Bohemian princes saw
advantage in continuing the conflict and were prepared to pay mercenaries to make it happen. Mansfeld shifted sides to the highest bidder
almost weekly, looting and raping throughout 1622. He took his army
into northwestern Germany, where Maximilian of Bavaria confronted
and pursued him, but could not defeat him. Along the way Maximilian
harried Protestants severely and reaped huge profits in the process,
including taking much of the 'Winter King's' Palatine lands and his
electoral seat and, of course, large sums from Emperor Ferdinand as
payment. Maximilian also preferred to keep the war going; Mansfeld
simply was a convenient excuse.

Meanwhile, Albrecht von Wallenstein (1583–1634) was doing the
same. A brilliant and enigmatic nominal Catholic mercenary of Protestant parentage from Bohemia, who, in the name of the emperor,
commanded armies which corresponded to no single concept of

Albrecht von Wallenstein, the enigmatic mercenary

nationality or religion, but were devoted to their leader because of his personal magnetism. Wallenstein far surpassed Mansfeld – but not Maximilian – in looting areas through which his armies passed, and he defeated Mansfeld in battle at Dessaubrücke on the Elbe when Mansfeld switched sides. By 1628 Wallenstein was maintaining an army of 128,000 on looted agricultural land, which meant that Ferdinand II was less out of pocket in terms of soldiers' wages. He was feared by everyone except the emperor, whom the mercenary leader presumably supported and obeyed. Indeed, Ferdinand's cause flourished in these years. Protestants were suppressed everywhere that he was victorious in battle, beginning with Bohemia; he redistributed territory and revamped Habsburg administration. And in the process, he came to believe that he could achieve what Charles V had failed to do: turn the Holy Roman Empire into an absolutist, sovereign, Catholic and Habsburg state with no limitations on the power of the emperor.

EDICT OF RESTITUTION

In 1629, Ferdinand ordered that all Church lands and possessions confiscated since 1552 be restored. That pleased the Church, certainly, but not also the princes, many of whom, Catholic as well as Protestant, had taken Church lands. And, those who had not also opposed the Edict, fearing that Ferdinand might take properties from them anyway to reward his powerful supporters, or they simply were at odds with expanding imperial power. They had reason to be fearful. In July 1629 Ferdinand took lands from the dukes of Mechlenburg-Schwerin and Mecklenburg-Güstrow which their families had owned since Carolingian times, and gave them to Wallenstein. Imperial Knights and other nobles were outraged; Ferdinand found himself under such pressure that in 1631 he suspended the Edict of Restitution and removed Wallenstein from his command.

GUSTAVUS ADOLPHUS

In 1630, Sweden entered the war. King Gustavus Adolphus (1594–1632) claimed that he came to rescue German Protestants; the Germans suspected otherwise, and their suspicions seemed confirmed when one of Sweden's first moves after defeating imperial forces in Pomerania was to impose control over the region. All the same, Gustavus gained enough support from an arrangement with Saxony and Brandenburg to field an army of 34,000. Then, Cardinal Richelieu, First Minister of Louis XIII of France, recognized that Sweden's presence could benefit France at the expense of the empire, and offered Gustavus one million livres per year, so long as he made vigorous and successful war against Ferdinand.

Gustavus did just that. In 1631 at Breitenfeld, he smashed an imperial army commanded by Johann Tserclaes Tilly and reversed many imperial gains made in the prior decade. He then sacked Bavaria with brutal thoroughness, and prepared to invade Austria, perhaps, it was speculated in some quarters, with an eye toward seizing the imperial throne for himself. That is as may be; but certainly at this point Gustavus had rescued Protestant states in northern Germany, and checked Habsburg ambitions virtually everywhere else. Then, in 1632, Ferdinand called Albrecht von Wallenstein back into service, and he took on the Swedish king at Lützen.

WALLENSTEIN

They met in a single vicious, cruel and bloody battle. At one point, Gustavus led a cavalry charge against Wallenstein's infantry, and disappeared into the dense cloud of gun smoke created by the fact that smokeless gunpowder had not yet been invented. After a while, the king's horse reappeared, riderless. The battle continued, and later, during a lull, the body of Gustavus Adolphus was found in the field among other dead. He had been stripped naked and mutilated. Enraged, the Swedish army attacked Wallenstein's forces and drove them from the field defeated, though not overwhelmed. Now neither side could quit, and neither side was strong enough to win nor weak enough to have to surrender.

In 1633, Wallenstein, who had intrigued behind the emperor's back since his dismissal in 1631, tried to open negotiations with Ferdinand's enemies. They did not trust him, however, and nothing happened – except that Ferdinand got wind of it. He again relieved Wallenstein of his command, had him tried *in absentia* for treason, and ordered him taken, dead or alive. The order was carried out in 1634 in Pilsen by one of Wallenstein's own officers, a Irish mercenary captain, who kicked open the door to his bedchamber and, in historian R. S. Dunn's words, 'speared his unarmed chieftain, rolled the bloody body in a carpet, and dragged it unceremoniously down the stairs.'

TO THE BITTER END

After 1634, French troops joined the Swedes and fought imperial forces across Germany; especially in Brandenburg, where Elector Georg Wilhelm backed the empire because Sweden had taken Pomerania. Cities were the principal targets: Marburg was occupied eleven times and Magdeburg besieged ten times, for example. Villages and peasant communities often were simply swept away. Sometimes town dwellers could withstand a siege, or even buy off a mercenary army; peasants could do nothing but run away, or die. Many Germans joined the mercenaries since military life was now much better than that on the civilian side. Occasionally they fought back with success; contemporary etchings depict peasants killing mercenary soldiers. All the same, the reverse was more often the case, indicated in other etchings depicting one mercenary killing a peasant while another drags his wife off to be raped.

The Peace of Westphalia

Peace negotiations began in 1644, in the Westphalian towns of Münster and Osnabrück. Agreement was reached in 1648, and the Treaty of Westphalia was signed. Calvinism was now recognized along with Lutheranism and Catholicism as a legitimate religion; and the Holy Roman Empire was politically more fragmented than ever before, as the *Kleinstaaterei*, the small German states and city-states, and more powerful states such as Bavaria, Saxony and Brandenburg, gained virtual autonomy within the empire. Even the Protestant son of the 'Winter King', now back from his service with Charles I of England, was made a Palatine prince with a seat on the Electoral council, now expanded to eight members. Fragmented and weakened; but the imperial structure remained the same, at least on paper.

The Thirty Years War encouraged European states to embrace the Balance of Power view of European affairs that would dominate for the next two centuries – and to recognize the destructiveness of war. In the eighteenth century, European wars tended to be fought on a limited basis by small armies engaged in carefully controlled battles with a minimum of bloodshed and a maximum of negotiation.

CHAPTER FIVE

From Desolation to Enlightenment, 1648–1789

The century and a half following the Thirty Years War was a time of recovery and redefinition in matters social, political and cultural, an era when new realities and new ideas were taking shape. It was the last great age of German particularism, which would end with the birth of the first real manifestations of a cultural, linguistic and ethnic German nationalism.

Germany Devastated

The war cost Germany nearly two-thirds of its population. Among the worst examples were Augsburg, reduced from 80,000 to 18,000 (143 of its citizens paid up to 100 guilders in taxes in 1617 but only 36 paid taxes at all in 1661), and the duchy of Württemberg, from 400,000 to 48,000 with more than 41,000 houses and barns destroyed. Elsewhere, Mark Brandenburg lost up to 60 per cent of its farms, Potsdam, Spandau and the town of Brandenburg lost 40 to 60 per cent of their populations, and Urach 75 per cent. In Stendal 2,980 children were born between 1600 and 1610, but only 969 in the 1670s. Meanwhile, mercenary soldiers roamed the countryside as brigands, and many Germans, uprooted by war, took to crime as a way of life. The decline of peasant rights that had begun in the sixteenth century continued, save in Bavaria where the scarcity of peasant workers forced the nobility to extend to those that were available more freedoms and a bigger share of agricultural profits. In Hohenzollern Brandenburg on the other hand, serfdom was reinstated in fact and in law after 1653. Many peasants simply fled to Poland in hopes of an improved status and way of life.

The war became a subject for literature and music. In *Simplicissimus* Hans Jacob Christoffel von Grimmelshausen depicts the life of a man who, driven from his home by plundering soldiers, becomes variously an imperial officer, a simple musketeer, a mercenary captain, a pilgrim, a traveller, a gigolo, and so on and so on, until he ends as a hermit on an island; clearly, man can live in harmony with God only if he turns his back on mankind and the depraved world around him. Dresden court *Kappellmeister* Heinrich Schütz experienced the war as both child and man, and composed such religiously inspired works as *Kleine Geistliche Konzerte,* which reflects his repudiation of a war that caused disease, famine and poverty and turned the Dresden court chapel into a virtual rubble heap.

The Ebbing of the Imperial Tide

In 1648 the empire covered nearly 700,000 square kilometres, but its power was diminished. There was no cultural or administrative centre: the Diet met in Regensburg, the Imperial Chancery in Mainz, and the *Reichskammergericht* (High Court of Justice) in Speyer, and after 1693, in Wetzler. Emperors were elected and crowned in Frankfurt, after which they resided in Vienna. The Habsburgs now saw their role as Austrian, Bohemian and Hungarian rulers as more important than that of being Holy Roman Emperors. The family court Chancery in Vienna now played a larger role in their affairs than did the Chancery in Mainz, which had the affect of reducing imperial authority and efficiency while increasing that of major principalities. When the Holy Roman Empire was abolished in 1806, 6,000 lawsuits were still pending before the *Reichskammergericht,* some dating from the sixteenth century. Also, the imperial army – beyond troops provided by allies and territorial princes under special circumstances – existed more on paper than in reality, and the income states were supposed to provide steadily shrank. In 1750 it was 58,000 gulden, a mere half of what the emperor had requested of the Imperial Diet. Imperial responsibilities were paid for largely out of Habsburg family pockets. That too undercut territorial commitments to the Empire, as did religious division that diminished imperial cohesiveness. Meanwhile, river trade was dominated after 1648 by the

English, Dutch, Danes and Swedes, who controlled the mouths of the Rhine, Elbe, Oder and Weser; and the some 300 petty principalities within the Empire imposed such tariffs upon river trade passing through their territories that it was rendered virtually ineffective.

Sweden, France and the Treaty of Westphalia

Sweden and France dominated making the Treaty of Westphalia. The latter took Habsburg possessions in Alsace plus the bishoprics of Metz, Toul and Verdun, which France had held since 1552, and the former took western Pomerania and the bishoprics of Bremen and Verden. They also imposed giving the German principalities, both large and small, a voice in all imperial decision-making, the right to coin their own money, maintain their own armies, and make alliances on their own with foreign powers. The Hohenzollerns of Brandenburg especially profited from this last provision, for it strengthened their position in the Prussian-Austrian rivalry of the eighteenth and nineteenth centuries over who should be the ruling power in Germany. Sweden and France also were given a voice in all important future decisions of the Imperial Diet, and guaranteed that the Empire would continue to exist. (Sweden later withdrew from this commitment, but Russia signed on as a guarantor in 1779.) The Rhenish Confederation was formed in 1654 composed of western German states, both Catholic and Protestant, and Sweden and France, to make the treaty work. It lasted until 1668, when Louis XIV (1638–1715) began asserting France as the dominant force in Europe.

The Victory of the Princes

Territorial princes now were looked to for leadership more than were the Habsburgs. It was the victory of particularism, so to speak, and they asserted their enhanced degree of independence by forming their own armies and bureaucracies, increasing the rights and powers of the nobility at the expense of the lower classes, and imposing royal absolutism upon all of their subjects; this while sitting in the Imperial Diet, which by its nature denied absolute power even to emperors.

PRINCES AND POWER

Louis XIV was the architect of applied royal absolutism, and the role model for German princes, whether they were rulers of major states such as Bavaria, Saxony and Brandenburg-Prussia, or petty states like the Archbishopric of Trier and the Electorate of Hannover, spelt 'Hanover' in England, of which the electors were kings beginning in 1714. German absolutist regimes, whether Catholic or Protestant, made 'Reason of State' – the interests of the State above all else – the sole principle upon which to base policy. Power was everything; the rights of the people, for which many Germans had died during the religious wars, were nothing. The social divide had never been wider. It was expressed in rigid class separation – even at royal balls nobles and burghers danced the *minuet* separated by a rope or a railing – and in the majesty and splendour of nobles and princes, who imitated the French in every way possible. German princes built versions of Versailles, spoke French at court, and emulated French *haute couture*. Elector Johann Georg II of Saxony maintained an opera house and orchestra with full-time conductors and Italian composers; in 1684 a French opera with ballet was performed for the court in Württemberg; it was obligatory for the sons of princes and high nobles to do a 'grand tour' of Versailles; and French fashion became the standard east of the Rhine, and French money wielded considerable influence in German politics. The princes also now included Jews at court, who 'played a vital part in the financial and business affairs of all the more important German rulers.' Among these was Joseph Süss-Oppenheimer at the court of Duke Karl Alexander of Württemberg (1689–1737), whose career Veit Harlan distorted in his 1941 Nazi anti-Semitic propaganda film, *Jud Süss*.

Francophilia had its critics, of course. Satirist Hans Michael Moscherosch wrote such lines as: 'Are you German? And you wear your hair like a Frenchman? Why do you wear that silly French kind of a beard? Is nothing good enough for you that is made in your own country, you despisers and traitors of your fatherland?' And journalist Johann Pezzl belittled the petty princes:

> There sits many a princeling upon a throne who would not be competent to rule over twelve chickens: but he wants to shine . . . to remain in step with

the grand princes; must have his own cooks, horses, dogs; his own viziers and troops, even if the entire army consists of four grenadiers, six musketeers, and two cavalrymen – and in order to bring all this into being, he fleeces his small herd of serfs mercilessly.

Pezzl might have added that 'fleecing the serfs' was not always sufficient to pay for all of this. Landgrave Frederick II of Hesse-Kassel (1760–1785), for example, sold 17,000 Hessian soldiers to Britain to fight against the Americans in their War of Independence, for which he received six million pounds. Many of the soldiers chose not to return to Germany when the war was over.

Absolutist Society

The princes also emulated Louis XIV as absolutists by keeping their subjects busy with endless festivals and social entertainments. Wrote Kurt Reinhardt: 'Marriages, baptisms, coronations, receptions, military victories offered a variety of occasions for colourful parades, processions, fireworks, ballets, masquerades and multiform other theatrical and musical divertissement.' Nobles were encouraged to engage in winter sleigh parties and carnivals, and in the summer, open air encampments (*Lustlager*) with ballets, concerts, military displays, and variations on the English sport of fox hunting. Some historians suspect that this endless plethora of activity may have created among princes a secret longing for solitude, which may explain such palace or castle names as 'Sans Souci' and 'Eremitage.'

THE NOBILITY

The urban nobility, both old nobles and urban patricians, were more inclined to participate in this life-style than were country nobles. The old nobles sat only with their own class at the theatre, had their own pews and burial vaults in church, and shunned education although they sent their sons to university, where they sat apart from commoners at lectures, save for learning to ride, fence, dance, play cards, carve at the dinner table, pay compliments, and behave properly at court balls. They did not consort with urban patricians such as merchants, military officers and state officials of common ancestry since their wealth often derived from trade, a 'dishonourable' occupation, and their titles, received from territorial princes or the emperor, were of recent derivation. The Old Limpurg Society in Frankfurt-am-Main would accept only members who could prove eight noble ancestors.

Again Reinhardt: country nobles, in particular those in the northeast, 'often differed little in appearance and work from their peasants.' They lived in timber and brick houses, castles in name but hardly in appearance, took little interest in anything beyond hunting, local affairs, and shooting parties, attended church on Sunday, acted weekly as local magistrates, and drank excessively, mostly beer and spirits of their own making. Their culture was maintaining their honour, which meant fighting duels and serving as military officers in time of war.

Meanwhile, fashion became increasingly important as a standard of place within this class-conscious, absolutist society. For men a periwig with curls flowing over neck and shoulder, a richly embroidered vest over ruffled shirt with necktie and cuffs of lace, silk stockings, buckled high-heeled shoes, and, of course, when in the street, an elaborate three-cornered hat and a rapier suspended from a wide cloth draped over the shoulder. For women a dress with richly pleated multiple skirts, train, lace embroidery and ribbons over a hooped petticoat known as the *Hühnerkorb* (chicken coop); the top was distinguished by a tiny waist and plunging neckline emphasized by a tight corset. Women's wigs were as elaborate as men's, and both genders wore exotic perfumes. This was made necessary by the virtual disappearance of bathing and personal hygiene. The public bath, so popular in the fifteenth century, was long since passé and, along with swimming in ponds and rivers, considered in bad taste if not actually immoral. Sexual misconduct on the other hand, was not, especially in the eighteenth century. In Reinhardt's words: 'Marriage ties were loosened to such a degree that adultery on the part of both sexes was considered a conventional rule rather than a deplorable exception.'

COFFEE, TEA OR TOBACCO?

Social norms particularly for the German middle class, took on a 'modern' look as the economy recovered in the late seventeenth and early eighteenth centuries. Germany became a market for new products brought from the Orient by English, Dutch and French trading companies: chocolate and coffee became as popular, or more so among burghers, as wine and beer. The first coffee shop opened in Hamburg in 1680, where gentlemen spent hours sipping coffee while reading the latest news sheet or playing billiards or cards. News weeklies (other than those produced by merchant princes such as the Fuggers) first appeared in Germany in 1609 in Strasbourg; the first daily, the *Leipziger Zeitung*, opened in 1660. By 1700 reading news sheets in coffee houses was a well-established habit, for the politically aware at any rate. Germany also participated in the tea trade – a substantial part of the 4,100,000 pounds of tea imported into Europe in 1721 went to Germany – and all social classes came to appreciate 'smoking and snuffing.' Tobacco growing was encouraged by the princes, and after 1700, was part of the economies of Alsace, the Palatinate, Hesse, Saxony, Thuringia, Brandenburg and Mecklenburg.

Imperial Wars

Absolutism and independence put some German princes on the side of Paris rather than Vienna when it came to imperial wars. Ferdinand II, who began the Thirty Years War, died in 1637 and was succeeded by Ferdinand III (1608–1657), who finished it. His 'timid and temporizing' son followed in 1658 as Leopold I (1640–1705), winning the Electors' support only by promising not to side with Spain against France. Leopold died in 1705 after having survived a half century of empire-threatening wars.

THE TURKISH PROBLEM

The Ottoman Turks were the first major difficulty, with Louis XIV's France not far behind. Since the mid-sixteenth century the empire had paid tribute to Ottoman rulers; this ended in 1606 when the Ottoman Sultan recognized the Holy Roman Emperor as 'the other world ruler,' after which Rudolf II (1552–1612) was able to strengthen the Habsburgs in the east. The Turks remained neutral during the Thirty Years War, owing to unrest at home caused by fractious janissaries. But in the

1660s quarrels over Transylvania caused Sultan Mohammed IV to launch an aggressive foreign policy that included invading Hungary in 1663 with a six-thousand man army, and subsequent rampages through Slovakia and Moravia. Clearly, the 'Turkish menace' had returned, and a Diet was summoned at Regensburg to grant aid to an imperial army. The Diet was now a 'closed corporation' of electors, princes and burghers. And, as the 'Turkish menace' remained a fixture in the minds of emperors and princes alike through the eighteenth century, it never again adjourned until Napoleon Bonaparte abolished the Holy Roman Empire in 1806.

SIEGE OF VIENNA

Though defeated by the empire in 1663, the Turks kept half of Hungary and two decades later were at it again, laying siege to Vienna. Brandenburg refused to support the empire, but Saxony, Hannover and Bavaria did, as did Poland, abandoning its friendship with France in response to impassioned pleas from both emperor and pope. This was a good thing for Vienna, for the siege was broken in 1683 by a Polish army under the command of King Jan Sobieski. The following year Leopold I agreed to French claims in Alsace so that the empire could concentrate on the Turks. Louis kept his end of the bargain and remained quiet while the imperial army drove the Turks out of Hungary and united it with Austria.

Breaking the siege of Vienna and Habsburg victories over the Turks elsewhere produced three results: first, further Ottoman expansion into Europe was curtailed; second, the empire was confirmed as Christian Europe's last line of defence against Islamic incursions (even as it had been under Charles the Great); and finally, in celebration of victory over the Turks, Viennese bakers produced a crescent-shaped bun in imitation of the symbol of Islam, which in time made its way to Paris. It is known throughout the world as the *croissant*.

THE FRENCH PROBLEM

Louis XIV was among the most manipulative European rulers. He lent French auxiliaries to aid the Habsburgs against the Turks in 1663; then in 1670 he aroused anti-Habsburg sentiments among Hungarian magnates. In 1668 he persuaded Leopold I to give France Habsburg possessions in western Europe, and then waged war against the Netherlands. Leopold considered this a betrayal, and declared war on France in 1674 as part of a coalition of the Netherlands, Spain, Sweden, Saxony, Brandenburg and Hannover. Louis also encouraged the Turkish assault on the empire in 1683. His ultimate ambition was French hegemony in Europe and disinheritance of the Habsburgs as Holy Roman Emperors; and in this, he had the sympathy of German princes who resented Habsburg power.

Wars, treaties and more wars followed involving France, the empire, the Netherlands, Sweden and Denmark: the 'War of Devolution,' the 'Dutch War,' and the 'War of the League of Augsburg.' James II of England favoured France and lent troops to Louis XIV, including the future Duke of Marlborough. Then in 1688 the English turned James out (the 'Glorious Revolution') over his insistence upon bringing England back to Rome, in favour of William of Orange, *Stadthalder* of Holland, who was crowned William III. William remained *Stadthalder* after becoming king of England, and brought his new realm into the continental wars. That probably was why he accepted the English throne in the first place.

THE GRAND COALITION

In 1688 France invaded and devastated the Palatinate, destroyed Heidelberg castle, and desecrated the tombs of past emperors in Speyer cathedral. The Grand Coalition then formed, now including Savoy, whose armies were under the most able command of Prince Eugen of Savoy, in whose honour an equestrian statue later was raised in front of the Hofburg in Vienna. War continued until the Treaty of Ryswick in 1697, which provided for territories to change hands on both sides. But that was hardly the end. In 1701 the 'War of the Spanish Succession' began, over whether a Habsburg or a Bourbon would succeed Charles II as king of Spain. Louis won the succession and his grandson ascended the throne as Philip V but lost the war, which dragged on until 1713, ending more or less with the Peace of Utrecht. Prince Eugen and the Duke of Marlborough were generals in this war whose brilliance in the field would not be equalled until the advent of Frederick the Great of

Prussia and Napoleon Bonaparte of France. Blenheim, Ramillies, Turin, Oudenard and Malplaquet were their most famous victories. Louis XIV died, in disgrace as many historians see it, in 1715; Leopold I had died in 1705, succeeded as emperor by Joseph I (1678–1711).

The German Mind in A Time of Troubles

After 1648 Germany seemed dominated by unreconciled opposites: rationalism and irrationalism, sensuality and spirituality, cynicism and mysticism, and stilted artificiality and the simplicity and harmony of nature. They applied to virtually every aspect of life and thought, shaping Germany one way or another into the nineteenth century.

RELIGION

Spiritual rethinking was a constant in this epoch; hardly surprising, given the century and a half of religious strife that preceded it. However, it was not radical departures so much as it was striving to find new and more relevant applications of long-standing religious traditions. Pietists rebelled against the practically minded, rationalist if you will, religion imposed upon Protestants by Luther and Melanchthon; Catholics stressed emotional and imaginative religion, which is to say a livelier version of mysticism. Procopius of Templic, a Capuchin, emphasized the yearnings of the individual soul in his hymns and pastoral poetry, while *Life of Christ* by Martin of Cochem, also a Capuchin, inspired a number of Passion Plays – not, however, that of Oberammergau in Bavaria, which is based upon much earlier texts.

Pietists also were mystics in their way, stressing subjective, personal and internal feelings regarding faith, advocating a personalized relationship between the Holy Spirit and the individual. While Pietism opposed the philosophic premises of Rationalism – 'I think, therefore I am,' as René Descartes phrased it in *Discourse on Method* – it nevertheless accepted that the divine could be understood empirically. Philip Jacob Spener's *Pia desideria* set Pietism in motion in Germany with its call for a 'practical' Christianity that penetrated the essence of human nature. The movement spread quickly, aided by such as August Hermann Francke's Pietist 'bible college,' opened in Leipzig in 1686, which inspired such enthusiasm among university students that city officials banned it. Elector Frederick III of Prussia (1657–1713) then brought Francke to Halle, convinced that Pietism would be of benefit to Junker military and civil service leaders. Pietists also were the first German immigrants to Pennsylvania colony in America, where their descendants would be known as 'Pennsylvania Dutch.'

Then there was Deism, an eighteenth-century conception of God that ran counter to virtually all existing Christian doctrines. Deists argued that God created the Universe, but then left it to look after itself, following fundamental laws of cause and affect. That applied to human beings as well, according to Hamburg theologian and Deist Hermann Samuel Reimarus, who were quite capable of directing their own affairs. This was 'natural' or objective religion which emphasized the human capacity to think. It was as removed from Catholicism and Pietism as could be imagined. Deism was the religion of Enlightenment intellectuals when they had religion, which in Germany included, among others, Lutherans Gotthold Ephraim Lessing (1729–1781) from Saxony, who published Reimarus' theologically critical *Wolfenbüttel-Fragmente*, and Immanuel Kant (1724–1804) of Königsburg.

Secret societies such as Freemasonry and its offshoot the 'Order of the Illuminati,' rejected religion altogether, except in Germany where they embraced belief in God and immortality. Freemasonry entered Germany in 1737 in Hamburg, where the first Grand Lodge was established. Frederick II of Prussia (1712–1786) and Emperor Joseph II of Austria (1741–1790) embraced Freemasonry, as did writers, philosophers and composers such as Lessing, Christoph Martin Wieland (1733–1813), Johann Gottfried Herder (1744–1803), Johann Gottlieb Fichte (1762–1814), Johann Wolfgang von Goethe (1749–1832), and Joseph Haydn (1732–1809). And of course Wolfgang Amadeus Mozart (1756–1791), whose comic opera *Die Zauberflöte* (Magic Flute) is an allegory of Freemasonry, full of Masonic symbols and rituals.

RATIONALISM AND ENLIGHTENMENT

Rationalism, derivative of both Humanism and Renaissance science, was the science of observation, description and experimentation (which need not lead to a particular conclusion, so long as that reached was logical, either inductively or deductively). It came into its own in the half century after the Thirty Years War and engaged German thinkers such as Samuel von Pufendorf (1632–1694) at the University of Heidelberg, and Gottfried Wilhelm Leibniz (1646–1716), first president of the Berlin science academy. Pufendorf argued in *De iure gentium et naturae* that human nature was the basis of all law and that human reason was its supreme authority. He also concluded in *The Christian Religion and its Relationship to Civic Life* that state absolutism was a good thing. This pleased Elector Frederick of Brandenburg so much that he made Pufendorf Privy Counsellor and Royal Prussian Historiographer.

Leibniz made his mark with *Monadology*, which depicted the world as 'a harmonically ordered system of monads – infinitely small, indivisible, and spiritual units, representing and reflecting the universe in varying and rising degrees of consciousness.' It also saw God mirrored in everything from minerals and plants to humans and pure spirits. Christian von Wolff popularized Leibniz's work at Halle University, until Pietists complained and King Frederick Wilhelm I (1688–1740) expelled him. Pietists notwithstanding, 'the principle of freedom in teaching' was proclaimed at Halle in 1711. After that Rationalism penetrated the curricula of schools across Protestant Germany. Students were to learn through 'practical applications, by experiment and demonstration.' Christien Weise, principal of the Gymnasium in Zittau, Saxony, was the leader in this regard.

In the eighteenth century, Rationalism gave way to the Enlightenment (*Die Aufklärung*), whose thinkers held that there is more to human nature than can be determined by pure reason, and that philosophical systems are not an end in themselves, but a means to an end with practical application. This was the point of *l'Encyclopédie* assembled by Denis Diderot and Jean d'Alembert in France. The Enlightenment was expressed through philosophy, literature, political theory, history, science and medicine, and in Germany, an expanding concern to improve the generally poor state of public education. Maria Theresa of Austria (1717–1780), for example, created a state committee to supervise the entire educational system. Leading representatives of the German Enlightenment included: Moses Mendelssohn (1729–1786), the Jewish grandfather of composer Felix Mendelssohn-Bartholdy and

Lessing's close friend; Lessing himself, author of *Nathan der Weise*, which clearly was inspired by Mendelssohn' life; Immanuel Kant, author of *Critique of Pure Reason* with emphasis on the ultimate subjectivity of knowledge; Friedrich Schiller (1759–1805), who repudiated preconceived standards for the study of history in *Ideas on the Philosophy of the History of Mankind*; and Friedrich Hahnemann (1755–1843), a Saxon physician whose *Organon of Practical Medicine* laid the foundations for homeopathic medicine. They and others had patrons the likes of Frederick II of Prussia, himself an author and composer, and Emperor Joseph II of Austria.

INTELLECTUAL WOMEN

Women now broke the traditional mode and found a place in the world of intellect as well. The 'scholarly woman' (*das gelehrte Frauenzimmer*) became a feature of German Baroque culture. Sophie Charlotte, a Hannoverian and the wife of Frederick I of Prussia, was close friends with Leibniz and mastered his work along with that of Descartes and Spinoza. Elizabeth Charlotte, from the Palatinate and married to the brother of Louis XIV of France, was noted for her originality, independence of mind, and keen observations on the frivolity of the

Dorothea Schlegel

society in which she lived. At the other end was Pietist Anna Maria Schurman (1607–1678) of Cologne, who reputedly mastered fourteen languages including the French in which she did her many writings. She had a keen interest in mathematics, history, philosophy and theology, as well as remarkable skills in wood carving, painting, etching and music. This was the age of the Salon in Germany as in France, where essays, poems, scientific treatises, satires and polemics were presented to sophisticated audiences. Salons increasingly were the domain of such intellectually, culturally and morally 'emancipated' women as Dorothea, daughter of Moses Mendelssohn and wife of Friedrich Schlegel, Carolina, wife of August Wilhelm Schlegel, Sara Levy and Amalie Beer. Levy and Beer were Jews who, unlike the Mendelssohn family, did not convert to Christianity.

Literature

The struggle – and choice – between Good and Evil, Heaven or Hell, and whether the individual could muster the will to choose, was essential to all German writers of this era, likely a reflection of ongoing struggles over religion and the devastation of seemingly endless wars. For example, Protestant Andreas Gryphius wrote gloomy sonnets portraying the transitory nature of earthly things, and a satiric play, *Horribilicribrifax*. All were the result, no doubt, of his having experienced the Thirty Years War as a youth.

THE SEVENTEENTH CENTURY

Some regard the Swabian Jacob Bidermann (1578–1639) as the best Jesuit playwright of the early Baroque period. His *Cenodoxus* had a Faustian theme; a self-styled 'superman' deals with the issues of life, death and judgment. It is said that several high-ranking courtiers were so moved by it that they altered their way of life entirely, and that the actor who played Cenodoxus became a Jesuit as the result of his experience. Other Catholic dramatists included Nicholas Avancini, a Jesuit from Tyrol, and Simon Rettenbacher, a Benedictine monk from Kremsmünster in Upper Austria. Among Protestants dramatists was the unschooled but brilliant Silesian shoemaker, Jacob

Böhme, whose work contemplated the relationship of God, mankind and the world. The drama of this era also necessitated new approaches in the art of stagecraft, theatrical architecture, stage design and stage decoration, requirements met first in Italy and then adapted to German theatre.

German novelists appeared at the same time as dramatists, and with similar themes. Daniel Casper von Lohenstein's hero in *Arminius* wins through by mastering the complexities of life. In *Assenat*, Philipp von Zesen depicts the Biblical Joseph establishing a 'planned economy' by reducing the people to serfdom, in an Egypt where royal despotism rests on a moral foundation. And *Roman Octavia* by Anton Ulrich, duke of Braunschweig, shows that the good are rewarded and the wicked punished – this theme was not exactly new.

THE EIGHTEENTH CENTURY

The often heavy seventeenth-century style now gave way to one lighter, more sentimental and thoughtful, and sometimes emotional. Christian Gellert, considered 'the most sensible of German men of letters,' stressed reason, sentiment and smooth elegance. Even Goethe appreciated the 'moral bases' of his writing, though he considered it mediocre in other regards. Ewald von Kleist was considered to be the most talented 'Anacreontic' poet, who wrote of an epicurean dream-world of wine, women and song. Christoph Martin Wieland was perhaps the most important German writer of the late eighteenth century, who evolved from a Pietistic sentimentalist into a sceptic with an eye for irony. He depicted 'a graceful and tolerant art of living' embodied in a refined humanism.

'STORM AND STRESS'

Then came 'Storm and Stress' (*Sturm und Drang*), a sentimentalist literary movement that carried into the early nineteenth century. It was inspired by Johann Georg Hamann's *Socratic Memoirs*, wherein an anti-hero is destined to tragedy and suffering for reasons beyond his control. The name derived from the title of a Maximilian Klinger play in which the hero rages about his 'lost generation' and prepares to volunteer for the American Revolution: 'I am going to take part in this campaign. . . .

There I can expand my soul, and if they do me the favour to shoot me down – all the better.' Herder, Schiller and Goethe were associated with the movement before they embraced Classicism; indeed Goethe's *The Sorrows of Young Werther* has been described as the standard for 'Storm and Stress' writers, many of whom ended their lives as 'dramatic suicides or poverty-stricken pariahs.' *Werther* also was an early example of the Romantic novel.

CLASSICISM

German writers of real depth left 'Storm and Stress' for Classicism, a movement predicated upon the forms of Greek antiquity. It sought an ideal for humanity to aspire to, and in the process, it might be argued, became difficult to distinguish from early German Romanticism. As a Classicist, Herder wrote *Letters for the Promotion of Humanity* and, in collaboration with Goethe and historian Justus Möser, *On German Arts and Customs*. Schiller (Goethe's close friend) protested against tyranny in *The Robbers*, celebrated the value of freedom of thought, self-sacrifice and loyalty in *Don Carlos*, and recognized history as the source for understanding the nature and destiny of humanity in *History of the Thirty Years' War*. Meanwhile, Goethe, born in Frankfurt-am-Main but the cultural icon of Weimar, is the most celebrated of the Classicists. His works include *Goetz von Berlichingen*, the story of a true German folk hero, *Egmont* and *Iphigenia*, inspired by the ideal of classical form, and *Wilhelm Meister's Apprenticeship* in which the aspirations of a talented youth are shaped. Goethe's most famous work is *Faust,* begun in the 1780s and completed only in 1831, the year before his death. Its point is the struggle between good and evil, at once a simple yet monstrously complicated issue.

Architecture, Sculpture and Painting

The arts generally were subsumed under the headings 'Baroque' for the seventeenth century, and 'Rococo' for the middle and later eighteenth. The former combined the spiritual form and natural fervour of the Gothic and Renaissance; the latter displayed their light-hearted degeneration. Princes continued, as they had in the Renaissance, to patronize artists, for to do so was to display power and sophistication and give the impression of having taste. Patronage often included giving whole cities, e.g. Mannheim and Karlsruhe, an architectural uniformity that replicated the absolutist regimes of the princes who ruled over them.

ARCHITECTURE

Germans copied the French and Italian models initially produced in Germany by French and Italian architects. In Munich, Agostino Barello of Bologna designed the Theatinerkirche, and François de Cuvilliés, a Walloon, the Residenztheatre, the Amilienburg and the interior of the Wittelsbach Palace. The style generally was spacious, illuminated by light from hidden sources, and with elaborate statues of St Mary and other sacred and secular women, surrounded by carvings of emanating rays of light. Rococo angels sometimes were laughing tots, coquettish girls or even effeminate men – the latter being the case with Ignaz Günther's 'Guardian Angel' in the Munich Bürgersaal. Church interiors emphasized white and gold, pillars decorated with angelic figures, and biblical scenes that made ceilings appear as 'the very gates of heaven.' White exteriors with various kinds of trim also was commonplace, but hardly new; St Severus parish church in Boppard-am-Rhine, for example, is white with brown trim, and it was built in the twelfth century. Secular buildings like town halls and palaces featured arched windows, decorative stonework, fountains, pools and elaborate, formally organized gardens.

German architects soon mastered the French and Italian style, and were busy across the empire. In Austria, Fischer von Erlach designed St Charles Church, Lucas von Hildebrandt Belvedere Castle, and Jakob Prandauer the Monasteries Melk and St Florian. In Bavaria, Joseph Effner built Nymphenburg and Schleissheim Castles, and Dominikus Zimmerman the churches Steinhausen and Wies (sometimes described as the most famous example of rococo in all of Germany). Michael Fischer designed the Zwiefalten and Ottobeuren churches in Swabia, while in Berlin, Andreas Schlüter was responsible for Berlin Castle. Georg Bähr and Daniel Pöppelmann worked in Dresden – Pöppelmann built the Zwinger there in a city that was a monument to both

Zwinger, Dresden by Daniel Pöppelmann

Baroque and Rococo architecture, until it was largely destroyed in the Second World War. Rococo connecting with the Classical is well represented by the stucco decorations, ceiling frescos, and white walls and columns trimmed in gold of St Ignaz church in Mainz, built by Johann Peter Jäger. So too the Abbey Church of Ottobeuren, begun in 1737 by Michael Fischer.

ART

Many critics saw German painting going downhill after the great age of Dürer and Holbein, certainly second rate compared to Baroque artists in Spain, Italy, Holland and England. Still, it provided the colourful, bright and radiant interior decoration suitable as context for Baroque and Rococo architects and sculptors. Portraiture, mostly realist with a romantic bent, was much sought after by princes, nobles, bishops and abbots, who wanted their image projected in heroic, glorious or sometimes contemplative, form. Johann Georg Ziesenis' royal portraits were exemplary in this regard. Meanwhile, goldsmiths, weavers and porcelain makers supplied churches, palaces and castles with elaborate and fanciful products, for example Johann Joachim Kändler's porcelain 'Scaramouche and Colombine.' Dresden, Meissen, Berlin, Vienna,

Ludwigsburg, Frankenthal and Nymphenberg became famous for their porcelain factories.

A Great Age of German Music

Nowhere was Germany better served in the Age of Absolutism than in the composition and performance of music. In that era, German music evolved from Baroque 'grandiose effects and highly ornamented details within elaborate structures and designs,' into the 'delicate, refined, and with aristocratic polish' style of the Classical.

JOHANN SEBASTIAN BACH

Born in Eisenach, Thuringia, into a family of professional musicians, Bach (1685–1750) became 'the towering genius' of musical composition in Germany and, indeed, in Europe. He was also notable for fathering twenty children, some of whom survived to achieve renown of their own as performers and composers. Bach was, variously, organist, cantor and church music director in Leipzig, court organist and concertmaster in Weimar, *Kapellmeister* at the court of Prince Leopold of Anhalt-Cöthen, honorary court composer for the Catholic Elector of Saxony, and a guest at the court of Frederick II of Prussia, where one of his sons was *Kapellmeister*. In his lifetime Bach produced literally hundreds of pieces of choral, orchestral, chamber, piano and organ composition, such as *The St John Passion* and *The St Matthew Passion* for choir, *The Brandenburg Concerti* for orchestra, and *The Well-Tempered Clavier* for piano. His last composition, *The Art of the Fugue,* was completed just before he died.

GEORG FRIEDRICH HÄNDEL

From Halle in Saxony, Händel (1685–1759) was Bach's contemporary and has been described as 'the foremost representative of a festive, majestic, and fully seasoned Baroque style.' He was as German as Bach in his compositions, despite spending a significant portion of his life in London. Händel began his conducting and composing career in Hamburg where he also became, in a bizarre way, a duellist. One night, he conducted the orchestra for Johann Mattheson's opera *Cleopatra,* in which the composer also sang the role of Antony. After Antony committed suicide and would not return to the stage, Mattheson decided to take over the conducting. Händel said no, Mattheson challenged him, and they duelled. No harm done; Mattheson's sword struck Händel's button and split in two. As Milton Cross put it, 'had it struck a more vulnerable spot, Handel's career would have ended before it began.'

After moving to London, Händel anglicized the spelling of his name to 'Handel.' Some of his most famous works were composed there: *Watermusic,* an orchestral piece for King George I; the oratorios *Israel in Egypt* and *Messiah,* the latter first performed in Dublin, Ireland in 1741; the opera *Radamisto*; and the orchestral *Concerto Grosse No. 6,* which compares well with Bach's *Brandenburg Concerti.* Altogether, he composed forty operas, thirty oratorios and Passions, and many pieces of orchestral and keyboard music over his long career. Handel (the English version) is buried in Westminster Abbey, and several London streets and squares are named after him.

CHRISTOPHE WILLIBALD GLUCK

German opera began effectively with Heinrich Schütz's *Daphne,* but was essentially Italian until the mid–eighteenth century when Christophe Willibald Gluck (1714–1787) changed it into something more serious and substantive; which is to say, more German. It did not take immediately. 'I have considered it my special task to try to achieve a beautiful simplicity and to avoid the mistake of parading clever technical tricks at the expense of clarity,' he wrote, and applied the concept to such works as *Orfeo et Euridice,* and *Alceste* (dedicated to Leopold, duke of Toscana and future emperor). However, these operas were failures when performed in Germany. Gluck's first triumph was in Paris in 1774 with *Iphigénie en Aulide*. All the same, with Gluck's work, a German concept of opera was born, and soon would take root back home.

JOSEPH HAYDN

German music embraced the Classical after 1760, beginning largely in Vienna. Joseph Haydn led the way in symphonic and chamber music which contained a 'childlike optimism ... revealing symbolically the placid beauty of the Austrian landscape and expressing the simple piety of the Austrian folk spirit.' His oratorios, though much influenced by Händel's style, included the naturalism that was part of the Classical mode.

WOLFGANG AMADEUS MOZART

Haydn's contemporary was Wolfgang Amadeus Mozart, the child genius from Salzburg. His father, Leopold Mozart, was a distinguished composer in his own right, and certainly encouraged his son. Wolfgang became interested in the harpsichord at age three, composed for it at age five, performed for the emperor at age six after which Empress Maria Theresa dandled him on her knee, had a Europe-wide reputation as a performer by age ten, and composed his first opera, *Mitridate, Rè di Ponto,* when he was fourteen. He never slowed down or looked back. When he died at age 35, Mozart had created 600 works, including symphonies, concerti, choral (the *Requiem* being among the greatest), quartets, piano pieces, and, of course, opera, both dramatic (*Don Giovanni*) and comic (*Cosi fan Tutti*).

The Beginning of the End for the Holy Roman Empire

There was a final round of imperial wars in the eighteenth century, which pitted the empire, or more precisely the Habsburg emperors, against Prussia. At stake was who would dominate the empire and under what conditions. This struggle was at once German and European, for both Prussia and the empire looked for allies not only among the German principalities, but among the British, French and Russians. Of course, it never would have happened but for the on-going battle between imperial centrism and territorial particularism, out of which Prussia emerged in the eighteenth century as the most particularist of all.

CHAPTER SIX

The Coming of Age of Prussia, 1640–1786

Between 1640 and 1786 Prussia grew from an imperial electoral principality into one of the five Powers that dominated European international affairs in the second half of the eighteenth century – and made the Habsburgs fear for their very existence.

The Origins of Prussia

For centuries, Prussia was in three parts: the Margraviate of Brandenburg between the Elbe and Oder, East Prussia beyond the Vistula, begun by the Order of Teutonic Knights in the thirteenth century, and Rhenish Prussia, a handful of petty principalities in the Rhine region which were absorbed by Brandenburg, a process begun in the 1400s and completed in 1866. Brandenburg was the oldest and most important, dating from the tenth century when the North March and the bishopric of Brandenburg began. It became the Margraviate of Brandenburg in the twelfth century, with capital and Margraves' residence at Tangermünde. As border rulers, the Margraves were more independent of imperial authority than other princes, and placed greater emphasis on military organization than might be typical in western Germany, in order to keep their conquered subjects under control. Over three centuries, beginning with the Ascanian, Albert the Bear (1100?–1170), in 1133 the Margraves tripled the size of their original territory, absorbed or drove out the Slav Wends, became imperial electors, and founded the *Junkertum* (landed nobility), the backbone of social power in Brandenburg. The 'twin towns' of Berlin and Cölln were founded between 1237 and 1244, on opposite banks of the River Spree. They were a transfer point between river and road for Hanseatic League trade goods in transit, and Berlin became the Margraviate seat in 1488. Meanwhile, housewife, lay mystic and anchoress Dorothea von Montau (1347–1394) was canonized in the fifteenth century as Prussia's first female saint. While the Margraves 'Germanized' Prussia by bringing in settlers from the Netherlands and Rhineland, it never lost its Slavic roots. 'Berlin' and 'Cölln' are both German versions of Slavic names, as are 'Quitzow' and 'Rochow'; and the name von Bülow, famous in the nineteenth and early twentieth centuries, derives from 'Bulowski.'

EASTERN PRUSSIA

The Teutonic Knights conquered and Christianized the Prusi, made war against the Lithuanians at Durbenforone, and (unsuccessfully) against the Grand Duchy of Muscovy. They founded Königsberg and made war (also unsuccessfully) against the Poles, who crushed them in 1410 at Tannenberg. The Peace of Thorn followed, in which the knights agreed to limits beyond which they could not expand. The Hanseatic Free City of Danzig then rose against them and claimed Polish protection. This led to the second Battle of Tannenberg (1466), and the division of Prussia between the East under Teutonic rule, and the West under Poland – ironically, almost the exact divide imposed by the Versailles Treaty in 1919.

Historians have viewed the Teutonic Knights very differently. For example, in 1915, J. A. R. Marriott depicted them as pious crusaders for civilization against the heathen Slavs; but in 1963, Norman Cantor described them as 'fundamentally a state in the guise of a religious order' which 'indiscriminately attacked Christians and heathens in eastern Europe.'

THE HOHENZOLLERNS

In 1412 Brandenburg passed into the hands of Frederick of Zollern (1371–1440), the Swabian Burgrave of Nuremberg. He came well heeled and well armed (including a large cannon allegedly named 'Big Bertha,' lent him by a relative and member of the Teutonic order), which was a good thing because the noble houses of Quitzow,

Rochow, Putlitze and Holtzendorf had no sympathy for the 'Toy of Nuremberg,' and revolted. Four years of war followed before these rebels were subdued. In 1417 Emperor Sigismund invested Frederick as Elector of Brandenburg and soon after that gave him suzerainty over Pomerania. Frederick was among the first in this family to add 'Hohen' (high) to the name, becoming thus Frederick of Hohenzollern.

CONSOLIDATION

Over the next two centuries the Hohenzollern dynasty consolidated and expanded control over what in time would become the Kingdom of Prussia. The dynastic principle was established in 1473 by a decree of Albert 'Achilles' (1414–1486). In this period, for whatever reason, Hohenzollern Electors liked to be known by heroic, or in this case barbaric, names. Hohenzollern lands could not be divided, but must be held by the law of primogeniture, which was a departure from German legal tradition. Meanwhile, by nibbling, negotiating, and making war, the Electors added towns and territories to their domain, closing many of the geographical gaps which in 1417 had made Brandenburg resemble an unfinished jigsaw puzzle. These included, among others, Lychen and Himmelpfort in 1442, Kottbus and Peitz in 1445, Wernigerode in 1449, Schwedt, Locknitz and Vierraden in 1472, Garz in 1479, Krossen, Zullichau, Sommerfeld and Bobersburg in 1482, Zossen in 1490, Ruppin in 1524, Havelberg and Lebus in 1548, and Buskow and Storkow in 1571. The Hohenzollerns inherited Mecklenburg in 1442, Grimnitz in 1529, and Liegnitz, Wohlau and Brieg, all in Silesia, in 1537.

Margrave Albert of Ansbach (1490–1568), a Hohenzollern, was elected Grand Master of the Teutonic Order in 1511. This placed East Prussia at least nominally under Hohenzollern control. Albert secularized the Order, Lutheranized its lands, and set in motion a process of establishing legal connections between Brandenburg and Prussia. The two were united at least in principle, when the right of succession in Prussia passed to the House of Hohenzollern in 1618. Now the Electors were vassals to both the empire (Mecklenburg) and the King of Poland (Prussia). And in 1610, the Hohenzollerns acquired at least partial control over the Rhenish states of Jülich-Cleves, Mark and

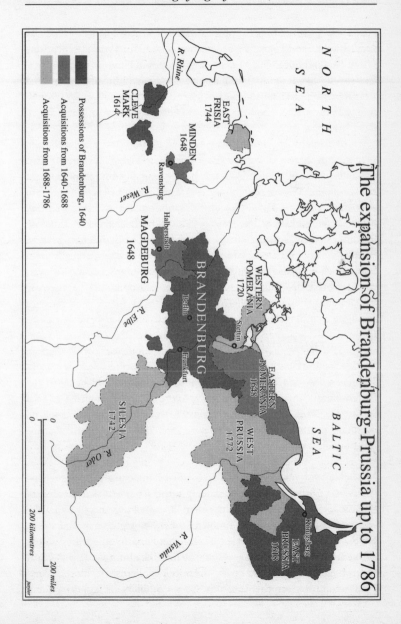

The expansion of Brandenburg-Prussia up to 1786

NORTH SEA

BALTIC SEA

R. Rhine

CLEVE MARK 1614

EAST FRISIA 1744

MINDEN 1648

Ravensburg

R. Weser

MAGDEBURG 1648

Halberstadt

BRANDENBURG

Berlin

Frankfurt

WESTERN POMERANIA 1720

Stettin

EASTERN POMERANIA 1648

SILESIA 1742

R. Oder

WEST PRUSSIA 1772

R. Vistula

Königsberg

EAST PRUSSIA 1618

Possessions of Brandenburg, 1640

Acquisitions from 1640–1688

Acquisitions from 1688–1786

0   200 kilometres

0   200 miles

jupiter

Ravensburg, while their territories in the north and east doubled. By 1650 Brandenburg was 697 square miles, and East Prussia 672. Ironically, Brandenburg was the smaller in population: about 260,000 compared to Prussia's 400,000, not least because Brandenburg suffered far more from the devastation of the Thirty Years War. Moreover, Königsberg was a major commercial centre well beyond any city in Brandenburg.

Hohenzollern expansion was complicated in the sixteenth and seventeenth centuries by the Reformation. Swabian Hohenzollerns remained Catholic, some Rhenish possessions split between Catholic and Protestant, and Brandenburg and Prussia split between Lutherans and supporters of Calvinist Elector Johann Sigismund. Here an irony intrudes: the nobles of the Prussian Estates did not relish the idea of submitting to a Calvinist master, nor did those of Brandenburg; most Prussians were Lutherans, and in any case, the Electors were 'a foreign dynasty, alien in religion, institution and ideas.' And yet, the descendants of these dissident Prussian and Brandenburg nobles became the backbone of the Hohenzollern dynasty.

The Great Elector

Frederick Wilhelm (1620–1688), the 'Great Elector,' reigned from 1640 to 1688 and laid the foundations of what would become the Kingdom of Prussia. His role model was the France of Louis XIV. That was true of other German princes as well – only Frederick Wilhelm did it better, becoming 'one of the main representatives of princely absolutism' in Europe.

ELECTORAL ABSOLUTISM

The Great Elector established princely autocracy, reaffirmed serfdom – 'Where serfdom exists and is customary it must by all means remain' – and took away the political privileges of the noble Estates and urban guilds. This included a decree that only he, and no longer the Estates, could summon the *Landtag* (Diet). When they protested, the Great Elector entered Königsburg and imposed the decree with an army. Meanwhile, he softened the blow to the nobility by granting them special status within society, the army and state bureaucracy, and economic privileges denied to the lower orders. Frederick Wilhelm like Louis XIV regarded himself as ruling 'by divine right' and would tolerate no rival to his authority. Having said that, it should be noted that he also worked at increasing the prosperity of the state and its people, claiming in an edict of 1686 that 'trade and shipping are the foremost pillars of a state.' Emulating the Dutch, he started a mercantile marine and attempted the founding of an overseas empire on the Guinean Coast of West Africa. The Dutch were not flattered by this 'emulation' and went out of their way to disrupt the Great Elector's efforts.

HUGUENOTS

Frederick Wilhelm also promoted religious toleration, including for Jews, at least up to a point; after all, he was a Calvinist in a predominately Lutheran principality. It was in his reign that the French Huguenots were introduced into Brandenburg, and became one of its most important minority groups. In 1685 Louis XIV revoked the Edict of Nantes, a decree of religious toleration, and the Elector responded with the Edict of Potsdam, which opened his realm to French Protestant refugees. And they came, especially to Berlin. The Huguenots were industrious, hard-working, innovative in trade, commerce and agriculture – and learned to their chagrin that the soil of Brandenburg was more barren than biblical Moab. Hence the name of the Moabit district of Berlin, where they tried with limited success to cultivate a mulberry tree. First World War eastern front commander General Hermann von François was descended from a Huguenot family.

FOUNDING BRANDENBURG-PRUSSIA

Frederick Wilhelm shaped his foreign policy according to the interests of his dynasty and lands. He made war regularly: for and against the empire, France, Sweden and Poland. His single most important military effort was when he fought for Sweden against Poland, 'winning renown for himself and his small army in the victorious battle for Warsaw,' and then switched sides and fought for Poland. The result was the Peace of Oliva in 1660, which though it did not win Swedish

Pomerania, did give the Duchy of Prussia independence from Poland. Thus was born Brandenburg-Prussia, the most powerful German state within the empire, and for all practical purposes, its most independent. War with Sweden resumed a decade later; he defeated the Swedes at Fehrbellin in 1675, and drove them out of East Prussia. Heinrich von Kleist recalled that victory in his play *The Prince of Homburg*, written in 1810, four years after Napoleon humiliated the Prussians at Jena. When England and the Empire formed the Grand Coalition against France, Frederick Wilhelm promised Brandenburg support, but died before that war actually began.

THE PRUSSIAN ARMY

A military system of discipline, reliability and superior fighting capability, inspired by the military system overseen by Louis XIV's war secretary, the marquis of Louvois, may have been the Great Elector's single most important contribution to the future history of Germany. The undisciplined rabble he inherited from the Thirty Years War simply would not do. Severe discipline was imposed which included warnings from clergy from the pulpit in daily religious services and from commanders addressing troops, that any act of plundering or harm done to an innocent civilian would be punished by hanging, and this in spite of Frederick Wilhelm being opposed to whipping or executing soldiers for desertion, punishments which became part of the military system under his successors. All recruitment was carried out in the Elector's name with artisans and peasants exempt from conscription. Emphasis was on recruitment of young men who would see the military as a profession as respectable as other professions and trades. This 'new army' remained small; even in wartime it rarely exceeded 30,000 men.

The Great Elector created the regiments and appointed their colonels, who in turn appointed subordinate officers. Louvois' model was again the model for a cadet corps to train future officers. Of course, Frederick Wilhelm did not trust the nobility entirely, so he balanced those drawn from the nobility (the base pool for the officer corps) with others who were not of old noble origin. It is said, though it is not provable, that his most outstanding commander, Field Marshal von

Derfflinger, was an Austrian of peasant stock – or perhaps he was a tailor's son. In any case, Frederick Wilhelm regularly met 'in council,' so to speak, with his senior officers. Historian H. W. Koch depicts these meetings as the origin of the Prussian General Staff.

BERLIN

Berlin and Cölln merged into Berlin in 1432. Elector Frederick II (1505–1571) built the first palace there, and the thought likely occurred to the burghers that Berlin was no longer a free city, but a seat of administrative power; in short, a capital. True enough. Elector Joachim II's palace, built between 1538 and 1540, was far more elaborate than Frederick's and was decorated by Lucas Cranach the Younger. Still, capital though it was, Berlin lagged culturally and morally behind the likes of Dresden, Munich, Nuremberg and Augsburg; in 1603 Elector Joachim Frederick issued a decree against the 'flourishing trade in prostitution and widespread fornication' in Berlin. And, when the Thirty Years War began, Elector Georg Wilhelm moved his court to far-away Königsberg. Just as well; Berlin had become part of the battlefield. General von Wallenstein made the Elector's palace his headquarters, and the general mayhem of war mixed with bouts of plague, reduced the population from 9,000 to 6,000.

It was for Frederick Wilhelm, the Great Elector, to begin restoration of Berlin after the ravages of war – and to turn it into a garrison town, which did not please the burghers. No Prussian ruler ever again would claim any capital other than Berlin. Under Frederick Wilhelm, new buildings went up and street lights were installed, an urban police force was created and two new urban districts, Friedrichswerder and Dortheenstadt, were established. And, one of Berlin's most impressive sights was laid out, the Avenue Unter den Linden. Andreas Schlüter's stature of the Great Elector stands today in the courtyard of the Charlottenburg Palace.

The King in Prussia

Elector Frederick III (1688–1713) sided with Britain and the Empire in the War of the Grand Coalition, and sent Prussian soldiers to fight at

Blenheim and in other famous battles. Yet he did not receive the respect from the Coalition that he thought he deserved; on the other hand, he achieved royal status for Brandenburg-Prussia.

FIRST ELECTOR FREDERICK III...

Uninterested in politics, Frederick left running the state to his first ministers, successively Eberhard von Danckelmann and Kolbe von Wartenberg, while he lived a life of indolent – and expensive – Baroque and Rococo luxury and display. His son and grandson later would depict him as wasteful and frivolous, though both approved of the royal throne he achieved for Prussia. Frederick also supported the intellectual and cultural interests of his second wife, Electress Sophia Charlotte of Hannover, which included founding the University of Halle in 1694, the first at which lectures were given in German, the Academy of Arts in 1696, and the Academy of Science in 1700. Its first president was her friend, the philosopher Gottfried Leibniz. Sophia's death-bed statement was a perfect epitaph for Frederick's reign: 'Do not grieve for me. I shall soon satisfy my curiosity about the cause of things, and give the king an opportunity for a wonderful funeral display.'

...THEN KING FREDERICK I

Frederick felt left behind: William of Orange became King of England in 1688, and Frederick Augustus of Saxony King of Poland in 1697, while he remained merely an Elector. And there was the etiquette factor. Kings reclined in what the French called *la chaise*, a chair with arms and a back, while lesser princes, including Electors, were consigned to *le tabouret*, a three-legged stool. In 1700, Frederick applied to Emperor Leopold I for kingship. And he got it, in return for military aid against France and accepting the designation king *in,* rather than *of,* Prussia so as not to offend the Poles, who still ruled West Prussia. Frederick was crowned in Königsburg on 18 January 1701, in a lavish display paid for by a special coronation tax and a 100,000 thaler donation from the Brandenburg Estates. He dressed in scarlet, placed the crown on his own head, picked up the orb and sceptre, and went to the queen's room and crowned her. A church service followed, and then a coronation dinner. In March Frederick returned to Berlin; the entire city was illuminated, and his entry celebrated by pealing church bells and artillery salutes. He was anointed by two Protestant bishops. Catholics were not even informed of his coronation. Still the Church got even: until 1787, the papal calendar listed the Kings of Prussia only as Margraves of Brandenburg. *And pic*

'DRILL SERGEANT' FREDERICK WILHELM I

Frederick Wilhelm I (1713–1740) was the opposite of his father. He focused on military expansion, and wore only military dress. 'I find pleasure in nothing in this world save the army,' he said, and began each day by parading his troops. Frederick Wilhelm established a military academy in Berlin for training officers, increased the military budget, increased discipline and punishment, and made military recruitment a national pastime. By 1740 he had created a formidable army of 80,000 life-time soldiers, including Prince Leopold of Anhalt-Dessau (1676–1747), 'the old Dessauer,' his good friend and among Prussia's most famous generals, and the famous Potsdam Grenadiers. This was a regiment of soldiers all over six and a half feet tall, with file leader Hohman more than seven feet. (The king himself was less than five and a half feet in height.) The one thing Frederick Wilhelm did not do was waste any of his hard-earned results by actually taking the army into war, save for a futile imperial campaign on the Rhine in 1734. Meanwhile, he expanded the powers of his state by increasing the bureaucracy, and himself working harder than anyone else in government in looking after the details of administration. He was a despot who once remarked that: 'We are, and remain, lord and king, and We do what We will.' His subjects' only duty was obedience. As he saw it, absolutism was the way to make Prussia even stronger and more independent; while claiming to be 'a good imperialist,' in fact Frederick Wilhelm trusted Austria no more than any other European state.

There was nothing of the French in Frederick Wilhelm I. He resented the Francophilic court created by his father, and he certainly was not a nice person. The king spoke German, ran a low-budget court, spent his evenings in jocular relaxation with his famous 'tobacco parliament' of officers and civil servants, over-ate, drank too much, hunted passionately, was abusive to his family, as verified in the memoirs of his daughter, Wilhelmina, and was said to have struck members of the *Landtag* with a stick when they disagreed with him. The idea of women's rights was beyond him – when he encountered a well-dressed woman on the streets of Berlin he would order her to get home where she belonged. The cultural and intellectual progress that had characterized his father's reign was reversed. In Robert-Hermann Tenbrock's words: 'The universities in Prussia lost their good name; the Prussian Academy founded by Leibniz languished; the intellectual life in the royal palaces was hardly distinguishable from that in the home of a Pomeranian country squire.'

Frederick the Great   Date of Birth?

No one knew the king's limitations or capacity for harsh behaviour better than his elegant and artistic son, Frederick, whom he regularly beat with a stick. The prince was a virtual slave to his father in regard to the strict, Spartan regimen set to prepare him for the throne. This included his education. In Frederick Wilhelm's words:

> Monday he shall be awakened at six o'clock.... From seven to nine Duhan shall work with him in history. At nine o'clock Noltenius shall come to instruct him in Christianity until a quarter to eleven.... He shall come to the King at eleven o'clock, with whom he shall stay until two o'clock.... Duhan ... will describe maps to him from two to three o'clock; he shall also explain to him the power and weakness of all European states, together with the size, wealth, and poverty of the towns. From three to four o'clock Frederick will work at morality; from four until five Duhan shall write German letters with him and help him acquire a good style.... On Saturday morning until half-past ten o'clock everything that he has learned during the entire week in history, writing, and arithmetic, as well as in morality, is to be repeated in order to learn whether or not he has profited therefrom.

And if Frederick had not profited, he had to spend four hours on Saturday going over everything again.

Hardly a surprise, then, that the prince was fed up. Also, he had homosexual tendencies and fell in love with Lieutenant Hermann von

Katte, also a cultured man and scion of an old and prestigious family. They fled Berlin for a new life in France, where the Versailles court had offered sanctuary. Only they were caught; Frederick was imprisoned and, on direct orders of the king, Katte was beheaded directly in front of Frederick's cell window. After this, Frederick 'bent the knee,' settling down to learn the business of kingship. Beginning at the bottom, he served as a clerk to government officials which, his father said, would make him understand how things really worked. He mastered every department of government including the army. On the king's order, though reluctantly, he even took a wife, Elizabeth of Brunswick-Bevern. 'She will be one more unhappy princess in the world,' Frederick wrote. No children resulted; it is doubtful in the circumstances that the marriage was ever consummated. They lived apart for most of the marriage.

KING FREDERICK

Frederick II, 'the Great,' was the most important Prussian ruler in history. Like his father, he operated on the principle of holding absolute power: 'All matters must be reported directly to me,' he once wrote, and in 1766 imposed excise taxes on tobacco, coffee and salt, the collection of which he placed in the hands of French officials, despite the objections of the General Directory, an administrative supervising council that had been established by Frederick Wilhelm I. As king, Frederick modernized and managed the Prussian State system according to his philosophy of top-down power exercised within a rational system. He wrote:

> A well-conducted government must have a system as coherent as a system of philosophy, so that finance, police and the army are coordinated to the same end, namely the consolidation of the state and the increase of its power. Such a system can only emanate from a single brain, that of the sovereign.... The sovereign is the first servant of the State.

Frederick also centralized and rationalized the Prussian court system, used mercantilist principles to institute what he regarded as progressive and expansionary commercial and economic policies, attracted new, skilled people to Prussia, encouraged the expansion of industry and agriculture through improvement and innovation such as introducing the new mould-board plough to Prussian peasants and personally showing them how to use it, improved the educational system across Prussia, at least at the elementary level, and retained and improved upon his father's bureaucratic organization and army. Frederick got rid of the Potsdam Grenadiers which he never liked, and increased the army in size from the 90,000 that he inherited, to 200,000.

Frederick also kept Prussia's Jews in their place. An edict of 1750 included these provisions: a wealthy Jew could leave his 'protected' status to only one child; a Jew must have at least ten thousand thaler to qualify for permission to live within the kingdom; certain categories of Jews could not marry or own rural property; and Rabbis and cantors were 'to be put up with.'

THE ENLIGHTENED ABSOLUTIST

Frederick was an 'Enlightened Absolutist.' That is, he ruled absolutely and regarded his subjects as nothing more than cannon fodder and a faceless rabble, but embraced many aspects of the Enlightenment. His mother, Sophia Dorothea of Hannover, encouraged his interest in music, philosophy and the arts generally, and he admired French *philosophes*, spoke French – 'I speak German like a coachman,' he once remarked – and regarded French literature, philosophy and culture as the essence of the Enlightenment, of which he was an active part. Frederick wrote books and poetry, composed music, was an accomplished flautist, conducted the orchestra of State from the Potsdam palace, and funded the building and performances of the Berlin opera house that opened in 1742, which a contemporary described as 'a model of its kind, over two thousand seats, parking for a thousand carriages, enormous entrances, spacious lobbies, rich interior décor with elegantly appointed boxes, perfect acoustics, special ventilation, expensive precautions against fire, advanced stage techniques.' Frederick also oversaw the planning and construction of Sans-Souci palace, completed in 1747 on the Weinburg, just beyond Potsdam gates. The king corresponded with French, Italian and Scottish intellectuals on such subjects as Isaac Newton's *Principia Mathematica*, and repudiated the religious fundamentalism of his father and became a

Deist, although he remained officially a Lutheran. Frederick once remarked that he was the Pope of the Lutherans, since he answered only to himself in matters secular or ecclesiastic. What he did not do was encourage the burgeoning German Enlightenment (*Aufklärung*). He largely ignored the work of such as Gotthold Lessing and Johann Winckelmann, and withheld from them the honours he bestowed on French intellectuals.

FREDERICK THE AUTHOR

Frederick was a prolific writer, beginning with *Reflections on the Present State of European Politics,* published in 1738. This work assessed the state of the European balance of power, which historians generally agree was the foundation upon which he based his foreign policy. *Anti-Machiavel* appeared in 1740, the year he took the throne, a moral homily written 'to inspire mankind with horror by the false wisdom of this policy'; that is, Machiavellian policy, derived from Niccolò Machiavelli's famous work, *The Prince*, and usually oversimplified to mean 'the ends justify

Frederick the Great and Voltaire

the means'. Voltaire (1694–1778), the giant of French intellectual life, edited and revised *Anti-Machiavel* before publication, and called it – tongue-in-cheek? – 'a book worthy of a prince.' In 1746 he published *Histoire de mon temps* (History of My Times) which reflected upon the first five years of his reign, and in 1748 *Les principes généraux de la guerre* (The General Principles of War), dealing with military strategy and tactics. Frederick also wrote on his forebears – a 'family history,' so to speak – in *Mémoires pour servir à l'histoire de la maison de Brandebourg* (A Dissertation on the History of the House of Brandenburg) published in 1751. Years later he began a two-volume history of the Seven Years War, which appeared only after his death.

VOLTAIRE

Frederick corresponded with Voltaire for forty years, and entertained him in Berlin on four occasions. Voltaire flattered Frederick shamelessly, writing on one occasion: 'You think like Trajan, you write like Pliny, you talk French like our best writers. . . . Under your auspices Berlin will be the Athens of Germany, perhaps of Europe.' So too Jean d'Alembert of *L'Encyclopédie* fame, who called Frederick 'a prince greater even than his fame, a hero at once *philosophe* and modest, a king worthy of friendship, in fact a true sage on the throne'; all of this because they wanted his patronage, which on the whole, they received. However, Voltaire eventually went too far, publicly demeaning Pierre Maupertuis, a Frenchman whom Frederick had named president of the Prussian Academy. They continued to correspond, but Frederick never forgave Voltaire and wrote of him: 'Voltaire is the most malevolent madman I ever met; he is only good to read.' Indeed over time, Frederick became disillusioned with all icons of the Enlightenment, and for much the same reasons. To his nephew and heir he said of them, 'the race of *Beaux Esprit* is an accursed one. They are a people insupportable for their vanity. Such a poet would refuse my kingdom if he were obliged to sacrifice one of his fine verses'; and, 'in the midst of my greatest misfortunes, I always took care to pay the *Beaux Esprit* their pensions' and then, 'these philosophers describe war as the most frightful folly – when it touches their pockets.'

Frederick perhaps also became disillusioned with the concept of perfection associated with the Age of Reason although he wanted it understood that when things went wrong, it was not necessarily his fault:

> With the best will in the world [the Prince] can make mistakes in the choice of his agents; he can be misinformed; his orders may not be punctually executed; injustices may never reach his ear; his officials may be too severe; in a word, the ruler of a large kingdom cannot be everywhere. Such is and such will be the destiny of things on earth that man will never attain to the state of perfection required for the happiness of the people, and therefore in governing, as in everything else, we must be content with what is least defective.

And, of course, war was a major feature of Frederick's reign from the beginning to the end, and he was not always in control there, either.

Frederick II and the Empire

All else taken into consideration, Frederick II's ultimate objective as king was to throw off all subservience to the Habsburg Empire, and, indeed, to replace Austria as the dominant force within Germany. This was possible in part because his East Prussian domain was not in the Empire, and in part because he was a military genius with no qualms about asserting himself against Austria. Under Frederick, Prussia emerged as one of the five European states to be termed Great Powers in the eighteenth century.

FOREIGN POLICY

Frederick's foreign policy was absolutist certainly, but not necessarily enlightened, save that he applied common-sense logic to it. He practised stealth, duplicity, rapacity and naked aggression rather than adhering to the principles of international law, universal morality and cosmopolitan unity. Even so, being both intelligent and articulate, the king expressed 'reasoned' and 'principled' justifications for his conduct:

> When one has the advantage, is he not to use it? Of all states, from the smallest to the biggest, one can safely say that the fundamental rule of government is the principle of extending their territories. . . . The passions of

rulers have no other curb but the limits of their Power. These are the fixed laws of European politics to which every politician submits.

Simply put, his criticism of it notwithstanding, Frederick practised *raison d'état* in a Machiavellian manner. He wrote: 'He whose conduct is best calculated triumphs over those who act with less consistency' in maintaining 'the fixed and lasting interests of the State.' Frederick also claimed, somewhat piously, that it was the 'evil ways' of his fellow rulers that compelled him to lower himself to their level when formulating his own policies.

The War of the Austrian Succession

Frederick's Machiavellian foreign policy went into effect immediately he became king, beginning with the 'War of the Austrian Succession' from 1740 to 1748. It began over Silesia, a Slavic region along the Oder southeast from Berlin and bordering on Bohemia.

FIRST SILESIAN WAR

In 1713, Emperor Charles VII (1697–1745) issued the Pragmatic Sanction, ratified by Prussia in 1726, which confirmed that Habsburg crown lands were indivisible, and that a woman could succeed to the throne. Upon Charles' death in 1740, Maria Theresa of Austria, who was married to Francis Stephen of Lorraine, became queen of Hungary and Bohemia, and, on the basis of the Pragmatic Sanction, claimed the imperial throne since there was no male heir. Frederick agreed to support her if she would cede Silesia to Prussia. She refused, Frederick occupied Silesia, and the war was on. Both sides won victories, and Prussia made alliances with France and other German states, while Austria allied with Holland and England. Then in 1742, Maria Theresa decided Prussia as ally was better than Prussia as enemy, and agreed to give Prussia Upper and Lower Silesia; Prussia then ended its alliance with France. Meanwhile, the German Electors voted for Charles Albert, Elector of Bavaria, rather than Maria Theresa, as Emperor Charles VII. A Wittelsbach, he was the only non-Habsburg to sit on the imperial throne between 1438 and 1806.

The Maria Theresa Thaler

SECOND SILESIAN WAR

Concerned about the security of his new possessions, Frederick took on Maria Theresa a second time in 1744, in alliance again with France and with Charles VII. Charles died the next year, and the war ended, more or less in a draw despite some Prussian victories. Over the next three years, alliances shifted back and forth on a regular basis making straightforward diplomacy virtually impossible; even so, Maria Theresa got Prussia to recognize her husband as Emperor Francis I, and in 1748, Prussia had its annexation of Silesia confirmed by international agreement at Aachen (Aix-la-Chappelle). Even so, the die was cast: Frederick now regarded the Empire as immaterial, and looked upon the Habsburgs simply as Prussia's rival for dominance within Germany. For their part, the Habsburgs looked upon Frederick as a challenge to the very survival of the Empire in its traditional form.

THE SEVEN YEARS WAR   *1756-1763*

This, the 'Third Silesian War,' resulted from the 'Diplomatic Revolution' of 1756, engineered principally on the one side by Frederick II, and on the other by Prince Kaunitz (1711–1794), the imperial foreign minister. Imperial policy since 1749 rested upon Kaunitz's plan to crush Prussia and restore Austrian hegemony in central Europe, which the loss of Silesia had compromised. He wanted to create an 'encircling coalition' with which to isolate Prussia. This required a strong and well-equipped Austrian military, and a more active Russian–Austrian relationship based upon the defensive alliance made in 1746 between

Maria Theresa and Empress Elizabeth of Russia. Secret articles in the alliance provided for restoration of Silesia to Austria, continuation of the Anglo-Austrian alliance created during the Wars of the Grand Coalition, and above all, Prussia detached from its alliance with France. In 1755 Kaunitz began to 'woo' France diplomatically, and induced Britain to make a subsidies (monetary aid) treaty with Russia which would make Russia an effective partner in this Habsburg-led 'encircling coalition.' However, Anglo-French relations were a major stumbling block: in 1756 they were shooting at each other in India and North America, a fact of which Frederick was fully aware.

Frederick reasoned that Anglo-French conflict gave both powers a compelling reason to disengage from central European affairs. In 1756 he signed the Treaty of Westminster with England, a neutrality pact inspired by George II's fear that Prussia might cooperate with France in an attack on Hannover. This treaty upset virtually all apple carts: Franco-Prussian relations deteriorated, Kaunitz talked France into a defensive alliance with Austria, and the Russians moved closer to the Austrian side, in the process forfeiting English monetary aid. Thus was made the 'Diplomatic Revolution' which turned the alliances of the Grand Coalition (1702–1713) upside down: Austria now sided with France and Russia against Prussia, while England moved to Prussia's side against France and Austria, and began providing Frederick with the funds that had been going to Russia. Now Frederick made his move: in August 1756, acting on the premise that France would be preoccupied with England, and that without England's financial backing Russia would stay out of central Europe, he invaded Saxony, took Dresden, and defeated the Austrians at Lobositz. The Empire officially declared war in January 1757.

This war did not quite work out as either Kaunitz or Frederick had hoped. France and Russia entered the war as Austria's allies, and Britain came in on the side of Prussia, but while both sides won victories, neither could gain the upper hand. France and Britain were preoccupied with India and North America – William Pitt's alleged comment: 'We shall win Canada on the banks of the Elbe' being a fair indication – and Russian armies did not coordinate well with Austrian forces. Even so, destroying the alliance one nation at a time was beyond

1761

Frederick's resources, which England stopped subsidizing following the accession of George III in 1760. A year later Berlin was attacked and burned, Austria occupied Schweidnitz and Russia Kolberg, and Frederick's back was to the wall; he was in danger of being taken captive.

THE MIRACLE OF ST PETERSBURG

Then, on 8 January 1762, Empress Elizabeth of Russia died, succeeded by Tsar Peter III, who was at best, strange; he once found a mouse in his quarters, and had it court-martialled and hanged, for treason. His wife, Catherine, detested him. 'When he left the room, the dullest book was a delight,' she once noted. Even so, Peter was a great admirer of Frederick II, whom he viewed as a military genius and role model. In March 1762 he declared a truce, and in May signed a treaty with Frederick that removed Russia from the war and restored to Prussia all lands taken by Russian armies. Prussia was saved, even though Catherine deposed her husband a few months later to become Empress Catherine II, and withdrew the Russian troops he had consigned to Frederick's army. She did not renew the war with Prussia however, and without Russia in the east forcing Frederick to divide his forces between two fronts, his enemies could not make the gains that would justify continuing the war.

The Treaty of Paris in 1763 ended the war. Prussia retained Silesia in exchange for which Frederick agreed to back Maria Theresa's son Joseph for imperial election when the time came. That was in 1765, and Frederick kept his word. Joseph was elected Emperor Joseph II, which was a mixed victory for in Austrian lands, he was only co-regent with his mother. Like Frederick, Joseph II was an 'Enlightened Absolutist'; however his many efforts at reforms for the people of the empire mostly failed. It has been said that his only truly lasting contribution was being one of Mozart's principal patrons. One additional Austro-Prussian conflict arose in 1778 when Prussia invaded Bohemia as an ally of Saxony. But it ended almost immediately when Maria Theresa initiated a personal correspondence with Frederick, the result of which was Prussia gaining additional territories and Saxony a greater degree of sovereignty.

Humour has always had a place in history, and the on-going conflict between declining Austria and rising Prussia in the eighteenth century was no exception. One joke that circulated during the Seven Years War was that a Prussian officer was captured by an Austrian. He sneered: 'We Prussians fight for our honour, but you Austrians fight only for money.' To which the Austrian replied: 'Why not? After all, each of us fights for what he needs most.'

The Partition of Poland

Frederick enjoyed a close yet tense relationship with Catherine II of Russia. They shared a high regard for Enlightenment culture and were absolutists. But both also were ambitious and did not trust each other; rightly so. Both regarded the expansion of territory and power as an essential part of their foreign policy. That made Poland an issue between them, beginning in the 1770s. The kingdom of Poland, which lay between them and once had ruled parts of both Prussia and Russia, now was in a state of serious decline. Catherine wanted a peaceful, docile Poland that would follow Russia's lead; Frederick wanted to expand eastward, which meant taking Polish territory. The Polish Diet enlisted Turkey as an ally in resisting efforts to impose a 'Russian order' on Poland, which led to the Russo-Turkish War of 1768–72. Frederick then suggested a deal whereby Poland would be partitioned between Russia, Prussia and the Habsburg Empire. As he put it:

> I pity philosophers who interest themselves in this people, so contemptible in every way. Their only excuse is their ignorance. Poland has neither laws nor liberty; the government has degenerated into licence and anarchy; the nobility exercise the most cruel tyranny over their slaves. In a word, it is the worst government in Europe except that of the Turks.

Russia and the Empire agreed, and in 1772, the first partition took place. Austria seized Zips, an enclave on the northern border of Hungary, and a portion of Poland bordering Hungary; Prussia then took territories west and south of Danzig, and Russia territories along the Davina and Dnieper. Poland lost five million subjects. Partition was completed in 1793 and 1795 in the reign of Frederick Wilhelm II

(1744–1797), again involving division between Prussia, Russia and Austria. After 1795 Poland disappeared altogether from the map of Europe – which turned the Poles into one of the most nationalistic ethnic peoples in all of Europe. They would not return as a nation until 1919.

End of an Era

Frederick II died in 1786, leaving behind a German state independent of the Empire that once had ruled it. He also had laid the foundations for the separation of the rest of Germany from the Empire, which would be accomplished in the nineteenth century. Of course, there was a great deal still to be done, and little did Frederick know as he lay on his death-bed that Prussia soon would have to deal with yet another French ruler of great power and pretensions.

CHAPTER SEVEN

Creating the Second Empire,
1789–1871

Frederick II would not have been wide of the mark had he uttered the famous line attributed to Madame de Pompadour (and he would have done in French): '*Après nous le déluge*' (After us the flood). In the century after Frederick, Germany experienced more change than at any other time in its history; and it began with the French Revolution and the Napoleonic wars that followed.

The French Revolution and Napoleon

Royal absolutism and aristocratic privilege were increasingly challenged by advocacy of constitutional government and mass democracy. The result was revolution in Paris in 1789. At the centre was an urban middle class, and a rank and file of *sans culottes* that well fit Karl Marx's concept of the Proletariat a half-century later.

THE GERMAN RESPONSE

Such German intellectuals as Immanuel Kant, Friedrich Klopstock, Johann Fichte, Joseph Görres, Friedrich Hölderlin and Georg Forster, hardly populists, saw the uprising as the Enlightenment transformed from theory into practice. 'It is glorious,' wrote Forster, 'to see what philosophy has ripened in the brain and realized in the state.' Britt Petersen described propaganda pamphlets, articles, poetry, songs and drawings in praise of the revolution that circulated throughout Germany and quoted a German woman who wrote: 'I do not know where to turn, for the papers contain such great and splendid news that I am hot from reading'; and also Johann Wolfgang von Goethe, who dis-

Johann Wolfgang von Goethe and Friedrich Schiller

missed it all as simply 'newspaper fever ... a bad case of an infectious disease.'

Enthusiasm faded when the revolution turned extreme. 'I am simply nauseated by the mindless brutality of those scoundrels,' was Friedrich Schiller's response to the 'September Massacre' in Paris, the trial and execution of Louis XVI and Marie Antoinette, and the 'Reign of Terror' which followed. Germans leaned toward constitutional monarchy over populist Republicanism, and supported an imperial ban on Republican propaganda. Ernst Posselt's book on the revolution was in Latin, in order to prevent 'any principles [being] circulated among the common people that could kindle the flames of revolution.' And there were conspiracy theorists, who argued that German Freemasons and the Illuminati were behind the French Revolution.

WAR

In 1791, German princes issued the Declaration of Püllnitz, a threat to invade France if any harm befell the royal family. France responded by declaring war on the Empire, and sent a revolutionary army to Valmy where it defeated the duke of Brunswick. Goethe witnessed the battle and made this observation: 'At this place, on this day, there has begun a new era in the history of the world; and you can all claim to have been present at its birth.' A Prussian officer was more blunt: 'You'll see how these little cocks will strut now. We have lost more than a battle.'

France was at war with the rest of Europe from then until 1815, first under Republican leaders seeking to spread revolution, and then under Napoleon Bonaparte (1769–1821) whose ambition was to build a French Empire that would stretch across Europe, including Germany. Napoleon was a great enthusiast for things German, cultural and otherwise. He admired Frederick II as one of Europe's greatest military geniuses, and his favourite novel was Goethe's *Sorrows of Young Werther*. When he met the author, he exclaimed: '*Voilà un homme!*' It is said that Goethe was not particularly impressed.

CONFEDERATION OF THE RHINE

Napoleon had dramatic impact upon both Germany and the Empire. His policy, simply put, was to enlarge Prussia relative to Austria, and create buffer states that would obviate union between the two. The Treaty of Lunéville in 1801 set the stage for the dissolution of the Holy Roman Empire by shifting a significant number of Rhenish territories from the Empire to France and various German principalities. In 1803, the Diet of Regensburg, now virtually independent of Vienna, at Napoleon's urging and with Russian backing created a commission to plan a Germany separate from the Empire and Prussia. The result was ecclesiastical states secularized and reduced in number from over 300 to less than 40, which deprived the German Catholic Church of most of its power and worldly possessions; forty-five imperial free towns and the territories of fifteen-hundred imperial knights were absorbed into such as Prussia, Baden and the newly created kingdoms of Bavaria (1805), Württemberg and Saxony (1806). Hannover also was elevated to a kingdom, in 1814.

In 1806, Napoleon dubbed this Germany, which excluded only Austria, Prussia, Brunswick and Hesse-Cassell, the 'Confederation of the Rhine,' and abolished the Holy Roman Empire. Francis II abdicated that throne, and took in its place the title Francis I, Emperor of Austria. The Confederation was, effectively, a 'Third Germany,' no longer even nominally under Austrian authority of Vienna, nor, for that matter, of Prussian. France soundly defeated Prussia in 1806 at Jena and Auerstadt, occupied Berlin, and forced relocation of the Prussian capital (again) to Königsberg. In 1807, the Treaty of Tilsit required Prussia to declare neutrality and cede territories to the newly created Grand Duchy of Warsaw, and to France all lands between the Rhine and Elbe – and still French-occupied Berlin.

PRUSSIAN REFORMS

Meanwhile, Prussia introduced sweeping reforms. Freiherr Karl vom Stein (1752–1831), imperial knight and chief minister, blamed the Frederician state system for Jena and Auerstadt. State Chancellor Carl August von Hardenberg (1750–1822) and writer-diplomat Wilhelm von Humboldt (1767–1835) were able to persuade not very reform-minded Frederick Wilhelm III (1770–1840) and the *Landtag* to take action: serfdom was abolished, tax collection put in the hands of elected bodies, state administration made more efficient, municipal governments strengthened, and burghers given more responsibility for running towns and cities. Humboldt also improved the educational system from elementary to university, founding the University of Berlin (Humboldt-Universität) in 1809. It became a principal rival to Ludwig-Maximilian University in Munich, created in 1826 by King Ludwig I (1786–1868) who detested Prussia.

Field Marshall August von Gneisenau and General Gerhard von Scharnhorst reformed the military. The officer corps now included middle-class officers of proven ability, the General Staff concept became a reality, and military tactics and the use of armaments were upgraded. This led directly to Napoleon's defeat at Leipzig in 1813, the so-called 'Battle of Nations' because the victorious armies came from across Germany. Actually, they were mostly Prussian, including the sixteen-year-old future German emperor, Wilhelm I. Simply put, Leipzig was a Prussian victory with German assistance. It also signalled the end for Napoleon, who was gone forever after Waterloo in 1815, and the Bourbon monarchy revived under Louis XVIII. Many in France preferred Napoleon; a Paris cartoon depicted an eagle leaving the Tuileries Palace while five fat geese waddled in.

Congress of Vienna

The Congress of Vienna, 1814–1815, restored German and imperial lands taken by the French, reorganized Polish and Saxon lands in the east, and in politics, re-established the Old Order (*Ancien Régime*) and the European Balance of Power. Meanwhile, Tsar Alexander I, once a 'liberal' but now a reactionary and religious mystic, persuaded Frederick Wilhelm III and Francis II to sign his Treaty of the Holy Alliance. The signatories were 'to be guided in their relations among themselves and their peoples by the principles of Christian morality.' Austrian Chancellor Prince Klemens von Metternich (1773–1859) was not impressed. He privately categorized the treaty as 'a loud-sounding nothing.'

Austria and Germany after Vienna

The Holy Roman Empire was not restored. Rather, a 'German League' of thirty-nine sovereign states was formed, with Emperor Francis II as 'president' of its now Frankfurt-am-Main-based Diet. Chancellor Metternich set internal policy for the member states. And why not; he really was a Rhinelander, his family having sought refuge in Vienna in 1792. His policy after 1815 was to stifle the growth of liberal ideas, nationalism or revolution – after all, the rise of nationalism would open the door to the disintegration of the Austrian Empire, which comprised many different ethnic groups including Germans. Also, in terms of state administration, never let the right hand know what the left is doing; after 1815 a state bureaucracy capable of making all matters disappear into a mass of paperwork characterized imperial government. Meanwhile, German states within and without the League sought to restore society as it had existed in the eighteenth century, with a pyramidal social and political structure that emphasized Church, military and administrative bureaucracy.

German Romanticism

The Romantic movement was the mind-set most common in post-Napoleonic Germany, at least until the 1840s. It turned away from

Reason and embraced emotion and imagination. As Goethe, Classicist turned Romantic, phrased it, 'we threw ourselves into living knowledge, experience, action and poetizing, with all the more liveliness and passion.' And, he might have added, into yearning (*Sehnsucht*), sometimes for death. at least in their writing. Friedrich von Hardenberg, 'Novalis,' used 'Sacred Night' as a metaphor for death in his poem *Hymns of the Night*: 'Sacred Night, with her unspoken mysteries, who draws me to her.... Night has aroused me to life and manhood.... What joys or pleasures can life offer to outweigh the chain of death.' Opposites also were a factor. Again Novalis: 'To the poet who comprehends the nature of his art to its centre, nothing appears contradictory and strange. To him all riddles are solved. By the magic of imagination he can unite all ages and all worlds.' Romantics admired nobles and peasants equally, alternated wild ecstasy with serene simplicity, and thought seriously while being dangerously irresponsible. Bettina von Arnim wrote: 'My soul is a passionate dancer. It jumps around according to inner dance music which only I hear and no one else....' Extreme, of course, was the lover of a minor German poet, who was convinced that not having suffered a soul-shattering sorrow was the cause of her darling's mediocrity; so, she committed suicide in order to provide him with one. Romantic characteristics also included individuality but not individualism – 'Everything I do I like to do in the company of others,' was one perspective – and search for the 'community soul' (*Volkgeist*). The latter motivated the Grimm brothers' collection, illustrated by Romantic artist Ludwig Richter, of German folk tales such as Cinderella and Snow White and the Seven Dwarfs. And there was pessimism. Philosopher Arthur Schopenhauer (1788–1860), weighing the amount of good and evil in the world, concluded that life is 'a business whose profits do not nearly cover its expenses.'

DRAMA, ART AND MUSIC

Romanticism also was expressed in drama, art and music. Heinrich von Kleist (1777–1811) drew upon the mysterious forces of nature and mind in *Käthchen von Heilbronn*, and upon passionate nationalism in *Hermannsschlacht*. The latter portrays Arminius (Hermann) liberating Germany from the ancient Roman Empire, 'a scarcely disguised call to arms against Napoleon, an outcry of passionate hatred and a document of excessive nationalism.' Artists concentrated on landscape and heroic portraiture. Romantics felt 'ever more distinctly that in every tree and flower there is hidden a certain human spirit, idea, or feeling.' Caspar David Friederich (1774–1840) was Germany's greatest Romantic landscape painter, his work combining the mystical with the 'softly melancholy.' In music, Franz Schubert (1797–1828) from Vienna was noted for Romantic *Lied* (song) and picturesque and lyrical quartet and symphonic music; his contemporary, Carl Maria von Weber (1786–1826) turned the fairy tale *Oberon* into the epitome of early Romantic opera. Felix Mendelssohn-Bartholdy (1809–1847) and Robert Schumann (1810–1856) dominated the next generation, the former with such work as the 'elfishly romantic' *A Midsummer Night's Dream*, and the latter with 'Spring' and 'Rhenish' symphonies. (Schumann's wife Clara Wieck (1819–1896) was a clear indication that women also could make a notable contribution to music given the chance.) These composers epitomized the lyrical, passionate and melancholy qualities characteristic of all Romantic composers. Meanwhile, Franz Liszt (1811–1886), a Hungarian, was most famous for 'Hungarian Rhapsodies,' and as *Kappellmeister* at Weimar and Richard Wagner's father-in-law.

ARCHITECTURE

German architecture had no genuine Romantic experience save, perhaps, for 'neo-Romantic' Neuschwanstein Castle, begun in 1869 for Ludwig II of Bavaria (1845–1886). Rather, it remained largely neo-classical, beginning with Berlin's Brandenburg Gate, created in the 1790s by Silesian architect Karl Langhans as the 'symbolic gateway to the metropolis of the soldier-kings of Prussia.' Nineteenth-century examples include Karl Friedrich Schinkel's Altes Museum and Berlin National Theatre *(Schauspielhaus)*, Friedrich Weinbrenner's remaking of Karlsruhe in Baden into a 'model city' of neo-classical form, and Leo von Klenze's neo-classical buildings in Munich, Regensburg and Kelheim, commissioned by Ludwig I of Bavaria. Schinkel also designed the *Pickelhaube*, the spiked helmet that became the trademark of the Prussian army and police. However, neo-classical, as Kurt Reinhardt

The Brandenburg Gate in Berlin

put it, 'was seen as foreign importations rather than as the manifestation of indigenous forces.' The German as opposed to foreign outlook in building and interior design was *Biedermeier,* the intimate and 'philistine' life-style of the middle class. It too was far from the Romantic.

The Rise of Nationalism

German nationalism reflected the passion and emotion of Romanticism. Whether it embraced liberty and equality, or authority and regimentation, nationalism was the 'Spirit of the Times' (*Zeitgeist*). Intellectuals and youth movements, in and outside of universities, were its earliest advocates, largely in the context of the War of Liberation against Napoleon. Ernst Moritz Arndt was an ardent propagandist for German unity against France; so too Johann Fichte. Ironically, when Fichte delivered his *Addresses to the German Nation* in Berlin in 1807, there were as many French as Germans in the audience. Nationalists themselves, they applauded Fichte's perspective – applying its principles to France, of course.

TURNVATER JAHN

Ludwig Jahn (1778–1852), '*Turnvater*' (Father of Gymnastics), was an early advocate of populist nationalism. He began the *Turnerschaft*, a student organization whose adherents dressed in open-throated tunics, wore daggers in their belts, stressed athleticism, used crude language and were aggressively anti-Semitic. They were the role model for the Hitler Youth of the 1930s. Meanwhile, in 1817 *Burschenshaften* (university fraternities) staged the *Wartburgfest,* a mammoth demonstration at Wartburg Castle near Eisenach where they proclaimed the rebirth of free thought and the liberation of the fatherland, burned books by 'reactionary' authors and symbols of absolutism and political conservatism. The following year Jahn invited them to embrace *Turnerschaft* principles. They did, swearing allegiance to 'freedom, honour and fatherland,' and taking as their colours the black, red and gold of Major von Lützow's 'Free Corps' of the War of Liberation against France.

Burschenshaften were usually 'left wing,' holding in contempt class privilege, sloth, complacency, bureaucracy and material things. They were easily led into extremism, as when Karl Sand was so moved by the fanatically nationalist Professor Karl Follen at the University of Jena that he sought martyrdom. And he found it: Sand murdered August von Kotzebue, an anti-radical nationalist writer whom students generally despised as a traitor to the cause, and paid for the crime with his life.

CARLSBAD DECREES

Metternich used the *Wartburgfest* to rouse recalcitrant princes against the dangers nationalism represented, and in 1819 got the Carlsbad Decrees through the Frankfurt Diet. The Decrees aimed at suppressing 'unsavoury ideas' such as liberalism, democracy, socialism and nationalism; but to no avail. A 'Festival of Freedom' was staged at Hambach Castle in 1825, where 25,000 people proclaimed their preference for liberal and national government. Metternich responded with still more censorship and the Diet with still more repressive laws, and he removed professors and other reformers from the universities when they spoke out against this suppression of free speech and dissent. The classic example was the 'Seven of Göttingen' which included, among others, historian Frederick Dahlman and the folklorists Jacob (1785–1863) and Wilhelm Grimm (1786–1859).

YOUNG GERMANY

Then there was the Young Germany movement, which advocated a national and more egalitarian Germany often through satire and denunciation. For example, Ludwig Börne on censorship:

> When the world catches fire and the fat begins to melt off the upper classes the police will make the announcement, 'Alarmists have spread the rumour that the world is overheated. This is an insidious fabrication. The weather was never cooler or finer. All people are cautioned against making ill-considered remarks and lounging about the streets.'

Heinrich Heine (1797–1856) also wrote satirically, and often with bitter sarcasm as when he raged against the 'nature philosophers' who would conjure up 'the satanic powers of old-Germanic pantheism.' When that happened, he warned, 'Thor with his hammer will rise up and smash the Gothic cathedrals.' Heine once claimed that he could write well only when breathing German air; this made it difficult for him, as he was an exile in Paris for much of his adult life. In 1835 the Frankfurt Diet banned all Young Germany writing.

Industrialization

The Industrial Revolution began in England and crossed into Germany in the first half of the nineteenth century. Many new German industries actually were started and operated by the English, because Germany lacked both capital and a work force with advanced technical skill. That soon changed. By the 1820s in Westphalia, Friedrich Harkort had established iron and copper works, built canals and railways, and promoted steam navigation in Westphalia. His contemporary, Friedrich Krupp (1780–1826), started the first German steel mills in Essen, which soon grew into one of the most powerful manufacturing cartels in Europe. It increasingly specialized in armaments, and after 1871 occupied a privileged place in the German Empire not unlike the Fuggers in the Holy Roman Empire three centuries earlier.

ECONOMIC NATIONALISM: *DIE ZOLLVEREIN*

Friedrich List (1789–1846), political economy professor at the

University of Tübingen, appeared before the Frankfurt Diet in 1819 to petition on behalf of an association of south German industrialists for the abolition of trade tariffs between the German states, Austria, Hungary, the Netherlands, Switzerland and Belgium; in essence, the concept of European economic union nearly a century and a half before the 1957 Treaty of Rome. The Diet refused. List went back to Tübingen and began writing *Nationales System der politischen Ökonomie* (National System of Political Economy) which called for a free market within Germany but protective tariffs against foreign competition, as the basis for building a German industrial economy. It was published in 1840, eight years after Prussia, which liked List's concepts from the start, had persuaded the German states (excluding Austria) to accept a *Zollverein* (customs union) that eliminated tariffs between the members and encouraged internal development. In 1835 Bavarian capitalists built the first German railway line from Nuremberg to Fürth, and in 1837 August Borsig founded Berlin's first engineering factory. Another step had been taken toward a united Germany.

KARL MARX AND GEORG FRIEDRICH HEGEL

Dramatic social change came with industrialization: a middle class and industrial working class emerged comparable in numbers and influence to those in Britain. For example: Silesian weavers rose up in 1844 demanding rights for labourers; and industrial capitalists proliferated, one of whom, Gerson Bleichröder, was Otto von Bismarck's banker. How would German society deal with such changes? In practical terms, it was handled through attempted – and failed – revolutions and in the later century, the development of trades unions. On a theoretical level, it was addressed most importantly by Karl Marx (1818–1883), creator of 'scientific socialism.'

Marx studied philosophy at the University of Berlin, specifically the metaphysical dialectic of Georg Friedrich Hegel (1770–1831) as laid out in *Phenomenology of Mind,* published in 1807. Hegel, a professor at the University of Jena, was so engrossed in writing this work that he was oblivious to the world around him. One day in 1806 he left his rooms for a meeting with his publisher and was surprised to find the streets full of French soldiers. Kurt Reinhardt described Hegel's perspective this way: '[The] understanding of opposites (theses and antitheses) leads to a synthetic comprehension of the nature of reality'; the individual is not a free agent but rather serves 'the still hidden designs of the ruling spirit of the universe'; and the State, from which ultimately derives the dignity and worth of humanity, is 'God walking upon the earth,' the highest and most perfect manifestation of the concept of Universal Reason. Over the nineteenth century, Hegel's process – though not necessarily his conclusion – was applied to virtually every venue of intellectual expression, especially historiography.

And to Marxism. Initially, Marx debunked Hegel, but over time came to embrace his work, turning it into 'dialectical materialism.' That is, thesis-antithesis-synthesis defined the process of social and economic history moving toward the day when the Proletariat would take control of economic, social, and political structure and activities. There Marx ended it. All humanity would then be merged into the Proletariat, so there would be no opposites left to synthesize. This was the concept Marx laid out in *Das Kapital*, first published in Hamburg in 1867. Of course, he had advocated Proletarian rule in *Communist Manifesto* in 1848, which argued that the workers have nothing to lose but their chains, and a whole world to win.

The Revolution of 1848

Radical republicanism and nationalism were the objectives of the European revolutions in 1848. They achieved neither.

THE EMPIRE

The revolution was Metternich's worst nightmare. He fled Vienna and cartoons depicted him sneaking out of the city. Ferdinand I (1793–1875) abdicated, and Bohemia and Hungary claimed their independence. Ferdinand, at least, was no great loss. A. J. P. Taylor depicted him as an incompetent figurehead (Metternich and Count Kolowrat ran the government) whose one memorable gesture was when he was served a dinner dish he did not like, and declared 'I am the Emperor and I *will* have dumplings!'

In Vienna, students, urban workers and the National Guard rioted and demonstrated, demanding Metternich's dismissal, freedom of the press, jury trials, civil rights, abolition of religious discrimination, academic freedom, full emancipation of peasants and a constitutional representative government. Concessions were made to these demands, and a succession of chancellors sat in place of Metternich, the most important being Prince Felix von Schwarzenberg, who remained in office until his death in 1852. But the revolutionaries were never satisfied, and the imperial court went to Innsbruck, and later to Olmültz, as a matter of security. So too the Imperial Diet for Kremsier near Olmütz, where it drafted a new constitution that was then proclaimed in Vienna.

Revolution spread to Venetia and Lombardy, backed by military forces from Sardinia. These provinces demanded independence from the empire and Italian unification. Meanwhile, Prague and Budapest rose up demanding independence and the creation of national states. Imperial forces retreated, and the wife of their commander, General Prince Alfred Windischgrätz, was killed by a stray bullet. This did not endear the revolutionaries to him. In Prague the plan was for a state comprised of the three lands of the ancient Bohemian crown, with Czechs playing the primary role; in Budapest a Republic was declared with the Magyars in control. War then raged between Austria and its imperial parts, for neither government nor emperor, now the eighteen-year-old Franz Joseph (1830–1916) who had succeeded Ferdinand in December 1848, would recognize these demands.

The empire won – and lost, for ethnic nationalism never went away. It won in the short term however. General Count Joseph Radetzky's army, situated in the Quadrilateral, a series of fortified cities in northern Italy, held out and in due course defeated the Sardinian army and restored order in Venetia and Lombardy. Windischgrätz took an army back to Prague and returned the northern Slav lands to direct imperial control. He then led an imperial army into Vienna, and with no 'sanctuary' left to them, the revolutionaries 'invited' the Habsburgs to return. They did. Emperor Franz Joseph repudiated the Kremsier constitution, agreed to the execution of hard-core revolutionaries, and restored the old order more or less as it had been. Windischgrätz then attacked the Hungarian Republic, and brought it down with the aid of

Russian forces. And that, concluded historian Robert Kann, 'sealed the fate of the Hungarian revolution and in the wider sense that of Hungary.' Internal disagreements also contributed to the failure of the revolution. Poles, Slovaks and Moravians did not accept Czech pre-eminence in the Bohemian State, and the Magyars' presumed dominance was unacceptable to Serbs, Croats and Romanians.

GERMANY AND PRUSSIA

In 1847 urban radicals in Offenburg demanded changes that included universal suffrage, a popularly elected German parliament, an armed populace, freedom of the press, religion and conscience, trial by jury, taxation according to income, education for all, protection of labour and the right to work, adjusted relations between capital and labour, abolition of all privileges, and government responsible to the people. Peasant organizations also made demands, a little different from those of Offenburg: destruction of the nobility, banishment of Jews from Germany, conversion of Germany to a free state on the order of the United States of America, and the execution of all government officials. In March 1848 the revolution began across Germany, with Berlin the most important centre of unrest. King Frederick Wilhelm IV (1795–1861) had summoned the Prussian Estates in 1847 who assembled as the United Diet (*Vereinigter Landtag*), to deal with funding for a railway project. It was their first summons since the Napoleonic wars, they were angry, and the project was rejected. For whatever reason, the king allowed their debates on the issue to be published, which led to public demonstrations demanding a Prussian constitution. On one occasion troops fired on the demonstrators, the situation became intolerable, and they turned into revolutionaries demanding both a constitution and German unification. Frederick Wilhelm tried to smooth things over by publically embracing the latter demand: 'I want German freedom and German unity,' and 'Prussia will henceforth be merged into Germany.' This infuriated Prussian Junkers who were *not* Germans, they *were* Prussians. They wanted the king to stand firm against revolution, and when events got out of hand and the queen told future Prussian minister-president and German chancellor, Otto von Bismarck (1815–1898), that the king was too upset to sleep, he replied: 'A king *must* be able to sleep.'

By May 1848 the revolution appeared to have triumphed across Germany. A 600-member *Vorpaliament* (pre-parliament) representing all of the German states and dominated by the middle class and academics, met at St Paul's Church in Frankfurt, for purposes of creating a National Assembly. The Prussians sent delegates reluctantly, and created their own Berlin Assembly. While the *Vorparliament* established the rules for creating a functioning parliament, a constitution was being drawn up in Heidelberg.

THE FRANKFURT PARLIAMENT

This was a government with its feet planted firmly in mid-air. Real power still lay in the hands of the princes, whose armies, police forces and bureaucracies remained under their own control – the Frankfurt military consisted of two river boats, donated by wealthy industrialists, armed with a single cannon each. The parliament also did not address basic social and economic issues: improvement in the situation of peasants and workers, and abuse of property rights, particularly in Prussia, by nobles who exhibited a lingering aura of feudalism. It did attempt to address the unification issue, however, and that led to a most interesting divide.

GREAT GERMANY OR LITTLE GERMANY?

The former would include Prussia and the Austrian Empire, both Germans and Slavs, and would be ruled by a Habsburg emperor, in essence, a recreation of the Holy Roman Empire of the German Nation. There was even a Habsburg archduke at Frankfurt to support those who favoured the plan. That did not include the Habsburg emperor, however, nor his government, which had no interest in the project. Nor did it include the Prussian delegates, who argued for a Little Germany that would exclude the Austrians and their holdings. The debate went on in Frankfurt; however, by the time Franz Joseph returned to Vienna and Frederick Wilhelm IV came out of the Royal Palace to retake control of Berlin, the issue had became a storm in a teacup. More important was the Schleswig-Holstein issue. Should these Danish provinces with preponderantly German and pro-German unification populations become part of a united Germany? Denmark said no, and a brief war followed, for which Frederick Wilhelm IV, momentarily embracing German nationalism, provided the troops. It ended when Britain intervened and got both sides to sign the Armistice of Malmö, leaving the provinces with Denmark. The Frankfurt Parliament repudiated the armistice, but to no avail.

THE 'CROWN FROM THE STREET'

By the spring of 1849 the revolution was over in Germany, and the Little Germany side in the unification debate had won the day. Or had it? A delegation from the Frankfurt Parliament went to Berlin to offer Frederick Wilhelm the crown of an Imperial Little Germany. He refused to receive the delegation, remarking: 'I will not accept a crown offered from the street.' And there was the Austro-Prussian Treaty of Ölmutz, signed in 1850, which required that Prussia stay out of involvement with the Germans of Schleswig and Holstein. Austria 'dictated' the terms, so to speak, and the treaty soon was known in Prussia as the 'humiliation of Ölmutz.'

The revolution was over; and it had failed. Many Germans expressed their disappointment by emigrating to the United States; one such was Karl Shurz, a Frankfurt Parliament member who was a Union army general during the American civil war, and was later Secretary of the Interior under President Grant.

Bismarck

Ölmutz became a rallying cry for nationalistic Prussians who wanted a Prussian-dominated Germany that did not include Austria. They got their wish, thanks to the Machiavellian policies of Prussian Minister-President, Otto von Bismarck.

YOUNG BISMARCK

Bismarck's background is central to understanding his perspective on German unification. He was born a Junker, and grew up on the family estate in Pomerania. His father was a typical landowner of the sort that had been around for centuries; his mother, on the other hand, was upper-middle class, bright and well educated, with strong Berlin connections. Bismarck regarded his father as a Junker role model, but disliked his mother – some historians say hated – for not being the female version of that model. In fact, Bismarck inherited most of his skills and talents from his mother, and had little in common with his father.

Prussian men of Bismarck's class had two career choices beyond managing the estate: the army or the bureaucracy. Bismarck chose the latter, to the extent that a foreign-service officer fits the description of a bureaucrat. But first, he went to school in Berlin, which he found routine and tedious, save, perhaps, for being friends with some Hohenzollern children, and not of sufficient interest to satisfy his generally excitable character, and then to university at Göttingen. There he initially was a *Burschenshaften* with a radical and even Republican point of view, but soon turned Right and became a typical *korpsstudent*, involved in scrapes, heavy drinking and running up debts. It is said that he once jumped into the Neckar river to escape a bill collector. In due course Bismarck finished with a degree in law and administration, having 'scraped by' his exams according to A. J. P. Taylor, or 'passed with distinction' according to Erich Eyke.

Young Bismarck was not a happy man. He lost his first love to a one-armed English colonel, a veteran of the Napoleonic wars, and returned to Schönhausen to take over running the family estate. But he was miserable, not at all fitted for the boring life of a Junker landlord, and became involved in riotous living, winning for himself the not complementary nickname, '*der Tolle Bismarck*' (The wild Bismarck). Enter Marie von Thadden, his second love: quiet, submissive and a Pietist – and engaged to a friend of his. The friend introduced him to Johanna von Puttkamer (1824–1894), also a Pietist. Bismarck demonstrated considerable diplomatic skills in convincing her father that he was sufficiently religious to qualify for her hand. Those who knew him well were not convinced. 'If Bismarck believes in his God,' said one acquaintance, 'then God himself must be a Prussian.' In fact, Bismarck's 'conversion' to Pietism was of great value later in gaining the trust, and therefore the support, of Pietist Junkers. In 1847 he married Johanna 'as a favour to Marie.' She proved the perfect wife for Bismarck's personality. She never interfered, never took an interest in his work, liked his friends and hated his enemies, and in due course provided a male heir. Simply put, she was 'a useful piece of furniture,' and that was exactly how he wanted it.

POLITICS

Bismarck became a member of the Prussian Diet, in 1847, where he courted unpopularity with inflammatory speeches attacking Liberalism. This brought him to the attention of the extreme Right, and a relationship formed that would help him ascend the political ladder. Then came the Revolution of 1848 in Berlin. Bismarck was indignant when Frederick Wilhelm IV appeared to cave into it. He was convinced that a stiff dose of police action would bring everything under control, and even offered to lead such an expedition. During the upheaval in Berlin Bismarck conversed with Crown Prince Wilhelm, with whom he later would form a most formidable partnership. Meanwhile, he blamed the king for letting events get out of control.

After the revolution, Bismarck was elected from Brandenburg to the newly formed Prussian parliament by the narrow margin of six votes. The king was not necessarily pleased, having once said that Bismarck was 'a red reactionary, smells of blood, only to be used when the bayonet rules.' Even so, Frederick Wilhelm made him Prussia's representative to the post-1848 Diet of the North German Confederation when it convened in Frankfurt in 1851.

In the 1850s Bismarck was part of a Right-wing Junker political action group organized around brothers Ludwig and Leopold von Gerlach, and cousins Edwin and Otto von Manteuffel, which worked against the idea of a constitution for Prussia. They caught the king's ear, won his support, and became the *Camarilla*, effectively an 'occult' ministry exercising the real power behind the throne. Bismarck was a principal contributor to their newspaper, *Kreuz-Zeitung*. Frederich Julius Stahl (1802–1861), Professor of Law at the University of Berlin, was the philosopher of the group. He invented the 'Theory of the Gap' (*Luckentheorie*) which was that if a dispute arose between king and parliament, and no rule existed in the ancient German constitution regarding the dispute, then the king could do as he chose. Bismarck put this to good use later on. Meanwhile, as a member of the parliament he spoke out against Austria – 'a worm-eaten and old-fashioned Man-of-War,' which had power because it was 'lucky enough to rule over foreign peoples' – and for Prussian self-reliance. 'The only sound basis for a great state is egoism, not romanticism,' he proclaimed in one speech. 'It is unworthy of a great state to fight for anything that does not form part of its own interest.' This made his comment to *Camarilla* member Victor von Unruh sound like a contradiction in terms: 'The sole reliable lasting ally whom Prussia could secure, if it set about it the right way, was the German people.' Unruh was shocked by this 'democratic' comment, but Bismarck reassured him that: 'I am the same Junker that I was ten years ago when we became acquainted in the Chamber. But I should have to be without eyes and brains not to see how things really are.' That is, Prussia had to connect German nationalism to the advance of Prussian interests.

Minister-President of Prussia

Wilhelm I (1791–1888) ascended the throne in 1861, the year the parliament rejected the Army Reform Bill, which called for extending the term of service and increasing the military budget by nine million thaler per annum. In 1862 Bismarck returned from Paris where he had gained 'deep and valuable insight into the political ambition of Napoleon III,' and Wilhelm named him Minister-President (prime minister) of Prussia. Bismarck knew a way around the Army Bill defeat: implement the provisions anyway, using the 'Theory of the Gap' as justification. Wilhelm did, the parliament could do nothing, and the Prussian military was strengthened. Meanwhile, the Minister-President called upon parliamentary deputies to regard their primary responsibility as educating their constituents in what government required, rather than representing what the constituents wanted. He also delivered his famous 'blood and iron' speech to the parliament, which effectively warned that Prussia would establish its position in Germany through armed force.

By 1863 Bismarck's policy for Prussia's future was clear: achieve Prussian dominance in Germany, and achieve Prussian and German security within Europe. Interestingly, in this era European colonialism peaked in Asia and Africa; Bismarck regarded colonies as a waste of time and money. What mattered was Prussia within Germany, and Germany within Europe.

The Wars of Unification

Bismarck had great confidence in the Prussian army. And why not; Army Reform Bill measures had been implemented, and the chief of the Prussian general staff was now Graf Helmut von Moltke (1800–1891), among the most competent military strategists of the nineteenth century.

DENMARK

The Schleswig–Holstein issue resurfaced in 1863. Denmark adopted a new constitution that called for the two provinces to be separated, with Schleswig incorporated into the Danish monarchy. Austria and Prussia objected that this violated the 1852 Treaty of London, to which both were signatories, which specified Schleswig would *not* be incorporated into Denmark. Danish troops used force to subdue riotous German protesters in Schleswig, and Bismarck seized the opportunity to intervene with force. Austria joined in, albeit reluctantly. Wilhelm I also was reluctant; however, once troops were dispatched, he began to 'smell the gunpowder' and became enthusiastic for war.

After nine weeks, Denmark was defeated and ceded Schleswig, Holstein and Lauenburg to the victors, Lauenburg going outright to Prussia. The Convention of Gastein was signed, mandating that Austria would administer Holstein, and Prussia, Schleswig, with this proviso: if either party reneged on any part of the Convention, its mandated territory would automatically revert to the other.

AUSTRIA

Bismarck demanded changes regarding control of Kiel harbour and the relationship of Schleswig and Holstein to Prussia. Austria would not agree, and Bismarck demanded that Austria be expelled from the North German Confederation. Meanwhile, he made a secret deal with Napoleon III guaranteeing that France would remain neutral in case of

war. He also spoke with the king of Northern Italy – no friend of
Austria – and with a Hungarian nationalist leader to whom he said: 'I
want to secure for Prussia the position which is her due in Germany as a
purely German state.... If we win, Hungary will get her freedom. You
may count on me.' Pushed to the limit by Bismarck's demands, Austria
demanded that the Confederation mobilize forces against Prussia;
Bismarck responded by sending Prussian troops into Holstein, and into
Hannover, Saxony, Hesse and Hesse-Nassau when they refused to
accept his plan for reforming the Confederation. Austria declared war
in the spring of 1866. Hungary refused to participate, and the war lasted
six weeks, ending when Prussian forces crushed the Austrian army at
Königgrätz on 3 July 1866. This was the *annus mirabilis*, as some historians put it, because the Prussian parliament passed the Indemnity Bill
which reversed its rejection of the Army Reform Bill. All military
expenditures undertaken since 1861 were approved retroactively.
Austrian power in Germany was now broken, and Prussian power was
paramount. Bismarck kept his promise to the Hungarians, and in 1867
the Austrian Empire became the Austro-Hungarian Empire. Hungary
had only to recognize Franz Joseph as its king-emperor, and submit to
the authority of the Austrian general staff in time of war.

FRANCE

Bismarck still needed to bring the remainder of Germany to Prussia's
side, and that required eliminating French influence among the
Rhenish states. The inspiration was the Hohenzollern candidacy for the
Spanish throne; the method was manipulating French official and
public opinion into an anti-Prussian war frenzy and to make it look like
the French started it all.

The king of Spain died without an heir in 1868, and Leopold of
Swabia, nephew of Wilhelm I, was put forward as a possible successor.
This bothered the French because with a Hohenzollern on Spain's
throne, France would effectively be 'surrounded' by Prussia. In fact,
Leopold was not the least interested, and Wilhelm would not give
permission as head of the family. The Spanish Cortes found another
candidate. Issue resolved, or would be as soon as Napoleon III was
given assurance that there never again would be a Hohenzollern can-

didate for the Spanish throne. In July 1870 Count Benedetti, French ambassador to Prussia, went to Ems where Wilhelm I was 'taking the waters.' He met the king on the promenade, and, according to the dispatch sent to Bismarck by Count Abeken, was told that the king could not commit himself 'for all time' to such an obligation, but that in the light of developments, Prussia clearly was 'out of the affair.' Wilhelm did not receive Benedetti again, but rather sent word to the effect that Prince Leopold confirmed that the Spanish throne had gone to another candidate. End of story.

Except that Bismarck rewrote the dispatch to make it sound as if Benedetti had made unwarranted demands on the king who in turn refused to submit to them and insulted the Count in the process. He released it to Berlin newspapers, while the Prussian ambassador to France did the same to Paris newspapers. It hit the fan in both capitals, and the Franco-Prussian war began on 18 July. It lasted for more than a year, and included the Prussian siege of Paris, the capture of Napoleon III who then abdicated the French throne, the payment of a five milliard compensation to Prussia when the war was over, and above all, the joining of the Rhenish states on Prussia's side. It was all celebrated by raising the Victory Column in the Tiergarten, distinguished by being partially constructed out of captured French cannons. A statue of Bismarck stands nearby.

German Unification

The war ended in May 1871. On 18 January 1871, Wilhelm I, King of Prussia, had become Wilhelm I, German Emperor – not emperor *of* Germany, for the Wittelsbachs and other royal houses would not accept that. He was proclaimed at, of all places, Versailles Palace, twelve miles outside of Paris, the symbol of French grandeur and power – and Prussian military headquarters during most of the war. The event was a slight to the French, and was intended so; and it was not forgotten. All the same, the Second German Empire was born, and unlike its predecessor, was comprised exclusively of German states and principalities. It would last exactly forty-eight years.

CHAPTER EIGHT

The Age of Bismarck,
1871–1890

Neustadt period?

Between 1871 and 1890, Germany emerged as the dominant military, diplomatic and economic power on the European continent. This was the 'Age of Bismarck,' and it made the rest of Europe uneasy.

Economic 'Take off'

The maturation of the German Industrial Revolution was an enabling factor. After 1871, Germany experienced, as historian Koppel Pinson phrased it, 'the change from a backward and predominantly agrarian nation to a modern and highly efficient industrial and technological one.' This reflected the rise in capital investment, expanding business and industrial organizations like Krupp of Essen, and modernization in technology such as Rudolf Diesel's engine, patented in 1892. By 1913 Germany was the leading economic competitor of Britain and the United States in trade, banking, insurance, industry and shipping, and the *Reichsmark* was the leading European rival of the English Pound. The impact overall on Germany was enormous.

POPULATION, URBANIZATION AND EMIGRATION

By 1913, the German population was nearly 68 million. In terms of population density, examples of extreme change include Silesia going from 48 to 130 inhabitants per square kilometre, the Rhineland 70 to 264, and Saxony 78 to 321. This reflected a simultaneous urbanization; by 1910 only 40 per cent of the population was rural, and cities had exploded in size. In round numbers, between 1820 and 1910 Berlin went from 200,000 to 2,000,000, Breslau 79,000 to 500,000, Cologne

55,000 to 600,000, Essen 4,700 to 410,000, Frankfurt-am-Main 41,000 to 415,000, Hamburg 128,000 to 950,000, Leipzig 37,000 to 645,000, and Munich 62,000 to 665,000. And emigration fell from a high of 83,000 per year in 1881 to 18,000 in 1912.

OCCUPATION AND INCOME

Also, in 1913 the Gross Domestic Product had grown to 43,500,000,000 *Reichsmarks*, and per capita 645 *Reichsmarks*. That was good news for the economy, though it did not notably improve the quality of life for workers. The bad news for the economy was that agriculture declined as industry expanded. Between 1851 and 1874 1,152 new *aktiengesellschaften* (corporations) were formed, and by 1914 over 50 per cent of workers were engaged in industry and crafts; those working in agriculture had dropped to 34 per cent. Wheat, rye, livestock, hops for beer, grapes for wine, beet sugar and tobacco production shrank relative to the rise in population, so that on the eve of the First World War, Germany was importing more than 20 per cent of its agricultural needs from neighbouring countries. In 1912 that included 200,000 cattle, 157,000,000 *Reichsmarks* worth of beef and bacon, and 907,000,000 *Reichsmarks* worth of milk, cream, butter, lard and various fats. This contributed to the value of German imports still exceeding that of exports by 1913.

INFRASTRUCTURE AND PRODUCTION

German industry depended upon an infrastructure of transportation, power sources and raw materials. By 1910 there were 60,000 kilometres of railway lines, and large shipping lines such as North German Lloyd in Bremen and the Hamburg-Amerika line in Hamburg, were in place for international trade. Coal production, mainly in the Ruhr, Saar, Silesia and Saxony, was 191,000,000 metric tons in 1913, 100,000,000 less than Britain. In 1910 pig iron production was 14,800,000 metric tons, 14,000,000 less than in the United States. Meanwhile, Werner von Siemens (1816–1892) and Emil Rathenau (1838–1915) pushed electricity production to the front of the pack, and by 1913 Germany produced more electrical products even than did the United States. So too in chemicals, where I. G. Farben and Bayer of aspirin fame stood out. And in armaments: Krupp employed 140 workers in 1846; by 1912 that number had risen to 68,000.

Of course, there were ups and downs. Sometimes industry over-produced, the money market over speculated, and crises followed. In 1873 the Vienna stock exchange went south, which made German investors nervous and caused difficulties for banks, the German stock exchange dragged its feet throughout the last years of the century, and German investors tended to look outside of Germany for opportunities. Meanwhile, increase in foreign competition inspired formation of *Verein deutscher Stahl-und Eisenindustrieller* (Association of German Steel and Iron Industrialists) in 1873 in Westphalia and the Rhineland, which campaigned for protective tariffs; it gained support across the nation. Organizer and strategist for this and other big business pressure groups was Heinrich Axel Bueck (1830–1916). Over time, the Navy and Army Leagues, Colonial League and Pan-German League formed and followed Bueck's example in both pressuring government and ignoring the parliamentary process.

THE SOCIAL IMPACT

Industrialists generally opposed trades unions and advocated the most work for the least pay possible. The mind-set was as Victorian as that in Britain. Wrote economic historian Hans Jaeger:

> ... they were thoroughly comfortable with the conventions of morality, decency, and authority prevalent in the late Victorian age. Strong person-alities, they expected obedient employees, wives, and children, although in their own eyes they were caring business leaders, fathers, and husbands. ... Their interests were largely confined to their businesses [and they] were also apolitical. Naturally they were nationalists, patriots, and anti-Marxists, but politics as such, they claimed, interested them only insofar as it affected their businesses.

Bismarck would have wanted it no other way; he was as unsympathetic to trades unions as any other German reactionary – such as Emperor Wilhelm II, who termed unions 'a mob not worthy of the name human.'

Still they were a presence, though initially not a large one. Christian unions and Hirsch-Duncker unions attracted very few members in the

1840s and 1850s, and even by 1875 unions associated with the *Sozial-demokratische partei* (Social Democratic Party, SPD) had less than one per cent of the national work force. However, this changed over time because improvements in the condition of labour did not keep pace with industrial expansion. In 1913 the average work week was 57 hours and the average annual wage 1,163 *Reichsmarks,* insufficient to sustain an adequate life. Industrial cities, inhabited in part by rural immigrants who were ill-prepared to deal with urban life, were overcrowded and poorly organized, and experienced regular outbreaks of contagious diseases such as tuberculosis and rickets; and, petty crime, alcoholism and domestic violence were commonplace. And factories, as historian Holger Holwig described them, 'were built as cheaply as possible: gray, ugly, unhealthy industrial barracks. . . . Noise, dirt, heat, cold, and physical as well as psychic brutality dominated the workplace. Chest and lung diseases flourished.' It is no wonder that trades unions began to play a major role in politics. By 1914 they counted 2,500,000 million members, and the SPD received 4,000,000 votes in the 1912 *Reichstag* elections. SPD deputies voted yes on war credits in 1914, largely with the expectation that the war would pave the way for a new, socialist, society. Only Georg Ledebour (1850–1947) voted no; but, then, he was a pacifist.

Bismarck's Empire

This was the reality of the empire that technically was ruled by Wilhelm I. He simply was too heavily under Chancellor Bismarck's influence for it to be said that he decided much on his own.

IMPERIAL STRUCTURE

The Imperial Constitution, crafted by Bismarck on the North German Confederation model, created a federated German empire based upon a dual constitution with separate powers for the empire and for the states – not unlike the United States of America. The empire oversaw customs, foreign policy and international trade, the military, postal service, and anything else that applied to the empire as a whole. Individual States oversaw their internal affairs, including the maintenance of law and order. The emperor had the power to declare *defensive* war – that point was made very clear – and was commander in chief of an imperial army only in time of war. That changed later when the States, save for Bavaria, Saxony and Württemberg, gave their military systems over to imperial control. The emperor also had the power to select and dismiss the chancellor, who in turn chose the cabinet ministers. This took control of the cabinet away from the parliament; the exact opposite of the British system, and at some variance with that of the United States.

The constitution also provided for a two-house parliament and a federal court system (individual States maintained their own courts for dealing with local affairs). The federal system included a supreme court which adjudicated between states, and lesser federal courts which dealt with matters involving federal law. The parliament was divided between the *Bundesrat* (upper house), with delegates chosen by State governments who also instructed them on how to vote, and the *Reichstag* (lower house), elected by 'the most progressive franchise in Europe: universal, secret, equal, direct, manhood suffrage.' Wonderful words, but in fact this nominally representative popular assembly had no real power to form policy or force choices on the imperial government; and until 1906 its members were unpaid.

PRUSSIA

Prussia remained special. The colours of the imperial flag were the black, white and red of the Prussian flag, the *Landtag* remained in place, elected by three estates – aristocracy, urban middle class and commons – and Wilhelm was both King of Prussia and German Emperor. With a single exception, Prince Chlodwig zu Hohenlohe-Schillingfürst, chancellors between 1871 and 1918 were also Prussian minister-presidents. Prussian delegates in the *Bundesrat* had the power of veto. Simply put, Prussia not only ran the empire, in a very real sense it *was* the empire.

Party Politics

Political parties came of age in the Age of Bismarck. They would play a key role in German politics ever after – save, of course, in the Third Reich, where only the one was permitted.

PARTIES

In the 1870s, the strongest party was the staunchly Protestant Prussian Conservative Party, the party of the Gerlachs, Manteuffels and other Junkers who had helped Bismarck scale the heights of political power, simply because it was Prussian. It favoured aristocratic balance in politics – the tradition of the landed Prussian nobility – was the party of imperial army leadership, and had the ear of the throne. The largest parties with regard to membership were the National Liberals and the Progressives, largely centred in the north and northwest. The National Liberals were essentially middle class and imperialist, though also pro-constitution, and advocated a state of laws and economic *laissez-faire*. The Progressives also were largely middle class, but more democratically oriented, demanding 'energetic action' by the imperial government on important issues, and 'responsible ministry' and wanted a cabinet answerable to the *Reichstag*. These parties faded in importance after the 1870s, owing to internal disputes, and the SPD and *Zentrum* (Catholic Centre Party) emerged as the most important; they alone would outlast the empire.

SOZIALDEMOKRATISCHE PARTEI (SOCIAL DEMOCRATS)

The SPD represented workers and the proletariat generally, but its leaders were elite middle-class intellectuals; this was customary on the left in the late nineteenth century. The party was a composite of Marxist and Lasallist, the latter referring to Ferdinand Lasalle (1825–1864), founder of the first German socialist party in 1863 which advocated a form of state socialism, and who, as a personality, had more in common with Bismarck than either liked to admit. The SPD had the best leadership, organization and bureaucracy of any German party; what it did not have was any support beyond the working class. Non-Socialist populist movements were alarmed by the SPD, fearing that its ultimate aim was radical revolution; which, of course, was precisely the aim of its Marxist supporters such as Spartacist League founders Karl Leibknecht (1871–1919) and Rosa Luxemburg (1870–1919). The party mainstream aimed only for a 'reformed' society. The SPD was usually in the political wilderness

Rosa Luxemburg, killed in 1919 by right-wing terrorists

where the *Reichstag* was concerned, and yet it was upon their position regarding public welfare that Bismarck based reforms between 1884 and 1889 that included national health insurance, worker's compensation, minimum wage and protection of worker's rights. In fact, Bismarck's real aim with these reforms was to undercut the trades unions. In 1878, when 'a deranged carpenter' took a shot at Wilhelm I, Bismarck had claimed that the SPD was behind the would-be assassin and tried to force a law through the *Reichstag* that would ban Socialism. It failed.

ZENTRUM (CATHOLIC CENTRE)

Centred in southern and southwestern Germany and overwhelmingly Catholic and international in outlook, the Centre embraced the 1870 Papal Bull of Pius IX (1792–1878) that proclaimed papal infallibility, along with the Church's desire to promote and control morality and its own educational system within Germany and to determine the criteria for marriage for German Catholics. All of this suggested to Bismarck less than complete loyalty to empire and emperor, and therefore a threat to German national security. That was all the excuse he needed to take on the Centre and force it to bend to the will of Protestant Germany.

KULTURKAMPF

In 1872, Bismarck launched the *'kulturkampf'* ('Struggle for Civilization') – the term was introduced during an 1873 *Reichstag* debate – a Catholic–Protestant battle for Germany. The 'struggle' began with an imperial decree suppressing the Jesuits in Germany, followed by the 'Falk Laws,' introduced by Minister of Religious Affairs Adelbert Falk, which ordered the arrest of Catholic priests and other clergy who disputed obedience to imperial rulings on any point. This was a 'war' that Bismarck could not win. Catholics resisted, arrests were made, and the 'image of uniformed Prussian policemen crashing through the windows of Catholic rectories while priests fled out the back doors' was more than most Germans could accept. No victory, but perhaps a compromise. Pius IX died in 1878 and his successor, Leo XIII (1810–1903), agreed to concessions on such issues as religious education. Bismarck in turn backed away from the Falk Laws.

German Catholics had much to offer the anti-Socialist Bismarck State, a fact of which he became increasingly aware in the 1880s. Father Adolf Kolping's *vogelsang*, a priest-run programme for helping the indigent, had evolved into a theory of social and labour interaction. It inspired the papal encyclical *Rerum Novarum* (1891) which directed Catholics along a middle path between capitalism and socialism, and between the material and the sacred. *Rerum Novarum* denounced class war and averred that the duty of workers was loyalty to enterprise, while the duty of property was responsibility to help the workers. After Bismarck lost National Liberal support in 1879, he relied on Conservatives and the Catholic Centre to support his policies. Of course, he fought constantly with Centre leader Ludwig Windthorst (1812–1891) and Liberal leader Ludwig Bamberger (1823–1899), both of whom he secretly admired. After all, he had to keep up appearances.

Rights for Women

Women in Imperial Germany did not have equality with men – hardly unique, for that was the case everywhere. 'Bismarckian Germany was a male-dominated society, and its male guardians were determined that it remain so,' noted Holger Herwig. Indeed, the Chancellor once remarked that he had 'a decided horror of clever women.' (His mother once again? Probably.) Women were barred by law from voting, and, save for in Baden, Württemberg, Bremen and Hamburg, from participating in political organizations and trade unions. Women also were denied access to *Gymnasium* and universities until the twentieth century although, bizarre as it sounds, women from foreign countries *could* attend German universities. In 1865, Luise Otto-Peters (1819–1895) launched the General German Women's Association and the German suffragist movement was underway. Socialist leader August Bebel (1840–1913) supported the movement; the SPD did not, and when he introduced a bill in the *Reichstag* in 1895 to grant female suffrage, it was rejected out of hand. Clearly, little real progress had been made over that thirty years, and at the time of Bebel's bill, Emperor Wilhelm II (1859–1941) publically advocated service to the three Ks, '*Kinder, Küche, Kirche*' (children, kitchen, church), as the proper role for women.

The struggle for women's rights continued all the same. In 1894, Auguste Schmidt (1833–1902) formed the Federation of German Women's Associations. Its newsletter, *Die Frau,* relentlessly advocated improvement in every aspect of women's lives. And changes were made. Women were identified as 'legal persons' for the first time in the Civil Code of 1900, and in 1901 the first German women were admitted to universities as full-time students. Various organizations campaigned for improved conditions for agricultural and industrial working women; but success was limited, and indeed opposition to women's rights began to rise among middle-class women. In 1912 they formed the League for the Struggle Against the Emancipation of Women which was predicated upon an incipient racism. The League advocated 'racial hygiene' on matters of reproduction, such as 'breeding the healthy' and thus maintaining 'racial health.' This position was endorsed by the likes of sociologist Max Weber (1864–1920), and, ironically, Sigmund Freud (1856–1939), physician, founder of psychoanalysis, and a Jew. One must wonder if he knew that a League supporter, the German National Commercial Employer's Union, linked the feminist movement to a 'Jewish world conspiracy.'

Bismarckian Foreign Policy

Bismarck's foreign policy corresponded to the views of the army, the agrarian elite, pressure groups such as the conservative Navy League – and even, on occasion, the emperor – but no one else. His objective was to maintain peace in Europe, and the security in Europe of Prussia and Germany. Unification had raised concerns among the powers regarding the former by tipping the Balance of Power in Germany's favour. Diplomatic juggling was needed; and no one was better at that than Otto von Bismarck.

THE FRENCH PROBLEM

France was understandably miffed at losing the Franco-Prussian War, a loss accompanied by paying Germany a huge compensation and giving up Alsace and Lorraine. From 1871 the French rallying cry was '*Revanchisme!*' (Revenge). However, the rest of Europe wanted peace; it accepted unification and even approved of German efforts at isolating France, so long as the Balance of Power was not endangered. Simply put, the Congress of Vienna mentality still lived, and Bismarck exploited it. In 1873 he introduced the *Dreikaiserbund* (Three Emperors' League) of Germany, Austria-Hungary and Russia, as a move to isolate France. In 1875, the French chamber of deputies voted for an arms increase, *Die Post* in Berlin published an article provocatively titled: 'Is War in Sight?', and the Imperial General Staff gave the appearance of being amenable to such an eventuality. Bismarck exploited this 'crisis' to isolate France even further, but failed. Austria and Russia preferred a mediated resolution, and Bismarck had to back down. It was clear that he could not have all of Europe on his side against France which, differences over colonial interests notwithstanding, was moving ever so cautiously towards closer relations with both Russia and Great Britain. Nor did the French repudiate *Revanchisme;* in 1878 the Boulangerists expressed decidedly hostile attitudes towards Germany, and in 1896, when Jewish French army captain Alfred Dreyfus was accused (falsely) of selling military secrets – to the Germans, of all people! – the public outcry was unprecedented.

THE RUSSIAN PROBLEM

Russia and the Ottoman Empire had been at odds for more than a century. They went to war in 1877 over the Straits of the Bosporus and Dardanelles, which linked the Black Sea to the Mediterranean and could provide Russia with a year-round warm–water seaport connecting its trading ships to European markets. Russia won, and imposed the Treaty of San Stephano, demanding huge indemnities from Turkey and control of the Straits. This would not do, claimed the western powers, for it endangered European security, that is, it endangered French and British Middle East interests, including the Suez Canal built by a Frenchman and funded by the British, which opened in 1869. Germany was not directly involved, so Bismarck seized the opportunity to play 'honest broker' by summoning the powers to the Congress of Berlin in 1878. Russia was forced to back off, and an independent kingdom of Serbia was formed in the Balkans, ostensibly to limit Russia influence there. However, Serbia posed a problem for the Austrian Empire which had considerable, and expanding, Balkan interests.

Russia never forgave Germany for the Congress of Berlin, and moved toward closer relations with Britain and France. Bismarck persuaded Russia to join in renewing the *Dreikaiserbund* in 1881, but this did not ease the growing tensions, which now included Austria. The reason was that the Pan-Slav movement was in full swing with Russia in the lead and applying pressure to Serbian and other Balkan Slavs, to come to Russia's side. As a result, Austro-Russian relations deteriorated while Vienna's connections with Berlin grew stronger. By 1886 the *Dreikaiserbund* was dead. Bismarck made a last-ditch effort in 1887, negotiating the Reinsurance Treaty (Austria excluded) in which both powers promised neutrality in a war involving either of them. It was dropped in the 1890s when Wilhelm II decided that such a treaty was inimical to German interests in Europe and the Middle East. Meanwhile, in 1882 Bismarck had negotiated the Triple Alliance of Germany, Austria and Italy, which was renewed in February 1887. A year later, in a *Reichstag* speech that dealt mainly with the Russian situation, Bismarck proclaimed: 'We Germans fear God, and nothing else in the world!' The terms of the Triple Alliance were made public for the first time immediately after.

GERMAN COLONIES

Germany had no overseas empire when Bismarck became chancellor, and he had no interest in acquiring one. 'As long as I am Chancellor of the Reich,' he vowed in 1881, 'we shall not carry on any colonial policy.' Many Germans disagreed. Missionaries, and Hansa commercial interests had been penetrating Africa since the 1840s; nationalist historian Heinrich von Treitschke (1834–1896) argued that without colonies Germany would remain a second-rate power; and organizations formed to promote colonization, notably the Colonial Union in 1882 in Frankfurt-am-Main, and the Society for German Colonization in 1884 in Berlin. Bismarck began to see that, in historian Gordon Craig's words, 'the political capital that might be derived from a colonial policy outweighed the risks involved,' and 'if properly directed, might even serve to strengthen the system of alliances. . . .' Angra-Pequeña provided the perfect opportunity.

ANGRA-PEQUEÑA

It worked like this. The British occupied Walvis Bay on the southwest African coast. In 1883, Germany requested that they provide protection for a German trader with a post at the port of Angra-Pequeña, south of Walvis Bay. The British claimed they had no authority to do so, since their jurisdiction did not include that port and, moreover, they would object to the Germans *or anyone else* laying claim to the territory in question. Bismarck had not even hinted that Germany might make such a claim; however, the British response suggested a way to drive a wedge between France and Britain and bring the former closer to Germany. Acutely aware of Anglo-French differences regarding Egypt, Bismarck sent a message to the French premier Jules Ferry urging France to 'take up a strong line' with Britain on Egypt, noting in the process that Germany too had 'quarrels with Britain,' specifically over Angra-Pequeña, and hinted that Germany was 'with France' against Britain. The implicit message of course was that if not opposed, Britain would seek to take over all of Africa.

Bismarck needed a 'coup' so that the naturally suspicious French would be persuaded. In 1884 he sent a deputation to London under his son, Herbert, to demand first the secession of Angra-Pequeña to Germany, and then the entire South West Territory. Bismarck was certain that the British would refuse, and in so doing, demonstrate the aggressive and acquisitive nature of their colonial policy. What was needed, he assured the French, was a 'league of all the secondary maritime powers, led by France' to keep the British empire in line. To Bismarck's chagrin, the British agreed to Germany's demands, and the French backed away, certain that he had been trying to finagle them into a conflict with the British. Anglo-French difficulties would continue in Africa, but the French were now even further away from resolving their differences with Germany.

The door was now open to a German colonial empire; by 1886, Germany claimed southwest Africa and protectorates in East Africa and Zanzibar, and by 1910, had established colonial claims in the Far East, the South Seas, the Near and Middle East and North Africa, although nothing like the British and French in those regions.

The Life of the Mind in Imperial Germany

German science, philosophy and historiography also 'took off'. Empiricism now was the foundation upon which rested the life of the mind; exploration and experimentation leading to new theories regarding how things actually are, was the order of the day.

SCIENCE

Germany was 'part of the package' of nineteenth-century empirical science, which focused on finding out how things work through research and then making practical use of the information. In the Napoleonic Era, Alexander von Humboldt (1769–1859), younger brother of Wilhelm, worked in scientific geography, the 'comprehensive analysis of climate, vegetation, and fauna in their relation to human activities.' After Napoleon, Karl Friedrich Gauss (1777–1855), astronomer and mathematician at Göttingen University, collaborated with his colleague Wilhelm Weber (1804–1891) in constructing the first electromagnetic telegraph. Medicine was revolutionized in the middle third of the century through the anatomical and biological research of such as Johannes Müller (1801–1858), Johann Schönlein (1793–1864) and Rudolf Virchow (1821–1902). At the same time, Justus von Liebig (1803–1873) laid the foundations for organic chemistry, Gregor Mendel (1823–1884) for genetic science, while Robert Koch (1843–1910) identified the bacterial sources of anthrax, Asiatic cholera and tuberculosis. And, of course, by the end of the century, Sigmund Freud in Vienna was beginning what his contemporaries regarded as the very scary science of psychoanalysis.

Appropriately, Austrian physicist-philosopher Ernst Mach (1838–1916) was then trying to interrelate physics and psychology in the context of scientific method. His contribution as a physicist to measuring the speed of objects relative to sound was more practically useful. In fact, the principle is named after him: for example, when at twice the speed of sound, a jet aircraft is flying at 'Mach 2.' Meanwhile, Wilhelm Roentgen (1845–1923) developed the science of X-rays, Max Planck (1858–1947), after whom a number of physics research institutes in Germany are named, articulated the quantum theory of energy, and between 1905 and 1916, Albert Einstein (1879–1955) advanced the theory of relativity, which radically changed the concept of the relationship between speed, time and space.

PHILOSOPHY

After Kant and Hegel, metaphysics were out, and empiricism – sometimes flavoured with existentialism – was in. Well, not entirely. At Marburg, Herman Cohen and Paul Natorp founded a neo-Kantian school as their own interpretation of the master's ideas which Nicolai Hartmann, of the generation after them, initially embraced but then turned against, at least to the extent of arguing ontology, a new, realistic metaphysics of being. He was encouraged by Moravian native Edmund Husserl (1859–1938), who laid out Phenomenology (emphasis on the analysis of 'pure consciousness') in his *Logische Untersuchungen*. Husserl founded a 'school' which enthusiastically opposed the 'social Darwinism' of Herbert Spencer's followers, and the 'exaggerated idealism' of the neo-Kantian Marburg school.

Friedrich Nietzsche

Then there was Germany's most complicated philosopher, Friedrich Nietzsche (1844–1900). He was at odds with everything conventional, including Reason. Nietzsche attacked Christianity, Judaism, democracy, nationalism, rationality, science and progress, and argued the intellectual limitations of women, while counting educated women among his most important intellectual friends. *Birth of Tragedy* equalled in importance and nobility the rational and nonrational aspects of human nature. *Also Sprach Zarathustra* denounced egalitarianism and Christianity, and proclaimed the death of the Judeo-Christian God which he viewed as the result of stultifying concepts of religion. Nietzsche then advocated creation of the 'Superman,' a being engaged in constant upward self-realization. Other writings argued for morality, against morality, and ... well, you get the idea. He also composed piano music, some of which has survived and been recorded. In his early adult years, Nietzsche was a friend of Richard Wagner, which often has contributed to interpretations of his 'Superman' thesis and criticism of Judaism as anti-Semitic. In fact, he later broke with Wagner, in part because of the composer's anti-Semitism.

HISTORIOGRAPHY

Historians were a major part of the German life of the mind, especially those with a political perspective. In *History of Prussian Politics* Gustav Droysen (1808–1884) advocated Prussian hegemony in Germany – he was a pro-Prussian member of the Frankfurt parliament in 1848 – and in his medieval studies, dismissed the 'Holy Roman Empire' as an ideological aberration. Theodore Mommsen (1817–1903), whose *Roman History* was regarded as a standard work on the subject, was politically active in the Prussian *Landtag* and the German *Reichstag*. And Heinrich von Treitschke's *German History in the Nineteenth Century* was an effective argument for Pan-Germanism. Treitschke described the French as 'half-educated barbarians,' and urged that it was time to rid Germany of Jews. 'The Jews at one time played a necessary role in German history, because of their ability in the management of money,' he wrote. 'But now that the Aryans have become accustomed to the idiosyncrasies of finance, the Jews are no longer necessary.' A bad omen, at the very least.

Without doubt the greatest German historian in the nineteenth century was Leopold von Ranke (1795–1886). His voluminous writings (fifty–four volumes) included a nine-volume *World History* that ended at the eleventh century, and studies of the Reformation and the Papacy reflecting Ranke's perspective as a devout Protestant. He interpreted each historical period in terms of its relationship to God and to the larger context of human history. Above all, he assigned to the historian responsibility for discovering '*wie es eigentlich gewesen*' (how it actually happened), a phrase that became a cornerstone of graduate-school seminars in history at American universities.

Art and Music

Neo-classical and neo-gothic remained the order of the day in German architecture. Painting was another matter. Rhinelander Alfred Rethel's frescos for the Aachen city hall, illustrations for the *Lay of the Nibelungs*, and woodcuts *Dance of Death*, introduced a new realism. However the greatest German realist was fellow Rhinelander Wilhelm Leibl (1844–1900). His idea was that: 'If we paint man as he is, his soul is included as a matter of course.' *Three Women in Church* was Leibl's most popular work, and perhaps also his best. Of course, classicism and romanticism did not disappear altogether, appearing in Anselm Feuerbach's portraits of *Media* and *Iphigenia*, and in the allegorical symbolism of Arnold

Böcklin's landscapes. Meanwhile, Adolf von Mentzel (1815–1905) from Silesia developed a 'luminous brilliance of colouristic pattern and composition' which was impressionist in all but name.

Romanticism remained a feature of German music until the turn of the twentieth century. Johannes Brahms (1833–1897), a Hamburger who finished his career in Vienna, the musical capital of the German world in the later nineteenth century, composed in the classical or romantic style in every genre except opera; Austrian Anton Bruckner (1824–1896) composed neo-romantic music reflecting Richard Wagner (1813–1883); and Gustav Mahler (1860–1911), musical director of the Vienna Court Opera, wrote romantically emotional symphonies and music for such German folk poetry as *Des Knaben Wunderhorn*. Then came Richard Strauss (1864–1949). His operas *Salomé* and *Electra* contained psychopathological elements underscored by particular tonal effects, which 'register and illustrate the most minute nervous reflexes.' And there was a hint of impressionism – an appeal to the senses rather than to realistic imagery – in *Der Rosenkavalier*, although it really was more reflective of operetta style made popular in Vienna by Johann Strauss and Franz von Suppé.

RICHARD WAGNER

The loudest noise in music in Imperial Germany was made by Richard Wagner of Leipzig. He led a 'colourful' life, beginning with his time as a duelling, carousing, womanizing *korpsstudent* at the University of Leipzig. He then became a composer, had many mistresses including Franz Liszt's daughter Cosima, who at the time was married to Wagner's friend and conductor Hans von Bülow, and with whom he produced three children before they finally married, maintained a bizarre relationship with Ludwig II of Bavaria who wanted to be his musical assistant, was outrageously anti-Semitic, and participated in the 1848 revolution in Dresden – it is said to get back at society for not recognizing his greatness. That led to thirteen years of exile, first in Weimar, then Paris. In the words of musicologist Milton Cross, Wagner was 'a liar, a cheat, and a hypocrite, without the slightest regard for ethics, morality, or personal honour. . . . [H]e always lived beyond his means, usually in regal style – "The world owes me a living," he said proudly.' Beyond that, he was indifferent to the feelings of others, regarded it a personal insult to be disagreed with, and would accept as friends only those who took him at his own evaluation. Perhaps this was another reason why Nietzsche ended their friendship. Again Cross: 'Wagner was an objectionable man in every way – except one: his attitude toward his art.'

Wagner's compositions included orchestral, song and operas, but the latter made his reputation. His operas were powerful, romantic, compelling, and ranged in subject matter from medieval romance to the celebration of Teutonic mythology. *Rienzi* 'took the audience by storm,' while *The Flying Dutchman* was a complete flop at the Dresden opera where Wagner was *Kapellmeister*. *Tannhäuser*, based upon the life of a thirteenth-century *Minnesänger*, also was a failure (pornographic, some critics complained), which put Wagner in the resentful mood that prepared him to join the 1848 revolution later. The *Lohengrin* premier was directed by Franz Liszt, but Wagner was then in exile and could not attend; he saw a performance for the first time a decade later. When his exile ended, the composer set up house in Zurich and began work on his grandest compositions, the *Ring of the Nibelungs,* which effectively tells the story of the Teutonic Gods from their beginning to their destruction: *Das Rheingold, Die Walküre, Siegfried,* and *Die Götterdämmerung.* To sit through The Ring takes approximately twenty-four hours. The importance of these works, at least historically, is that they connected Wagner to the rising tide of German ethnic nationalism that contained a virulent strain of anti-Semitism.

Along the way, Wagner composed *Tristan und Isolde,* a love story inspired by his passion for Mathilde Wesendonck, one of his many lovers – and married to a Wagner supporter – and *Die Meistersinger,* appropriately set in Nuremberg where Wagner's greatest twentieth-century German admirer, Adolf Hitler, staged Nazi party mass rallies. The Wagner festival theatre in Bayreuth, Bavaria was designed and built with performances of the Ring in mind. Everybody who was anybody was there for the opening in 1876: Tchaikovsky, Saint-Saëns, Gounod, Grieg, Liszt, Bruckner, to name a few. And they loved it.

Wagner ended his career with *Parsifal*, a story of the search for the Holy Grail, which is to say Redemption; something Wagner sorely needed.

Literature

Realism and naturalism replaced romanticism in German writing in the second half of the nineteenth century. Poets Annette von Droste-Hülshoff (1797–1848) and Adalbert Stifter (1805–1868) were inspired by their deep Catholic faith, but also by the natural world. Silesian Gustav Freytag (1816–1895) wrote historical novels in a realist style, and satiric comedies which poked fun at the daily press, politicians and political party leaders – certainly a form of realism. Otto Ludwig (1813–1865) and Friedrich Hebbel (1813–1863) relied on descriptions of their surroundings 'as they really were,' and engaging in 'exhaustive character analyses.' Ludwig gave his work an innovative psychological slant, while Hebbel developed a 'pan-tragic' approach in which humans had to deal with antithetical contradictions, but could not do so successfully. These contradictions represented the irreconcilable dualism of time and eternity, the natural and the moral, male and female, and life and death. Naturalism was the essence of Gerhart Hauptmann (1862–1946) characters, who were both the products and victims of circumstances beyond their control. He owed much to French writer Emile Zola in this regard.

Meanwhile, impressionism was the format for dramatist, poet and librettist Hugo von Hofmanstahl (1874–1929), and symbolist-impressionism for Rhenish author Stefan George (1868–1933). George repudiated the 'vulgarity of form and content' of naturalism, and embraced the aristocratic separatist attitude contained in the dictum: 'I hate the profane crowd and keep away from it.' Then there were the brothers Heinrich (1871–1950) and Thomas (1875–1955) Mann from Lübeck who addressed the contrast between art and life. Heinrich passed through Bohemianism and then Expressionism, in such works as *Die kleine Stadt* and *Der Untertan*; Thomas 'made the journey' by demonstrating in *Buddenbrooks* how the 'virus' of art and culture threatened physical and mental health, and then by exploring the life-hungry artist in *Tonio Kröger* and an artistic culture embracing social responsibility in *Königliche Hoheit*. It was, when all is said and done, a brilliant age which extended from the time of Bismarck through the Wilhelminian epoch and beyond.

The Fall of Bismarck

Bismarck's career ended shortly after Wagner's death; appropriate, since both thought in terms of power and display. So too, unfortunately for Bismarck, did Wilhelm II.

WILHELM II

Frederick III (1831–1888) ascended the throne in 1888, died 100 days later, and was succeeded by his son, Wilhelm II. The new emperor was an imperialist and monarchist who had no patience with constitutionalism, political parties or independent political participation by any but the wealthy and aristocratic. 'There is only one master in the Reich,' he once said, 'and that is I, and I shall tolerate no other.' This included his chancellor.

AGE AGAINST YOUTH

In 1890, Bismarck was in his seventies, tired, content with the status quo and wanting nothing more than the settled process of day-to-day existence: no more social legislation or territorial expansion. The diplomatic situation in Europe was set, and could be maintained indefinitely to Germany's advantage. However, the emperor thought otherwise, and determined to find a chancellor more to his liking. Bismarck himself provided the opportunity and excuse.

The issue was Bismarck's anti-Socialist regulations, up for renewal by the *Reichstag* in 1890. He had hoped to provoke the Socialists into violent resistance, thus providing an excuse to crush them, including the SPD, presumably, by military force. The consequences were likely to be horrendous, a fact clear to both mainstream German conservatives and the new monarch. Bismarck had his way, initially; a bill was introduced in the *Reichstag* authorizing local governments to expel all Social Democratic Party leaders from villages and towns. Wilhelm ordered that the bill be defeated. It was. Meanwhile, in foreign policy, he demanded closer ties with both Austria and Russia, which Bismarck opposed. It was crunch time.

CRISIS AT THE SCHLOSS

Bismarck dug out an old royal order from 1852 by which King Frederick Wilhelm IV had required all cabinet ministers to consult with the Minister-President *before* consulting with the king. This, Bismarck contended, applied also to the imperial cabinet. His point was to isolate the emperor from all ministerial advice save his own, which, if implemented, would give him the emperor's ear without interference – just as he had the ear of Wilhelm I. Wilhelm II's response was his worst nightmare. Bismarck was ordered to draw up a repeal of the royal order for the emperor's signature, or resign.

What happened next is the stuff of dramatic historical film. Bismarck faced Wilhelm and said he would do no such thing. The emperor reminded him none too kindly, that Ludwig Windthorst, the Centre Party leader, had been seen coming to the Chancellor's apartment during the crisis over Socialist legislation; clearly, if the Chancellor was going to entertain opposition leaders, he could not be trusted. Bismarck understood this to mean that Wilhelm wanted no powerful minister around him, but only ciphers who would be mere spokespersons for the crown. He drew himself up and reminded the emperor of all that he had contributed to making the German empire. Wilhelm responded by throwing an inkwell at him. That did it. Bismarck, stiffly, tendered his verbal resignation, which the emperor accepted. Then he withdrew. To his supporters later, Bismarck proudly said: 'I cannot serve on my knees.'

The emperor had won. The Iron Chancellor was apparently not missed. Wrote *Die Vossische Zeitung* in March 1890:

> [N]ot a finger had been lifted, not a pen taken up so far as individuals and journals in an independent position are concerned, to advocate Prince Bismarck's continuance in office. The Iron Chancellor had lost his sureness of touch, he had begun to vacillate, while the will of the youthful and energetic ruler was coming more and more strongly into play.

Still, given what lay ahead for Germany, perhaps Bismarck was just as well off out of it. He spent the last years of his life writing his memoirs, which were classical Bismarck: reality manipulated with sufficient skill as to make it appear that he had planned, and controlled, virtually everything that happened between 1862 and 1890. Wagner could not have done it better.

AFTER BISMARCK

None of Bismarck's successors down to the end of the Great War were in his league: Leo von Caprivi, a general and man of some principle, was unable to cope with Wilhelm's strong will; south German aristocrat Prince Chlodwig zu Hohenlohe-Schillingfürst was nearly eighty when he took the post, and spent most of his time sleeping off his lunch and dictating his voluminous memoirs; Prince Bernhard von Bülow was a Junker reactionary, a tool and an anachronism who thought the empire should be based on agriculture rather than industry; and Theobald von Bethmann-Hollweg was a man of potential, but was outnumbered, outflanked and finally overturned by the war and its commanding generals; and his war-time successors, Georg Michaelis and Count von Hertling, were completely at the mercy of the General Erich Ludendorff (1865–1937), advisor on the General Staff to Field Marshal Paul von Hindenburg (1847–1934).

CHAPTER NINE

The Age of Wilhelm II, 1890–1918

Emperor Wilhelm II was born with a withered left arm. As a growing child, he wore braces, clamps, a medical boot, and was given shock treatments to make the arm grow into normality. Nothing worked. The arm appeared to atrophy, and as portrait photographs make clear, it remained shorter than his right arm his entire life. The deformity may have given him an inferiority complex, contributing to his 'bully-boy' expansionism of the pre-1914 era. A theory only; yet Wilhelm pushed with an 'in your face' attitude for a German colonial empire, challenged British naval supremacy, and revelled in being Commander-in-Chief of the largest German army in history.

Germany After Bismarck

The sacking of Otto von Bismarck as Chancellor, pictured in a London *Punch* cartoon as the emperor 'dropping the pilot' of the German ship of state, opened the door to Wilhelm calling the shots as Head of State. And he did for the most part with the support of the system under which Germany functioned in Bismarck's era: the Prussian aristocracy set the standards for the army, western German industrialists ran the economy, and aristocrats, also mostly western, dominated the imperial bureaucracy.

'THE MOST BRILLIANT FAILURE IN HISTORY'

What was he like, the new German emperor, grandson of Queen Victoria of England? He was twenty-nine, full of himself, and in the view of Portuguese diplomat and writer José Maria Eça de Queiroz, a man of many faces. In 1891 he described Wilhelm as, variously, a Soldier King who put changing the guard over all matters of state, a Reform King concerned only with capital and wages, a King by Divine Right 'haughtily resting his sceptre on the backs of his people,' a Courtier King, worldly and pompous, and a Modern King, 'dreaming of a Germany worked entirely by electricity.' Queiroz opined that what he actually was, or would be, was anyone's guess.

In fact, the bottom line for Wilhelm was imperialism, absolutism – to the extent the constitution allowed – and militarism. He was contemptuous of *Reichstag* leaders, whom he called 'Sheep's Heads,' and 'Night Watchmen,' and once remarked that if Centre Party leader Ludwig Windthorst ever came to the Palace, 'I would have him collared by a subaltern and three men and thrown out.' Wilhelm began his first public address as emperor 'To my Army,' rather than 'To my People.' His military policy was to increase the army and armaments, for in his view, and that of the Imperial General Staff, an expanded *Reichswehr* (imperial army) was essential for Germany to achieve the great things 'divinely' ordained for it. He once remarked that: 'Our Lord God would not have taken such great pains with our German Fatherland and people if He did not have still greater things in store for us'.

Not everyone was impressed. Walter Rathenau (1867–1922), executive of the electoral cartel AEG and architect of Germany's economic mobilization in the First World War, complained of

The Reichstag Building by Paul Wallot

Wilhelm's 'dilettante foreign policy, romantic conservative internal policy, and bombastic and empty cultural policy.' And a 1903 edition of American magazine *Harper's Weekly* published a poem in Wilhelm's 'honour,' which read in part:

> Kaiser, Kaiser, shining bright,
> You have given us a fright!
> With your belts and straps and sashes,
> And your skyward-turned mustaches! . . .
> Kaiser, Kaiser, Man of War,
> What a funny joke you are.

Dividing Europe

Wilhelm's foreign policy was *Weltpolitik*, a 'new course' to making Germany a world power with a large, modern navy as part of the military establishment. Chancellor von Bülow echoed the emperor's views in his first *Reichstag* speech:

> We do not desire to put anyone else in the shade, but we want our place in the sun. . . . The sea has become a factor of more importance in our national life than ever before in our history. . . . It has become a vital nerve which we must not allow to be severed if we do not wish to be transformed from a rising and youthfully vigorous people into a decaying and aging one.

Bülow and other 'New Course' advocates were influenced also by the fact that expanding German industry now needed a world rather than a European market.

COLONIES AND NATIONALISM

Colonialism was the answer, and historian and nationalist Adalbert Wahl was among its enthusiasts: 'Germany needed colonies . . . in order to provide a field of activity for the German people overflowing with the spirit of enterprise and energy and to help create a new and less commonplace type of German.' Moreover, this Germany 'must not be hemmed in,' thus articulating the concept of *lebensraum* (living space) later used by the Nazi regime to justify expansion eastward. Meanwhile, future Weimar foreign secretary Gustav Stresemann (1878–1929) waxed romantic on colonies as 'a piece of the German soul.' By 1914 the German colonial empire covered more than 1 million square miles, with a population of 12,000,000 native peoples and 24,300 Europeans – German emigration to the colonies was a non-starter – and an investment value of 505,000,000 *Reichsmarks*. Not much compared to the British Empire, nor overly competitive with that of France; but it was a start.

Colonialism was inevitably linked to nationalism, xenophobic and racist among both Germans and Austrians from the start, but even more so in the Age of Wilhelm. In 1905 students in Vienna rioted against the presence of 'foreigners' in the University, while the Pan-German Association emphasized an early form of Aryanism echoing Heinrich Class, a former Prussian Ministry of Justice official, who recommended reducing democracy, expanding German power abroad, and removing 'Jewish influence' from German affairs. Meanwhile, the German Conservative Party espoused anti-Semitism, and in the years before 1914, Vienna mayor Otto Lueger systematically exploited anti-Semitism as a political weapon within the city.

THE ANGLO-GERMAN NAVAL RACE

In 1890, the German fleet ranked seventh in the world in size and capability. In 1896 Wilhelm II proclaimed Germany a *Weltreich* (World Power), and in 1897 ordered that American Admiral Alfred Thayer Mahan's writings on the importance of sea power be translated into German and distributed as pro-navy propaganda. The same year naval expansion enthusiast Admiral Alfred von Tirpitz (1849–1930) was appointed naval affairs secretary. Tirpitz understood the value of propaganda, and in 1898 launched the *Flottenverein* (German Navy League) to promote naval expansion and lobby support for it in the *Reichstag*. Within a decade the League had over 1,000,000 members, and its official newsletter circulated to more than 370,000. Industrial and commercial leaders, backed by university professors, enthusiastically supported naval expansion, which in their view was linked directly to expanded international trade. Only Progressives, Socialists, Poles, Guelphs (a small *Reichstag* party dedicated to hatred of Prussia), and a minority section of the Centrist party opposed it. The first naval expansion bill passed the *Reichstag* in 1898; subsequent bills passed in 1900, 1906, 1907 and 1908.

The British were not pleased. They were already suspicious because in 1893 Germany had opened the Kiel Canal connecting the Baltic Sea with the North Atlantic, fortified the North Sea island of Heligoland, and entered as preamble to the 1900 navy bill: 'Germany must have a battle fleet so strong that, even for the adversary with the greatest sea power, a war against us would involve such dangers as to imperil her position in the world.' Could this have any other purpose than to challenge the British Empire or perhaps to stage a sneak attack on Britain? That was Erskine Childers' view in his novel *Riddle of the Sands,* published in 1903. Nonsense, countered Wilhelm in a 1908 interview with the London *Daily Telegraph.* The German navy was to protect German commerce, not threaten Great Britain, and the English were 'mad, mad as March hares' to think otherwise. In any case, he went on, Britain had made building a German navy necessary in the first place.

And so, the naval race was on. Encouraged by First Lord of the Admiralty Sir John Fisher, Parliament passed appropriations bills for naval expansion, and in 1906 Britain launched the first fully modern battleship, the 17,000 ton *Dreadnought.* It had ten twelve-inch guns, eleven-inch armour plating, and a speed of twenty-one knots. Of course, it was not cheap at £1,600,000, and compromise had to be made on the number built. Winston Churchill and David Lloyd George led the 'We want eight and we won't wait' campaign in 1908, but had to settle for four. All the same, by 1914 Britain had eighteen battleships and Germany thirteen.

Triple Alliance, Triple Entente

At issue in the First World War were imperial, colonial, national, military and economic concerns with central Europe on one side, and western Europe allied with the Russian Empire on the other. While the course of events that shaped this divide sometimes resembled chaos, there was a certain mad logic to them all the same.

CRISES IN AFRICA

The South African War, traditionally referred to as the Boer War (1899–1902), was fought between Great Britain and the Boer Republic of Transvaal. Wilhelm II took a keen interest because German Southwest Africa was next door, and made public his 'moral support' for the Boer side. That included the congratulatory telegram he sent to Transvaal president Paul Kruger on the occasion of successfully fending off the Jamison Raid on Transvaal in 1895, which set the stage for the Boer War. British soldiers showed their 'appreciation' for the German emperor by demeaning him in public. Meanwhile, in 1898 Britain and France faced off over Fashoda in east Africa, but stopped short of war and began discussing ways to satisfactorily divide their interests in northern and eastern Africa. Wilhelm's bellicosity was raising hackles in both nations, and in 1904 they settled their territorial differences over Egypt, Morocco and elsewhere in Africa, Canada, and Asia, and formed the Entente Cordial. The Entente was not a military alliance, but it was understood that one could be arranged in case of need. Germany challenged the Entente, which resulted in the First Moroccan Crisis in 1905. Wilhelm (on the urgent advice of his chancellor and foreign minister) visited the Sultan of Morocco and insisted that Germany should have a share with Britain and France in Moroccan economic affairs. The Sultan then convened a conference at Algeçiras, where France and Britain persuaded Germany to back off in exchange for certain considerations. Wilhelm returned home and claimed in a public address that 'Germany is the friend of the 400,000,000 Moslems in the world.' He may actually have said 'only friend,' though that is not clear; if he did, it certainly was meant to provoke the French and British.

RUSSIAN PROBLEMS

Britain's alliance with Japan in 1902 strained Anglo–Russian relations. St Petersburg saw Japan's rising and admittedly aggressive power in the Pacific as a threat to eastern Siberia, not to mention to Russia's imperial interests in China. The result was the Russo–Japanese War in 1905, which Russia lost, and which triggered the unsuccessful 1906 workers' revolt in St Petersburg. Now Russia was in a spot and turned back to

Britain for support in dealing with both Japan and the European powers. Britain welcomed the reconciliation, largely out of fear that otherwise Russia might turn to Germany, which would shift the continental balance of power in Germany's favour. France agreed, though with reservations, and joined Great Britain and Russia in 1907 to form the Triple Entente.

After that Russia turned its attention from Asia to the Balkans, where it encouraged, and assisted, Serb expansion. This focus on the Balkans simply carried forward Russia's long-standing effort to connect its only western warm-water ports (the Black Sea) with the Mediterranean. Austrian annexation in 1908 of Bosnia-Herzegovina, which shared a border with Serbia, was as much a move against Russia as against Serbia. Germany backed Austria and warned Russia not to interfere. Meanwhile, Italy withdrew from the Triple Alliance, which had the effect of bringing Germany and Austria-Hungary even closer together; Italy's place in the alliance was filled by Turkey in 1913.

MOROCCO AGAIN

The Second Moroccan Crisis came in 1911. Wilhelm II charged that prior agreements regarding German interests were not being respected, and ordered the German battleship *Panther* to drop anchor at the port of Agadir. Much to-ing and fro-ing followed between Germany, France and Britain, and though war was narrowly avoided, relations remained tense and the pace of European armaments speeded up. In 1913 British Foreign Secretary Lord Haldane undertook a mission to Berlin to persuade Germany to join Britain in pushing for a general European disarmament, or at least a downscaling of the arms race. Wilhelm refused even to discuss the issue. 'I and my 21 Army Corps will decide Europe's future,' he brusquely informed Haldane. Europe was now divided in every way imaginable.

The Austro-Serbian Factor

The First World War had many causes, 'entangling alliances' being high on the list. One also could refer to economic and colonial competition, the arms race and the 'accidental bungle,' which was historian A. J. P. Taylor's favourite. And that leads us to the 'Austro-Serbian factor.'

MURDER IN BELGRADE

In 1903, King Alexander and Queen Draga of Serbia were assassinated in the royal palace in Belgrade, their mutilated bodies thrown from a second-storey window. The act was perpetrated by the Black Hand, a militant, ultra-nationalist Serb organization the aim of which was to create a Greater Serbia by adding such regions as Croatia, Slovenia and Bosnia-Herzegovina to the Serb kingdom. The rivalry between the Obrenovitch and Karageorgovitch families, reaching back to the early nineteenth century, also was a factor. Austria-Hungary had backed King Alexander Obrenovitch because he supported Austro-Hungarian Balkan policy, which was to oppose both Serb expansion in the region and the penetration of Russian influence. Consequently, Greater Serb nationalists, with Russian backing, favoured the traditionally anti-Austrian House of Karageorgovitch, now represented by Prince Peter Karageorgovitch. After the assassination, Peter took the Serbian throne and Austro-Hungarian relations with Serbia, and with Russia, deteriorated even further.

THE BALKANS

Nationalism was anathema to the Habsburgs, as it always had been, owing to the multi-ethnic make-up of the Austro-Hungarian Empire. The imperial throne was the only 'nation' tolerable; when Tyrolean Andreas Hofer led a peasant army to victory in 1809 over the French in Brenner Pass and was described to Leopold II as a 'patriot,' the emperor responded: 'But is he a patriot for me?' In 1910 the imperial population of more than 51 million included Germans, Magyars, Czechs, Moravians, Croats, Serbs, Poles, Ruthenians, Romanians, Slovenes, and Italians, most of whom now saw their ethnicity in nationalist terms. Germans and Magyars together were just over 40 per cent of the population, and while the Magyars shared running the empire with Austrian Germans, they still thought of themselves as Hungarians first – just as they had in 1848. The stage was set for the summer of 1914.

MURDER IN SARAJEVO

On 26 and 27 June, the Austrian army carried out military manoeuvres in Bosnia. Archduke Franz Ferdinand (1863–1914), heir to the throne and Inspector General of imperial armed forces, was present with his wife, the Archduchess Sophie. Together on 28 June they visited the Bosnian capital, Sarajevo, for a mayoral reception at City Hall. In anticipation of the visit, the Black Hand had organized an assassination plot. The first attempt was a bomb thrown at the royal car – a touring car with the top down, hardly designed for security against assassins – as it drove into the city. The bomb missed, and the archduke and archduchess arrived at City Hall alive and well. The reception was tense because of the bomb attempt, even though the archduke managed to joke about it. Everyone was relieved when the imperial party left for a luncheon at the Governor's Residence. It had been decided, for security reasons, to drive through the city to the Residence along the Appel Quay, a wide boulevard on the bank of the River Miljacka, rather than drive through the old medieval city centre as originally planned. Military Governor General Potiorek climbed in the front seat with the archduke's driver, and off they went with the mayor's car leading the way.

Unfortunately, no one had informed the mayor's driver of the changed route. When he reached Franz Joseph Street, he turned off and headed into the city, and the archduke's chauffeur followed. 'No, no,' Potiorek shouted. 'Wrong way! Straight along the Appel Quay.' The chauffeur stopped and tried to back up, and, according to some reports, the engine stalled. Meanwhile, Gavrilo Princip, a Black Hand assassin who thought he had missed his try at the archduke, was wandering disconsolately along Franz Joseph Street when he ran into an old acquaintance, with whom he engaged in conversation. At some point, Princip looked up and to his astonishment, saw that the archduke's car was stopped in the street directly in front of him. He seized the moment. Princip leaped onto the running board and fired his pistol point blank at the royal couple. Sophie was killed instantly; her husband died within the hour.

WAR ON SERBIA

Clearly, concluded Vienna, this was a plot concocted with the approval and knowledge of Belgrade, and provided a golden opportunity to have it out with Serbia once and for all. This would be a war that could be blamed on the Serbs and that Austria-Hungary, with its much larger and better equipped army, could win hands down. On 5 July, Vienna informed Berlin that the origin of the conspiracy 'had been firmly traced to Belgrade.' The Austro-Hungarian government would issue an ultimatum, and if it was not met, imperial troops would march into Serbia. Wilhelm II, with the concurrence of Chancellor Bethmann-Hollweg (1856–1921), responded by issuing a 'blank cheque': Germany would support Austria-Hungary to the hilt, whatever was necessary. There is no clear indication that he expected this to mean war, however; Wilhelm apparently doubted that any European power would intervene on Serbia's behalf, not even Russia. Meanwhile, clamour for war against Serbia was rising in Austria.

The ultimatum went out on 23 July. It demanded that the Serbian government condemn anti-Austrian propaganda, admit that Serbian officials had been spreading it, punish them for having done so, and agree to Austro-Hungarian authorities participating in the suppression of irridentist movements in Serbia. To Vienna's surprise, the Serbian government accepted the ultimatum – save for the last item. In fact, the Serb government did arrest and execute Colonel 'Apus' (Dragutin Dimitrijevitch), founder and leader of the Black Hand, who had ordered the assassination and also had orchestrated the assassination of King Alexander and Queen Draga in 1903. Vienna ignored the suggestion that a European conference might settle the matter, and declared war on 28 July. Wilhelm reaffirmed the 'blank cheque' by ordering mobilization of the *Reichswehr*. This set in motion the 'ripple affect' that led to the First World War; and all because of a wrong turn on the Appel Quay in Sarajevo.

MOBILIZATION

A London newspaper cartoon portrayed the member states of the two major alliances as chess pieces knocking one another over. This was mobilization, each state claiming that it had to mobilize because everyone else was doing it. In international law, military mobilization was a *de facto* declaration of war. Russia required longer than anyone else to mobilize – from 21 to 25 days – and so gave the order on 29 July. Germany immediately demanded that Tsar Nicholas II back down, and when he refused, declared war on Russia on 30 July which technically began the war on the Eastern Front. Having declared war on Russia, Germany looked also at war with France; what better opportunity, indeed, to resolve once and for all, Franco-German differences left over from 1871.

The first step was to demand that Belgium permit the passage of German troops through its territory when war was declared on France. If it refused, 'Germany would be obliged, to her regret, to regard the Kingdom as an enemy.' The second was Germany's declaration of war on France on 3 August. Belgium then refused military passage, and in the dawn hours of 4 August, units of Uhlan cavalry crossed the Belgian frontier. Britain demanded that they withdraw, and when Berlin did not respond, reluctantly declared war on Germany. The British had hoped to escape involvement in this continental fraças altogether; however, they had been committed since 1839 to the guarantee of Belgian neutrality, and the Triple Entente did have clauses requiring its signatories to come to each other's aid in case of war.

The First World War

The war lasted more than four years, engaged the European powers, many of their colonies, the United States, and Japan, and made the Napoleonic wars look like a minor scuffle. No one had expected or wanted it – which is why the French called it *la bavure* (the 'cock-up'). All the same, in August 1914 the streets of Berlin, Paris and London were full of patriots cheering the regiments as they marched off to the front. Walther Rathenau was not among them. One autumn day in 1914, he stood with Prince von Bülow looking through a window in the Hotel Adlon at leaves falling on the Unter den Linden. Pointing toward the Brandenburger Tor, he remarked:

Can a monarch of such arresting personality, so charming and human a man, so utterly inadequate as a ruler, as is the Emperor Wilhelm II – with an impossible chancellor like Bethmann and a frivolous chief of staff like Falkenhayn – ever expect a triumphal return through that arch? If he gets it, history will have no meaning.

THE SCHLIEFFEN PLAN

The fuss over Belgian neutrality was quite simple, really. In 1905, the Imperial General Staff put together the Schlieffen Plan (named for General Alfred von Schlieffen whose idea it was) to be deployed in the event of war with France: German troops would advance through Luxembourg and Belgium, turn south in a 'huge wheeling movement,' a 'hinged hammer,' so to speak, and smash through the French army deployed around Paris. They then would encircle the city, trap the French army deployed between Paris and the German border, and force France to sue for peace. The whole operation should not take more than six weeks.

The plan was put in motion on 4 August 1914 with one and a half million troops divided into seven armies, the lead army commanded by General Alexander von Kluck. It failed. First, Kluck departed from the original plan to pursue a French army in retreat; second, the British Expeditionary Force counterattacked the advancing Germans with sufficient success to convince General Helmuth von Moltke, Chief of the Imperial General Staff, that he must divert troops from the 'head' of the hammer in order to protect its 'hinge'; and third, the French despatched 14,000 troops from the Paris garrison (some by taxi, some on bicycles) to reinforce the divisions engaged against the Germans. The German advance was stalled at the Marne, and by the end of October, both armies were digging in, starting the trenches that eventually would stretch some four hundred miles from the English Channel to Switzerland, and define the war on the Western Front.

THE WAR

There was an 'Eastern front,' a 'Western front,' and a 'Naval front,' the latter including German submarines attacking American and British ships – the *Lusitania* most famously – and the Battle of Jutland in 1916. On that occasion the German High Seas Fleet fought the British North Seas Fleet to a draw; the High Seas Fleet then sailed back to the Kiel and Wilhelmshaven naval bases, which the British blockaded, and never again sallied forth to do battle.

The Eastern Front was much more of a 'war of movement' than that in the West. It was only in the East that Germany won, owing in part to the November Revolution of 1917. In January 1918, the Bolshevik government made the Treaty of Brest-Litovsk, which gave the Ukraine to Germany. Now the Germans could concentrate on the Western Front, or so they thought; partisan warfare broke out in the Ukraine immediately the treaty was signed, and Germany had to deploy troops desperately needed in the West to hold on to it. Moreover, Germany's firepower was shrinking. It has been suggested that by mid-1918 the Entente armies had twenty times the ammunition available to the *Reichswehr*. Meanwhile, food shortages ravaged the civilian population. In the winter of 1915 alone, more than 1,100 Berliners died of malnutrition.

German resolve was slipping. In 1914, the *Reichstag* had passed the *Burgfrieden* (truce) – pacifist Georg Ledebour the lone dissenting vote – by which all political parties agreed to give full support to the war; now in July 1917, a resolution calling upon the government to pursue a course of peace was passed though with a large minority vote opposed to it; *Reichswehr* leaders ignored it. In the debate, Independent Socialist Hugo Haase (1863–1919) spoke out against 'wars of conquest' and demanded that the government seek a peace of reconciliation. Then in August 1918, the enemy broke through German lines in a tank-led attack, and German troops began falling back toward the Rhine. Meanwhile, Germany's allies – Turkey and Austria-Hungary – were in a state of collapse (Italy had declined to enter the war at all in 1914, and had joined the Allies in 1915). 'We have reached the limit of our endurance,' said General Ludendorff. 'The war must be ended.' And it was, when Centre party leader Matthias Erzberger signed the Armistice for Germany in a railroad car in Compiègne, at the eleventh hour of the eleventh day of the eleventh month of 1918.

A WAR LIKE NO OTHER

This was the first truly 'mass war' in history. Entire economies went on a 'war footing,' women worked in munitions factories for the first time, and armies, 'conscript' rather than 'professional,' numbered in the millions. At the height of the conflict Germany had six million men in uniform, and Russia 12 million. In 1916 Britain introduced military conscription for the first time in its history; and propaganda was disseminated. Historian Philip M. Taylor makes clear in *Munitions of the Mind* that propaganda has always played a role in war; however, that role expanded to an unprecedented degree with the advent of mass war in 1914. Recruiting posters, war bonds posters, posters depicting the heroism of soldiers in the context of the monstrosity of the enemy, and public rallies to raise money and encourage recruitment were commonplace in every belligerent nation; so too were films depicting the enemy as evil, depraved, weak, and/or cowardly. Siegfried Kracauer described German 'staged propaganda films in which extras put into British uniforms surrendered to valiant German troops,' which were then distributed both at home and among neutrals. There was even propaganda poetry, as in *Hasslied* (Song of Hate) by Ernst Lissauer which called upon the Germans to hate England in particular.

War ordnance also was new and more sophisticated than in any previous conflict: tanks, airplanes, poison gas, submarines, dreadnoughts, long-range rifles with steel-jacket bullets, and field guns with more power, range and accuracy than ever before, were the order of the day – all produced by such industrial cartels as Krupp of Essen who profited greatly as a result. The Germans bombarded Paris with an artillery piece called 'Big Bertha' (probably in honour of the siege cannon used by the Hohenzollerns to subdue Brandenburg ca. 1415) mounted on rails. It was capable of firing a one-ton shell eighty miles. And of course the machine gun, first introduced in the nineteenth century, had evolved by 1914 into probably the single most important weapon of the war. Soldiers in the trenches were bombarded by artillery for hours on end; then they piled out of their trenches to cross the one or two hundred yards of 'no man's land' to attack the enemy in their trenches, which took them straight into a barrage of machine gun fire. The results were usually catastrophic. The 1916 Battle of the Somme alone resulted in more than a million casualties on the two sides combined, vast numbers of which were victims of machine guns. No war in history had produced such losses: Britain suffered more than

900,000 fatalities, France nearly 1,400,000, Russia 1,700,000, Germany 1,800,000, and Austria-Hungary 1,200,000.

And for what? In 1914 no one had clearly defined war aims. Eventually the Central Powers decided that they were fighting for hegemony on the European continent, while the Western allies announced – with great propaganda value – that they were opposing monarchial and aristocratic institutions (among the losers, at any rate), and supporting the self-determination of peoples (save for those in French and British colonies). And they wanted this war to pave the way for a world 'safe for democracy,' and to make a peace that would guarantee that it had been, as it was described in the West, the 'war to end all wars.' When the Armistice went into affect, everyone was relieved to have it over.

The Fall of the Austro-Hungarian Empire

The Austro-Hungarian Empire not only was defeated in the war, it ceased to exist as a result. Franz Joseph died in 1916, replaced by Charles I (1887–1922). By then, Vienna was feeling the strain of the war, but was not yet overwhelmed by it. Curiously, despite their growing ethnic nationalism, Hungarians, Czechs, Poles and others fought bravely and endured much hardship in the name of the empire. This did not mean that they gave up on their desire for independence.

REVOLUTION IN AUSTRIA-HUNGARY

In May 1915 the Yugoslav Council was set up in London, and a year later the Czech National Council in Paris. Thomas Garrigue Masaryk orchestrated the latter and worked successfully to attract American support for an independent Czechoslovakia. President Woodrow Wilson's Fourteen Point Doctrine issued in January 1918, called for the autonomy of all ethnic peoples in the empire, rectification of the frontier with Italy, and creation of an independent Poland. 'Our programme is justice for all peoples and nationalities, be they strong or weak,' the document read – which raised British eyebrows since that language could apply to their colonials. By June 1918, dissidents in

Vienna opposed the war and continuation of the Habsburg monarchy, Hungarians demanded independence, and Croats, Serbs and Slovenes advocated formation of a South Slav state (Yugoslavia.) Also in June, the Czech National Council in Paris was 'formally recognized as the provisional government of a Czechoslovak State.'

As late as October, a rag-tag imperial army still fought against the allies in northeastern Italy. But to no avail. The war was over for them as for others, and when disintegration began, it was swift: 3 November, an Armistice was agreed between Austria–Hungary and the allies; 12 November, Emperor Charles I abdicated and left for exile on Madeira, off the coast of Portugal; 13 November, the Republic of Austria was declared, which then banned all Habsburgs with claims to the throne from Austria; 16 November, the Hungarian Republic was proclaimed under Count Michael Karolyi; and 24 November, representatives from Croatia, Slovenia, Serbia and Montenegro announced the United Kingdom of Yugoslavia, with King Peter I of Serbia on the throne.

A note: in the United States, a town populated mostly by descendants of Czech immigrants to America took its name from President Wilson in gratitude for his contribution to the making of Czechoslovakia. It is called Wilson, Kansas.

The End of the Age of Wilhelm II

Disillusionment with the war spread in Germany beginning in 1916; by 1918 agitation for ending it and for remaking the German political system was rife, particularly among such Majority Social Democrat leaders as Frederick Ebert (1871–1925) and Philipp Scheidemann (1865-1939) and Independent Socialists behind Hugo Haase. The Spartacists led by Karl Leibknecht and Rosa Luxemburg, with the support of pacifist Social Democrat Georg Ledebour, were even more determined for radical change. They wanted a Bolshevik-style revolution, and on 2 November 1918 presided in Berlin over a committee meeting of 'revolutionary shop stewards' who called for mass strikes and demonstrations to occur on 4 November. Ledebour promised 75,000 workers to answer the call.

REVOLUTION IN GERMANY

Meanwhile, on 28 October the Admiralty ordered the High Seas Fleet assembled at Wilhelmshaven to raid the British Grand Fleet. To sailors there and at Kiel (already demoralized by strict food rations, harsh discipline, no expectation of improvement, and the command of officers much better treated than themselves) this order 'seemed a lunatic gesture designed to appease fanatical officers and likely to endanger the armistice negotiations.' Their response was open revolt. A sailors' council issued an ultimatum that they would go to sea only if the British fleet attacked them first. There was genuine fear that rebellion might spread beyond the navy to include the army, and arrests were ordered. On 3 November, military units fired on a mass demonstration of sailors; eight were killed and twenty-nine wounded.

The government was fully aware how dicey the political situation had become, and began cooperating with the Social Democrats to stave off the extremists. Haase and Gustav Noske (1868–1946), a Majority Socialist leader, were asked to go to Kiel and calm things down. Noske later recounted that when he arrived in Kiel and a soldier jumped on the running-board of his car shouting 'Long live freedom!', the crowd in the street merely laughed. But that was 4 November; on 5 November the spark ignited by sailors in Kiel spread across the country

Friedrich Ebert, *Reichspräsident* until his death in 1925

to such cities as Lübeck, Hamburg, Bremen, Hannover, Magdeburg and Dresden. In Berlin, the Majority Socialist executive committee presented Chancellor Prince Max von Baden (1867–1929) with a demand that Wilhelm II abdicate, and a warning that if he did not, Berlin would be subject to a general strike. Prince Max did not act upon the demand. Then on 8 November, Kurt Eisner led an uprising of workers, soldiers and peasants in Bavaria that deposed the Wittelsbachs and proclaimed a Bavarian Democratic and Socialist Republic separate from Germany. A disgruntled Bavarian populace acquiesced. It was now clear to Prince Max and *Reichswehr* leaders in Berlin how large the crisis was. The next day, demonstrating factory workers filled the streets of Berlin, Spartacist leaders urged a Communist revolution, and a deputation of Majority Socialists led by Ebert and Scheidemann called upon Prince Max to demand the abdication of Wilhelm. Field Marshal Ludendorff and General Wilhelm Groener (1867–1939) understood that the 'imperial jig was up' and urged the Prince to give in. He did, declared the emperor and the crown prince abdicated, and handed over his office to Ebert. It was Prince Max's hope that Ebert would represent a peaceful government transition that would avoid revolution, which, indeed, was Ebert's intention. For the moment, he signed himself 'Imperial Chancellor' as a symbol of continuity. Meanwhile, Wilhelm did not want to abdicate, and demanded that he at least be left with the title King of Prussia. That too was denied (General Groener at one point suggested that the emperor might go to the front, place himself at the head of a counterattack, be killed, and go out like a hero), and the now ex-emperor packed his bags and left for exile in Holland, never again to set foot in Germany. The Age of Wilhelm II was over.

What happened next was typical of the era. The German Republic was born on 9 November – by accident. At 2 p.m., 100,000 demonstrators filled the square in front of the *Reichstag* building. Philipp Scheidemann addressed them from a balcony, concluding his harangue by saying: 'Workers, Soldiers, the German people has triumphed all along the line. A large part of the garrison has joined us. The Hohenzollerns have abdicated. Long live the great German Republic!' All well and good, except that he had no authority from his party, and certainly not from the new 'imperial chancellor,' to make such a claim.

Ebert was furious and shouted at Scheidemann: 'You have no right to proclaim a republic. What becomes of Germany – whether she becomes a republic or something else – a Constituent Assembly must decide.' But the damage was done, and the stage was set for the birth of what would be known as the Weimar Republic.

The Paris Peace Conference

The war ended on 11 November without Germany having been invaded by allied armies. The *Reichswehr* marched home looking like anything but a defeated army. Meanwhile, the victorious allies prepared for the international conference that would make treaties to officially end the war. Germany was the real issue; the other Central Powers were but small fish in a large pond. The allies, particularly Great Britain and France, were determined that Germany should pay a stiff price for the war.

SETTING THE STAGE   Fourteen Points

Paris was the obvious location for the peace conference, and delegates began assembling there in January 1919, two months after the Armistice. The principals were Britain's prime minister, David Lloyd George, who wanted Germany to 'pay until the pips squeak' for the costs of the war; French premier Georges Clemenceau, who wanted revenge against Germany and had no doubt but that the French nation was behind him; and US President Woodrow Wilson, who wanted his idealistic Fourteen Points Doctrine – which included the League of Nations that could end war by resolving all international conflict through discussion – to be the basis upon which a treaty would rest. Vittorio Orlando of Italy was also part of what came to be known as the Big Four, but was of minor significance compared to the other three. And there was disagreement from the start. Lloyd George and Clemenceau viewed Wilson as too idealistic by half. As Clemenceau put it: 'God gave us Ten Commandments we could not keep. Now Wilson gives us Fourteen.' They and other critics saw him as the 'New Messiah,' and it was not meant as a compliment. Even so, the opportunity to perhaps create a 'New Europe' had considerable popular appeal, and Wilson's pre-conference tour of France was well received.

CONGRESS OF VIENNA *REDIVIVUS*?

Delegations to the Paris conference represented thirty-two allied and associated nations from around the world; comparisons have been drawn with the Congress of Vienna in 1814–1815. True, both conferences drew representatives from many countries, and both aimed at resolving political and diplomatic upheavals and dislocations caused by a major European war. Also, like Vienna Paris was dominated by a handful of Great Power leaders. However, delegations to Paris in 1919 included experts in economics, international and domestic politics, geography, demography and ethnography – for example, John Maynard Keynes, perhaps the single most important economist of the twentieth century, was part of the British delegation. Further, Paris was predicated upon democratic representation: no monarchs were present, and where Vienna had been traditional 'secret diplomacy,' Paris was 'open diplomacy', at least for a while. That proved unworkable in the end, because daily press releases became instant propaganda material, and that made reaching agreements almost impossible. 'Open diplomacy, openly arrived at' had to be abandoned for 'closed diplomacy, secretly arrived at.' That, at least, was 'Vienna *Redivivus*.'

TERMS OF THE TREATY

First there was argument over the Covenant of the League of Nations. It could not work, argued the critics, for national rights and international agreements made between individual states might have to be sacrificed. Not so, replied Wilson: 'Nothing in the Covenant will be deemed to affect the validity of international engagements, such as treaties of arbitration, or regional undertakings ... for the securing of the maintenance of peace.' Finally, in exchange for compromise on the issue of self-determination of peoples Wilson had his way, and the Covenant became the first 26 Articles of the Versailles Treaty with Germany.

The conference then proceeded to matters of territories, armaments and reparations. While neither Lloyd George nor Clemenceau got all

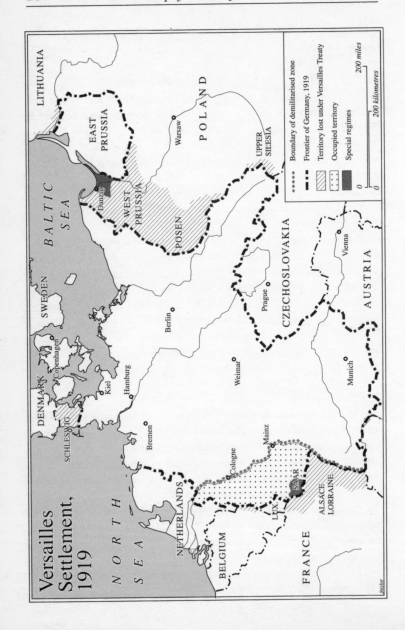

Versailles Settlement, 1919

they wanted, Germany suffered considerable setbacks in each area. Alsace-Lorraine went to France, Eupen-et-Malmédy to Belgium, Posen to newly recreated Poland, Memel to Lithuania, all German colonies to allied states – there were limits to 'self-determination' after all – Danzig was made a free city under League of Nations mandate, and a 'Polish corridor' reaching to the Baltic Sea separated East Prussia from the rest of Germany. Clemenceau wanted the Rhineland to be a separate state independent of Germany, but had to settle for a demilitarized west bank. Meanwhile, the Saar was made a French protectorate for fifteen years, when it and Schleswig-Holstein, southern East Prussia and Silesia would hold plebiscites to decide their future. Altogether Germany lost 1/7th of its territory, 1/10th of its population, half of its iron ore and a quarter of its coal reserves.

Germany also lost most of its navy, which was reduced to 15,000 men and officers, six cruisers, twelve destroyers, twelve torpedo boats, and no submarines or battleships. It became, in short, a coastal defence force with no allowance for future expansion. Meanwhile, long-range artillery such as 'Big Bertha,' military aircraft, tanks and poison gas were banned, and the *Reichswehr* was reduced to a 100,000-man 'defence force.' The General Staff was disbanded as well – at least officially; in fact, it remained quietly in place and continued to operate more or less as it had in the past.

Reparations was the real sore point from Germany's point of view. Clause 231 of the Treaty, known as the 'War-Guilt Clause,' forced Germany and its allies to accept responsibility 'for causing all the loss and damage to which the Allied and Associated Governments and their nationals have been subjected as a consequence of the war imposed upon them by the aggression of Germany and her allies.' Germany was to pay for these damages, and pay compensation for loss of life to the widows and families of allied soldiers killed in battle. An initial sum of about £1,000,000,000 was to be paid by 1921, and other amounts later, to be determined by subsequent Reparations commissions. The initial sum was roughly the equivalent of the indemnity Germany exacted against France in 1871. In addition to money, Germany was to turn over 60 per cent of its coal production through 1930, 90 per cent of its shipping fleet, half of all river shipping, all foreign investments and

patents, half of all dairy herds, one quarter of chemical and pharma-
ceutical output, and a significant amount of locomotives and rolling
stock. France was given exclusive rights over the use of the terms
'champagne' and 'cognac' to designate sparkling wine and brandy.
Finally, if Germany failed to meet the Reparations requirements, the
Rhineland 'will be re-occupied immediately by the allied and associated forces.' Meanwhile, a 'War Crimes' provision, which would
have demanded bringing Wilhelm II and other German leaders to trial,
never got off of the ground.

THE GERMAN RESPONSE

The treaty was presented to the German delegation, headed by Count
Ulrich von Brockdorff-Rantzau, on 7 May 1919. He refused to sign, as
did Scheidemann, who resigned from the delegation and returned to
Berlin, where he also resigned as Chancellor. There, before a crowd in
the same Berlin University hall where Johann Fichte had delivered his
Addresses to the German Nation, Scheidemann condemned the treaty and
pleaded with the National Assembly to reject it: 'What hand will not
wither that delivers us into such chains?' he declaimed. On 19 June, the
Cabinet split seven to seven over signing the treaty; then, advised by the
army that failure to sign would result in an allied invasion of Germany
which the *Reichswehr* could not defeat, the seven dissenters gave in.

The Treaty of Versailles

On 28 June, Hermann Müller and Johannes Bell signed the treaty for
Germany in the great Galerie des Glaces (Hall of Mirrors) in the
Château de Versailles twelve miles outside of Paris. They also signed
their political death warrants. Soon the treaty was being referred to in
Germany as the '*dictat*' (dictated peace), and those who signed it as
'criminals' who had 'stabbed Germany in the back.' This phrase may
have begun with Field Marshal Paul von Hindenburg who swore
before a *Reichstag* committee hearing in November 1919 that 'Germany had never been militarily defeated but "stabbed in the back" by
certain pacifist and socialist elements – Jews and Marxists.' Simply put,
the treaty was not severe enough to cripple Germany, but it was too

severe to be acceptable, in particular the 'war-guilt clause.' Still, Germany officially accepted it; ironically, the United States did not, despite Woodrow Wilson's exhausting campaign of persuasion when he returned home from Paris. Rather, the US simply declared in 1921, that the war with Germany 'was over,' and that was that.

OTHER TREATIES

Germany's war-time allies also were dealt with, in separate treaties named, as was Versailles, for places in or around Paris. St Germain (1919) recognized Austria as a separate state of 6,000,000, of which 2,000,000 lived in Vienna, and the transfer of former imperial territories to Czechoslovakia, Italy, Yugoslavia and Romania, among others; Trianon (1920) transferred territories from Hungary to the newly formed Slav states; Sèvres (1920) dismembered the Ottoman Empire and turned over most of its Middle Eastern holdings to Britain as 'protectorates'; and Neuilly (1921) shifted territories from Bulgaria to Greece and Yugoslavia.

The war was over, peace had come, and the German and Austro-Hungarian empires no longer existed, defeated on the field of battle and put in their place. Or were they? So far as Austria was concerned, yes; at least so long as it was left on its own. As to Germany, not at all, despite the efforts of such Weimar Republic statesmen as Gustav Stresemann. French Field Marshal Ferdinand Foch spoke far better than he knew when he dubbed the Versailles Treaty a 'twenty-year armistice.'

CHAPTER TEN

The Weimar Republic,
1919–1933

'The Weimar Republic, Germany's first bid for democracy, failed,' wrote Holger Herwig. Why? Because the military and bureaucracy remained unchanged from the Second Empire, class interest and factionalism took precedence over national interest in both the political process and *Reichstag* proceedings, divisive economic issues were never fully resolved, and resentment over the Versailles Treaty, the 'Germany was stabbed in the back by traitors at home' argument, was never laid to rest. In the end, Weimar Germany accepted an Austrian, Adolf Hitler, as its leader.

Making the Republic

Wilhelm II abdicated on 9 November 1918. Chancellor Prince Max von Baden handed his office over to Majority Socialist leader Friedrich Ebert, and the Weimar Republic was born.

CONSTITUENT ASSEMBLY

Eighty-three per cent of eligible voters turned out for the general election on 19 January 1919. The object was creation of a constituent assembly to both make a new constitution and govern the new Republic. The results revealed a divided Germany. No single party or even a coalition emerged with a majority: Majority Socialists won 165 seats, Independents 22, German Democrats (for which Albert Einstein voted) 75, the Centre 91, German Nationalists 44, and Populists (National Liberals) 19. Even so, on 10 February the assembly gave Ebert the presidency of the Republic by a margin of 277 to 51. He then formed the 'Weimar Coalition' by assembling a government with members from left and centre.

Making a constitution was the first item on the constituent assembly agenda. Law professor and liberal Hugo Preuss was assigned to get things started. He did, emphasizing democracy and parliamentary representation 'with a high degree of centralization.' This did not suit everyone, and the debates were fierce and divisive. The particularism that had been part of German history for more than a thousand years was far from dead, and the constitution finally agreed upon and ratified on 11 August 1919 combined a unitary state with recognition of at least the existence of individual states. The unitary principle was central to the first clause, titled 'Reich and States,' which opened with a line that to Herwig sounded like 'a formula worthy of *Alice in Wonderland.*' It read: 'The German *Reich* is a Republic. Political authority emanates from the people.' The clause went on to specify that the German States (twenty-five in number and referred to as *Länder*) were required to submit to the authority of the *Reich*, to institute republican state governments, to recognize that sovereignty was concentrated in the nationally elected parliament, and to accept direct taxation being in the hands of the *Reich*. The States would retain control over the administration of local education, police, the church and indirect taxation.

THE WEIMAR CONSTITUTION

The constitution also established the governmental system, and certain rights for the people. It called for a president and two-house legislature, the former to be elected by popular vote for a term of seven years with the power to represent the *Reich* in foreign affairs, and to appoint and dismiss military and civil servants including the cabinet and chancellor. Both of these were responsible to the *Reichstag* but not required to be members of it. The legislature was the *Reichstag* and *Reichsrat,* delegates to the former elected by popular vote every four years, and to the latter appointed by state governments. Universal suffrage was established for both men and women beginning at age twenty, and a Bill of Rights guaranteed personal liberties, freedom of religion and the right of assembly. Marriage and family were protected by law from state interference. Judges were appointed for life, which proved to be not such a good thing, since in Weimar, they tended to be hard on the Left and lenient on the Right.

The constitution also provided for dealing with emergencies. Article 48 gave the president the power to issue emergency decrees whenever he deemed it necessary in the interests of public order:

> If a *Land* fails to fulfil the duties incumbent upon it according to the Constitution or the Laws of the *Reich*, the *Reich* President can force it to do so with the help of the armed forces.
>
> The *Reich* President may, if the public safety and order in the German *Reich* are considerably disturbed or endangered, take measures as are necessary to restore public safety and order. If necessary he may intervene with the help of the armed forces. For this purpose he may temporarily suspend, either partially or wholly, the Fundamental Rights established in Articles 114, 115, 117, 118, 123, 124 and 153.

This was a loaded gun waiting to go off. Ebert used the article 134 times in the five years before he died in office; Adolf Hitler used it to destroy the Republic. Still, in principle the Weimar Constitution was not a bad thing; applying it to a nation with a limited democratic tradition, on-going state particularism, economic and political uncertainties left over from the war and the November Revolution, proved difficult. And, there were practical shortcomings: the people voted for party lists rather than for individuals, which separated them from their *Reichstag* representatives. Prussia, despite constitutional limitations that deprived it of the special status it had enjoyed under the emperors, still controlled three-fifths of German land and population, which gave it far too much power in the legislature. Then there was the fact that before 1930 Germany had up to forty political parties, ranging from the Majority Socialists to the Farmers' Party. It became impossible to have a *Reichstag* majority, and power had to be achieved through coalitions, which often meant negative compromise.

WOMEN'S RIGHTS

Women now were more independent than ever before: equal rights with men, including in marriage, jobs in the civil service, competition in the market place, suffrage, access to universities and professional schools, and membership to political parties. Women flocked from agricultural to urban employment; admittedly, the least skilled earned as much as 40 per cent less than men, but the gap was much smaller among the highly skilled. By 1931, 16 per cent of university students were women who upon graduation became teachers, nurses and physicians. Meanwhile, women were activists and politically involved in ever increasing numbers. The Union of Rural Housewives had 90,000 members, the Imperial Union of German Housewives, 100,000, and the Trade Union League of Salaried Employees, 100,492. The Evangelical Women's Union had 1.5 million members, and its political wing, the German Evangelical Women's Federation (linked to the German National People's Party), 200,000. The Catholic Women's Federation volunteers who supported the Centre Party had 250,000 members, and 1.6. million women belonged to various Church lay organizations. Ten per cent of Social Democrat *Reichstag* deputies were women, though the majority of women voted for the Centre Party, the German National Peoples Party, and the German Peoples Party. Gertrud Bäumer (1873–1954), leader of the Federation of German Women's Associations, worked with both Social Democrats and the Centre to pass laws decriminalizing prostitution as a way to crack down on the spread of sexually transmitted diseases.

Meanwhile, women were 'caught up' in the trend toward modernity, which not everyone regarded as a positive thing. Wrote Holger Herwig: 'Wearing casual clothes, bobbing their hair, and smoking cigarettes, modern women joined the white-collar labour force at levels three times those of the prewar period. . . . Magazines, newspapers, and film celebrated them as young, elegant, and sexy; by 1930 cinemas were selling 6 million tickets per week.' Women also became involved in gymnastics in unprecedented numbers. And, of course, sexual promiscuity and divorce rose, along with illegitimate births. Sexual literature was wildly popular; for example, Theodore Van de Veldes' *Eroticism in Marriage* went through eleven printings in just three years.

A Time of Chaos

Given the upheavals between 1919 and 1923 it is a miracle that the Weimar Republic survived at all. Even as the constitution was being shaped, and the Ebert government was settling in, or trying to, Germany was engaged in civil war, political rebellion and economic disaster.

CIVIL WAR

Ebert cracked down hard on the extremist 'revolution' attempted by Kurt Eisner in Bavaria and Karl Leibknecht and Rosa Luxemburg in Berlin. He had to; and not only because he disagreed with them. On 10 November 1918, Ebert made a pact with General Groener: the army would come home in orderly fashion and defend the provisional government, which would rely on the traditional officer corps and put down Bolshevism. The crisis effectively began in Berlin when the German Communist Party was officially established on 31 December. On 5 January radical German workers called for a revolution, and the 'Spartacist Uprising' began the next day. It was over by 13 January. These pro-Bolsheviks were incompetently organized and managed, and had little popular support; the First German Congress of Workers' and Soldiers' Councils, for example, rejected the idea of 'government by soviets' by a vote of 400 to 50, while the civil service and army gave their loyalty to the provisional government. The uprisings were easily smashed by a combination of imperial army troops and *Freikorps* (Free-

Government troops on top of the Brandenburg Gate, about to fire on the Spartacists in Berlin, 1919

Corps) units, the paramilitary force put together by Gustav Noske consisting of ex-soldiers. It was not unlike the Black and Tans whom the British sent into Ireland to put down the Irish Republican Army rebellion at about the same time, behaving with much the same kind of brutality and disregard for regular army discipline. The *Freikorps* captured Leibknecht and Luxemburg on 15 January, murdered them, dumped their bodies into a Berlin canal, and claimed that they had committed suicide.

Kurt Eisner was murdered in Bavaria by a right-wing extremist, but a 'Soviet Republic' was proclaimed all the same, support for which 'ranged from radical farmers to anarchists and from confidence-men to psychopaths.' On 1 May regular army and *Freikorps* troops invaded Bavaria, crushed this rising, and established – sort of – republican government. This 'Bavarian civil war' cost six hundred lives; ever after, Bavaria was the Mecca of right-wing fanatics, sometimes represented by 'regional combat leagues' with names like Bayern and Reich, Oberland, Viking, Young German Order, and so on. In 1920 the National Socialist German Worker's Party (Nazis) was founded by Adolf Hitler, in Munich.

KAPP *PUTSCH*

Meanwhile in Berlin, Wolfgang Kapp, co-founder of the Fatherland Party, staged a *putsch* (power seizure) in protest against the *Reichswehr* demobilization clause in the Versailles Treaty. He was supported by disgruntled army and navy personnel who had refused demobilization. They entered Berlin through the Brandenburger Tor, where they were met 'by chance' and welcomed by retired imperial general, Erich Ludendorff. General Hans von Seeckt, army chief of staff, just happened to be on sick leave at the time. Ebert and other government officials fled to Stuttgart, once more confused and uncertain upon whom they could rely.

The active resistance of Berlin workers and trades unions – a general strike was called – and the passive resistance of government bureaucrats brought the *putsch* to an end. Kapp went into exile in Sweden, Seeckt miraculously recovered from his illness, and the government returned to Berlin. Even so, street violence and demonstrations continued, and it was not until 1921 that the Ebert's authority as president was more or less established and accepted. Even then political violence did not go away. By the end of 1922, there had been 376 political murders, including Matthias Erzberger and Walter Rathenau. Meanwhile, the number of paramilitary organizations such as *Stahlhelm* (Steel Helmet) and Adolf Hitler's *Sturm Abteilung* (SA) were on the rise despite new laws passed by the *Reichstag* to deal with them. The court system tended to be lenient when political crimes were committed by those on the Right.

CRISIS IN THE RUHR

At the end of 1922, the French government charged that Germany was defaulting on reparations payments, and ordered French troops to occupy the Rhineland, in accordance with the reparations enforcement clause of the Versailles Treaty. George Clemenceau's failed attempt during the Paris conference to have the Rhineland established as a state no longer part of Germany was revived. The occupation force replaced some 19,000 Berlin appointed officials with pro-separatists, and evicted 147,000 German workers. Pro-Germans retaliated with a policy of passive resistance – mine workers went on strike, for example, and circulated anti-occupation propaganda calling upon Rhinelanders to resist the 'invaders.' Coal production in the Ruhr dropped by fifty per cent.

And there was the inflation factor, a plan to drive the French out by flooding the Ruhr region with *Reichsmarks* having no standard monetary backing, which would result in massive inflation and do harm to the franc. The author of this scheme was not thinking clearly, for the *Reichsmark* was the currency for *all* of Germany, not just the Rhineland. Inflation hit the Ruhr, and then spread across the rest of Germany. By December 1923, 400,338,326,350,700,000,000 *Reichsmarks* were in circulation, their value having virtually disappeared: one pound sterling, for example, was worth 15,000,000,000 *Reichsmarks*. The effect was devastating: savings wiped out, inflation beyond comprehension, and the German economy effectively destroyed. On 23 September, recently appointed Chancellor Gustav Stresemann called a halt to the 'resistance movement' and promised Paris and London that reparations payments would resume; on 23 November French premier Raymond Poincaré accepted the promise to resume payments, and ordered troops to withdraw. The monetary disaster was ended by suspending the *Reichsmark* and replacing it with the *Rentenmark*, a temporary currency issued in limited quantity with a set value, and not backed by gold.

THE BEER-HALL *PUTSCH*

During the Ruhr crisis, separatist movements resurfaced from Schleswig-Holstein to Bavaria, and Upper Silesia to the Palatinate, all crying out against Berlin. Those that occurred in Rhenish cities such as Bonn, Mainz and Wiesbaden, among others, were supported by French and Belgian troops. Also, in Saxony and then Thuringia, state minister-presidents appointed Communists to their cabinets 'to pre-clude a military dictatorship by big business,' and Soviet agents came in to train 'proletarian legions' in anticipation of a working-class revolution. Of course, Bavaria took the opposite direction, as Minister-President Gustav von Kahr proclaimed a conservative national monarchist government and called a meeting at the Bürgerbräukeller in Munich to demand restoration of the Wittelsbachs. Adolf Hitler and twenty of his Nazi Brown Shirts disrupted the meeting, demanding a 'National Revolution' instead, and the next morning, with Erich Ludendorff at his side, Hitler led a Nazi march through Munich. Police broke it up with gunfire, and Hitler was arrested. He used his trial as a propaganda platform and persuaded the court that the Brown Shirts ultimately were acting out of patriotism. Hitler was sentenced to five years in prison for this 'beer-hall *putsch*,' as it came to be known. He served only nine months, during which time he wrote *Mein Kampf*, the 'bible' of the Nazi movement.

A strong element of conservative-to-extreme right politics ran throughout the Weimar period. When Ebert died in 1925, his elected successor was former Field Marshal Paul von Hindenburg. Many voters hoped that Hindenburg would turn back the liberal elements of the constitution, and move towards re-establishing the monarchy under Crown Prince Wilhelm. However, Hindenburg was nothing if not committed to duty, and once he was sworn in as president and took the oath of loyalty to the Republic, there was no question in his mind but that he would follow the rules. Which he did, with only an occasional lapse in favour of rightist political action groups.

STRESEMANN AND GERMAN FOREIGN POLICY

Gustav Stresemann left the Chancellory on 30 November 1923 to become foreign minister, a post he held until his death in 1929. He was the real power in the Weimar government. Opportunist, skilled diplomatic tactician – Bismarckian, in a sense – and convert from monarchist annexationist to democratic-minded republican, Stresemann brought Germany into a better relationship with the rest of Europe than had existed since the end of the war. The United States played a role in this, despite having never ratified the Versailles Treaty. In November 1923, Germany requested that reparations be reconsidered, given the present economic crisis. The Reparations Commission responded by forming committees to look into stabilizing the German economy. American Charles Dawes chaired one of the committees, which published its report, the Dawes Plan, in April 1924, which provided for adjusting reparations payments to Germany's economic capability of meeting them. Stresemann accepted the plan, though he regarded it as 'no more than an economic armistice.' Meanwhile, the United States was making major investments of capital in German industry.

The Dawes Plan was a start. In 1925 came the Accords formally signed in Locarno, Switzerland. This was Stresemann's greatest diplomatic triumph, coming at a time when Britain and France were backing away from evacuating the Ruhr because they perceived Germany simply ignoring aspects of the Versailles Treaty. The *Reichswehr* was nowhere near meeting the mandated 100,000 man limit, for example. General European disarmament had been under discussion since 1919, but had made little progress owing in particular to French fears regarding security relative to Germany; in 1925, it looked as if disarmament efforts would break down altogether. At this point, Stresemann, encouraged by the British ambassador to Weimar, proposed that the powers with direct interest in the Rhineland, that is Germany, France and Belgium, with Britain and Italy seconding them, should solemnly declare that they would never go to war again over their common western frontier. The initiative pleased both Britain and France; fear of an anti-German coalition eased, complaints about German rearmament were dropped, war was renounced, and the Ruhr was evacuated. And, by 'cutting its losses' in the west, Germany opened the way for manoeuvres in the east and primarily the future of the Polish Corridor. While France might complain about the east, it was not in a position to intervene in the way it could with regard to the Rhineland. Stresemann had won the day.

Meanwhile, in 1927, Germany became involved in the general disarmament talks, a positive factor that encouraged America to press for further reparations revisions. The result was the Young Plan, the result of talks in 1929 chaired by American banker Owen Young: Germany would pay reparations until 1988, only at a much reduced rate and with a total that was less than a third of the sum agreed in 1921. Further, the Reparations Commission would be dissolved, all foreign control over reparations ended, and German railroads and industries would be freed of all mortgage burdens. Reparations henceforth would be solely the responsibility of the Weimar government. Alfred Hugenberg (1865–1951), former Krupp director, publisher and film magnate who also was a radical nationalist, orchestrated a right-wing campaign against the Young Plan; all the same, the plan was accepted. Sadly, Stresemann, exhausted and stressed from overwork, suffered a fatal heart attack before the negotiations were over and did not live to see the outcome. It was a triumph for him all the same. Stresemann was a German statesman ahead of his time, who talked of a future democratic 'United States of Europe.' Had he lived, he might have defeated both Hitler and Hindenburg in the general election of 1932.

A Troubled Culture

Weimar's culture was in conflict no less than its politics and society. Writers, artists, film makers and philosophers were controversial and critical, even negative, about virtually everything. They rarely could agree on what was 'good' and what was 'bad': the war had been a horror or a heroic venture; the Weimar Republic did not go far enough

or it went too far; and there was no agreement on what 'art' meant.
Holger Herwig put it well:

> Art and literature became political battlefields, polarized into extremes:
> beauty versus degeneracy, belief versus putrefaction, nature versus asphalt,
> manliness versus effeminacy, martial music versus 'nigger' music (jazz),
> countryside versus city, discipline versus indiscipline, night versus day.

Weimar was a cultural 'golden period' in the sense that it was filled with
exceptional writers and film makers; however, Herwig continued, 'the
general public by and large ignored the avant-garde in favour of the
traditional.' At the same time, young Germans, nonplussed by war,
revolution, unemployment and the new democracy that did not seem
to work all that well, turned to the right, joined the Free Corps in great
numbers, and at universities tended toward anti-democratic fraternities.
By 1931 student governments at Erlangen, Greifswald, Berlin, Breslau,
Giessen, Jena and Rostock were controlled by Nazi youth; in 1933
Hitler appointed one of them, Baldur von Schirach (1907–1974), to be
'Youth Leader of the German Reich' with authority over everything
from fraternities to Boy Scouts and Girl Scouts.

LITERATURE

Weimar readers mostly preferred patriotic commentary and adventure
stories, the latter favourite being the American Old West novels of Karl
May, who lived in Dresden and never actually visited the United States.
All the same, serious writers abounded. Heinrich and Thomas Mann,
'rational' republican in outlook, were disillusioned by the horrors of
war and the inadequacies of the society which came out of it. Heinrich
was overshadowed by his brother, who, with Hermann Hesse (1877–
1962), was an exemplary left-wing writer. Thomas Mann's *The Magic
Mountain* and Hesse's *Steppenwolf* pilloried middle-class hypocrisy and
stressed the importance of individuality. These writers supported the
Weimar Republic, but were not overly pleased with it. So too Max
Weber, though he died in 1920, well before it was clear just how the
Republic would play out.

Whether left or right, Weimar literati tended to denounce, and thus
undermine, the Republic. In Hesse's words, it was a 'rotten and

spiritless state created out of the vacuum, the exhaustion after the war.' This view was shared by such as Gerhart Hauptmann, Harry Count Kessler and Austrian literary giant Hugo von Hofmannsthal, who found the German and Austrian Republics equally depressing or, perhaps, simply 'boring and dull'. Meanwhile, satirist Kurt Tucholsky and playwright Bertolt Brecht (1898–1956) demeaned the Republic respectively in *Deutschland, Deutschland über alles* and *Threepenny Opera*. Many Weimar writers went into exile in the Nazi period. Erich Marie Remarque (1898–1970), for example, who led out in the anti-war literary movement with *All Quiet on the Western Front,* which sold 640,000 copies in three months, and was made into an award-winning Hollywood film in 1930, emigrated to the United States. Remarque was notoriously unpopular with the right because of his pacifism. Nazi demonstrators included his novel in book burnings, and smashed up cinemas where the film version was being shown.

Writers on the Right were equally – or even more – unhappy with Weimar. Arthur Mueller van den Bruck's *Third Reich* called for a neo-conservative alternative to the Republic, and in 1924 Oswald Spengler (1880–1936) described the Republic as 'a five-year orgy of incompetence, cowardice and vulgarity.' He had already published *Decline of the West* in which he predicted the replacing of western degeneracy with 'brainless but brutal dictators,' and *Prussian Socialism* where he denounced Marx and called for a socialism that would reflect the Prussian military tradition. And Ernst Jünger, veteran of the Great War, wrote *Storm of Steel*, a novel which called for 'national resurrection' in the aftermath of 'decay and decline.' Writers such as these helped sew the seeds for the Nazi movement although, as Holger Herwig phrased it, when Hitler emerged in 1933 they were 'terribly disappointed in the herd-like mentality and hysterical oratory of his mass movement.' Meanwhile philosophers Martin Heidegger, Karl Jaspers and Max Wundt expressed despair and hostility towards the Republic, while historians Friedrich Meinecke, Hans Delbrück and others, accepted it – in Delbrück's manner: 'One serves the Republic, but one does not love it.' These historians looked back longingly to the age of Bismarck and denied any guilt on Germany's part for the Great War.

ART AND ARCHITECTURE

Revolts against the artistic establishment that began a decade before the First World War continued in Berlin, Dresden, Munich and elsewhere. Abstract forms such as expressionism, cubism, fauvism, and others were the focus. Expressionism led the way, reflecting the Freudian unconscious, the 'sorrow and anguish of human existence,' and the misery of the artist's surroundings. Expressionism often was the 'art of alarm, entreaty and accusation.' When the economy collapsed in 1923, Käthe Kollwitz drew a poster titled 'German children are starving'; Georg Grosz caricatured the 'moral depravity' of cabaret society and political demagogues, including Adolf Hitler; and the horror of war filled paintings by Carl Hofer and Otto Dix. Cubism was less pessimistic and was the essence of the Bauhaus Movement, begun in Weimar in 1919, and moved to Dessau in 1925. Leading Cubists included Paul Klee, whose 'factory murals' fused art and architecture, Wassily Kandinsky, Lyonel Feininger and Oskar Schlemmer, among others. Schlemmer's 'Staircase in the Bauhaus' was somewhere between Cubist and Impressionist. Again the idea was to be unconventional, to challenge artistic tradition – and it was, and they did. The Right condemned the Bauhaus as a haven for 'Bolshevik Jews.'

Architecture was probably the best known result of the Bauhaus experience. Two the most famous names in innovative architecture in the world were Walter Gropius (1883–1969) and Ludwig Miës van der

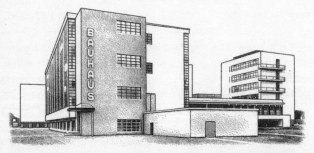

The Bauhaus glass and steel complex in Dessau built by Walter Gropius in 1925–6

Rohe (1886–1969). Gropius designed the Bauhaus School in Dessau, which was completed in 1926. Miës van der Rohe produced, among other things, a design for an all glass skyscraper in 1921, the Werkbund Housing Exposition in 1927, and in 1968, the year before he died, the New National Gallery in Berlin.

THEATRE AND CABARET

Brecht's *Threepenny Opera,* score by Kurt Weill, was a highly critical commentary on 'the evils and hypocrisies of bourgeois society' in a tongue-in-cheek style, and was a powerful hit in Berlin. The Carl Zuckmayer comedy *The Captain of Köpenick* satirized Prussian military traditions, and was made into a film in 1931 (and again in 1956). However, this was the beginning of the end for 'left-wing' Weimar theatre. In the 1930s classic theatre took over, such as Goethe's *Faust,* for which 1932 was the centenary year. Meanwhile, Tucholsky, Brecht and Walter Mehring wrote material for cabaret performances, in which social satire, rooted in the social, political and cultural life of Weimar, was a staple. Of course, cabaret also was light entertainment in song and dance. African-American Josephine Baker, a permanent resident in Paris after 1925, occasionally performed exotic dances, partially in the nude, at Berlin cabarets. Again, the Right regarded cabarets as dominated by the 'racially inferior': Jews, blacks, homosexuals and other deviants; in short, anyone different from themselves.

MUSIC

Historian Walter Laqueur observed that Weimar music patrons other than cabaret audiences faced an '*embarras de richesses,*' in both extant classics and prolific contemporary composers – save, perhaps, for Richard Strauss, whose *Die Frau ohne Schatten* and *Arabella* were not up to the standards of such pre-1914 works as *Salomé,* based on the Oscar Wilde play. Austrian Alban Berg's opera *Wozzeck* was expressionist, Hans Eisler wrote choral works for workers' massed choirs, Brecht and Weill's *Mahagonny* attacked a corrupt society, and Ernst Krenek's jazz opera, *Jonny spielt auf,* 'encountered both enthusiastic acceptance and violent rejection.' Once again, the standard for the Weimar period: discontent.

FILM

Innovation, variety and controversial themes were nowhere more prevalent in Weimar culture than in film. This relatively new invention had the potential for mass audiences going far beyond theatre, opera, art-work, or for that matter, readers of a controversial novel. German film first appeared in the Berlin Wintergarten in 1895, but only came into its own on the eve of the First World War when theatre director and producer Max Reinhardt led a movement of stage artists into film. Most film was then comedy or farce, save for such as *The Student of Prague* and *Der Andere*. When the war began, Germany had 2,000 well-attended cinemas, and UFA (*Universum Film Aktiengesellschaft*) was founded in 1917. It would became the primary source of Nazi propaganda films overseen first by Alfred Hugenberg and then by Joseph Goebbels (1897–1945).

'The nightmarish quality of the expressionist drama held a mysterious appeal to the tortured German soul during this period,' wrote film historian Ephraim Katz. Much early Weimar film was Expressionist: sets that resembled Expressionist paintings, distorted shapes and twisted minds. Major Expressionist film makers and examples of their work include screenwriter Carl Mayer, *The Cabinet of Dr Caligari*, director-producer Fritz Lang, *Dr Mabuse the Gambler*, director F. W. Murnau, *Nosferatu*, and director-art director Paul Leni, *Waxworks*. However, Expressionism faded after 1925, though its psychological and artistic elements remained in such films as Lang's 1927 masterpiece, *Metropolis*.

Historic epics with huge crowd scenes and historic costume dramas were also a feature of Weimar period film. Examples include Ernst Lubitsch's *Madame Dubarry/Passion* and *Anna Boleyn/Deception* and Lang's *Die Nibelungen*. Other popular genres included 'street films,' 'mountain films,' and films with a specifically political purpose. Street films were psychological melodramas, at which G. W. Pabst was a specialist. Mountain films 'exalted the beauty of nature and celebrated the triumph of the human body and spirit over the environment'; Leni Riefenstahl (1902–) was a leading performer in this genre with *Peaks of Destiny* and *The Ski Chase* before emerging as Joseph Goebbels' favourite Nazi propaganda film director. Pabst street films included *The Street of Sorrow* and, related to the genre at any rate, *Pandora's Box*. Not all German film stars or directors were German; Louise Brooks, the female lead in *Pandora's Box,* was a native of Cherryvale, Kansas in the United States, and *The Blue Angel* was directed by Josef von Sternberg, born in Vienna but from the age of seven, resident and then citizen of the United States. And political films were, well, political, an expected genre in an era of turmoil and uncertainty. *Metropolis* (1927) confronted the issue of labour vs capital, *Westfront 1918* explored the futility of war, and *Kameradschaft* suggested that Germans and French actually could get along, if they worked at it. These were films by directors on the Left, as were Leontine Sagan's *Mädchen in Uniform* with a lesbian sub-theme, Richard Oswald's film version of Zuckmayer's play *The Captain from Köpenick*, and Slatan Düdow's *Kühle Wampe*, which dealt with the impact of economic depression on Germany. Films from the nationalist Right included historic dramas about famous German leaders, soldiers and patriots, such as Gustav Ucicky's *Flute Concert at Sans-Souci* and *Yorck*, and Luis Trenker's *The Rebel*. These were UFA films, with propaganda themes.

The Rise of National Socialism

Which brings us to Adolf Hitler (1889–1945) and the National Socialist German Workers Party (Nazi). They came to power in 1933 and began turning Germany so far as it was possible, into a totalitarian dictatorship predicated upon racist and militarist premises.

ADOLF HITLER

He was born in 1889 in Braunau-am-Inn, the son of Alois Hitler, a minor Austrian customs official, and his third wife, Klara. The family was Catholic, lower middle class, and lived variously in Braunau, Passau, Lambach (where Adolf served as choir boy and acolyte at a nearby Benedictine Abbey), and after Alois died, in Linz. Alois was the illegitimate son of Maria Ann Schicklgruber, a domestic servant; father unknown, though one improbable theory is that it was a Graz Jew named Frankenberger in whose household Maria is said to have worked. Maria later married Georg Hiedler, an impoverished ne'er-do-well. Alois never knew his real father, and at age thirty-nine dropped the name Schicklgruber for 'Hitler', a variation on Hiedler. Just as well, opined historian Robert G. L. Waite: 'It is a bit difficult to cry with fanatic intensity "Hail Schicklgruber!"'

Not that anyone was 'hailing' young Adolf. An intelligent child, he received high marks in elementary school, but lost interest when he reached *realschule,* where he did poorly. Teachers described him as 'a gifted underachiever and a moody, antisocial loner given to day-dreaming.' He left school at age sixteen without a diploma. His academic failure likely was rooted in his family and home life, where Alois abused him with regular and severe whippings, for which Klara tried to make up by being overly indulgent. The latter may have deprived him of emotional stability and self-discipline, while the for-mer filled him with a desire for revenge, 'the still-unformulated search for an enemy to punish and destroy.'

In Linz, Hitler visited museums, attended operas (Wagner's *Rienzi* was his first), avidly read newspapers and Karl May's American Wild West novels, and day-dreamed about being a great artist – or a great politician, depending on the day of the week. In 1907 he tried for, but was denied, admission to the Viennese Academy of Fine Art; a blow to his ego, certainly. That was followed the same year by an even greater blow when, just before Christmas, his mother died of cancer. An important point here is that her physician was a Jew, Edward Bloch, who tried unproven procedures in treating her. Hitler apparently blamed him for her death; indeed for hurrying it. Soon after, he left for Vienna to become an artist, refusal by the Academy notwithstanding, carrying with him a growing resentment against Jews. In fact, Hitler had been anti-Semitic in Linz; Vienna, with a large Jewish population, simply expanded it.

In Vienna, Hitler slipped into the populist and nationalistic sub-culture of the city which was driven in part by racial hate and anger against Jews, Marxists, Freemasons, pacifists, and women from all social strata. Hitler avidly read *Ostara*, published by the renegade Catholic priest Adolf Lanz, alias Jörg Lanz von Liebenfels, which ranted about blond heros and 'racial hygiene,' blue-eyed 'Aryans' and 'swarthy ape-men,' and the need to 'deport, sterilize, and liquidate' the latter sub-species. He was exposed as well to the Pan-German preaching of Georg von Schönerer which advocated uniting Europe's German-speaking peoples, and embracing the virtues of Germanic culture, blood and soil. Hitler learned the 'hail' greeting from Schönerer. And, of course, there was Karl Lueger, Vienna's popular and demagogic anti-Semitic mayor. He learned from them all.

In 1913, Hitler fled to Munich to avoid military draft, was arrested, turned over to Austrian authorities, and, to his delight, failed his physical examination. He remained in Munich and tried to resume his 'artistic life.' Then came 1914 and war: Hitler eagerly volunteered for the German army, and this time, passed the physical. He served in a combat zone as a message runner between headquarters and the front lines. This was the first time, wrote Donald Wall, that he had 'a structured life, a sense of purpose, and close relationships that did not invade his privacy.' Hitler was wounded twice, promoted to lance corporal, and awarded the Iron Cross, First Class, on the recommendation of regimental adjutant Major Hugo Gutmann. Irony of ironies: Gutmann was a Jew.

BECOMING A NAZI

Hitler was posted to Munich in 1919 as a *Reichswehr* political instructor. His task was to 'inoculate' new army recruits against 'contagion' by socialist, pacifist or democratic ideas, and to investigate radical right-wing organizations. The latter included the German Workers Party, connected with the racist Thule Society, and headed by Anton Drexler (1884–1942). Hitler attended a meeting in September and spoke out against Bavarian separatism; the members liked it so much that he was invited to join. He did, officially listed as the seventh board member in charge of recruitment and propaganda. Hitler took charge of the party, changed the name to the National Socialist German Workers Party (Nazi) which had much wider appeal, and co-authored with Drexler the 25 Point Programme. In 1921 he replaced Drexler as official party leader, and soon was being addressed as *Der Führer*, a title reflecting his 'charismatic oratory, inspirational leadership, and fund-raising skills.' It all worked; by 1922, the Nazi party had 6,000 members and money.

THE PARTY

It also had the SA, whose job was to intimidate critics and hecklers at public meetings, and engage in street warfare against Communists and Socialist trades unionists. The *Schutzstaffel* (SS) was added in 1925 as an elite bodyguard unit for Hitler. Meanwhile, the party's inner circle formed around him: notably Herman Goering (1893–1946), Wilhelm Frick (1877–1946), Julius Streicher (1885–1946), Dietrich Eckart (1868–1923), Rudolf Hess (1894–1987) and Heinrich Himmler (1900–1945). Some of these joined Hitler's cabinet when he became German Chancellor in 1933. 'At best second-raters,' wrote Holger Herwig, 'these men were given an outlet only by Hitler's movement.' Streicher started *Der Stürmer*, a magazine filled with 'anti-Semitic pornography,' and Eckart organized the party newspaper, *Völkischer Beobachter*. Led by Hitler, they built the political movement that ended the Weimar Republic and established the Third Reich.

THE CRASH OF 1929

The economic disaster of 1929, which started with the Wall Street crash in New York and spread across industrial Europe, was a boon for the Nazi Party. *Reichstag* elections were an indicator: in 1924 the party took fourteen seats, and only twelve in 1928; then in 1930, with unemployment rising toward six million, they took 107. Meanwhile, politics had moved to the streets where chaos, violence, murder and polarization between extreme Left and Right was undercutting the democratic Centre. Non-unionist workers, agrarian labourers, white-collar workers, craftsmen and artisans, and women moved to the Nazi side in increasing numbers. Hitler left no doubt as to what the party intended for the future. At the trial of three Nazi hooligans in Leipzig in 1930 he testified:

> I stand here under oath to God Almighty. I tell you that if I come to power legally, in my legal government I will set up state tribunals which will be empowered to pass sentences by law on those responsible for the misfortunes of our nation. Possibly, then, quite a few heads will roll, legally.

He also told a Leipzig press reporter that he favoured the 'brutality' of the proletariat to the 'aestheticism' of the bourgeois, who simply reflected the decadence of cabaret society and 'are lost to the German nation!' And, in 1930, he orchestrated the ousting of Gregor Strassor (1892–1934) and his supporters from the Nazi party, ending a dispute over philosophy and direction that had persisted since 1925. Strassor led the genuinely Socialist part of the party, in opposition to Hitler's 'Big Money faction' supported by Joseph Goebbels (who had broken with Strassor in the late 1920s), Hermann Goering and others. Simply put, Hitler viewed wealthy supporters such as Alfred Hugenberg and industrialists Emil Kirdorf and Fritz Thyssen as a more useful road to power than idealistic nationalist socialists.

The Crisis in Weimar Politics

Recognized as a rising political force, Hitler was invited in October 1931 to consider entering the government. Nothing important, mind; Postmaster General was the offer on the table. After all, both the Nazi movement and Hitler – referred to by the president and his circle as the 'Bohemian corporal' – were regarded as abhorrent. It simply was a way to 'disarm' him, so to speak. Of course Hitler refused, and two weeks later presided over a mass demonstration of 100,000 SA with planes circling overhead trailing Swastika banners. In 1932, after much to-ing and fro-ing on the issue, Hitler decided to run for president. He lost to Hindenburg, but the Nazi party won 230 *Reichstag* seats; not a majority, but it was a plurality and gave the Nazi Party effective control over the parliament.

POLITICAL CRISIS

1932 was the year of reckoning. Hindenburg used Article 48 of the Weimar Constitution with regularity, and was surrounded by an increasingly reactionary collection of advisors, including Elard von Oldenburg-Januschau, who once remarked that it ought always to be possible to dissolve the *Reichstag* by sending a lieutenant and ten enlisted men to do the job. Chancellor Heinrich Brüning (1885–1970) lost favour with Hindenburg and was replaced by Franz von Papen (1879–1969), nominated by wannabe power-broker, General Kurt von Schleicher (1882–1934), the newest member of Hindenburg's inner circle. Papen at once lifted the ban Brüning had imposed on the SA and SS, which led to an immediate 'civil war' between Nazis and Communists that over five weeks produced 500 clashes with 99 dead and 1,125 injured. He also commuted the death sentences of five Nazis who had broken into the home of a Communist trade unionist and kicked him to death. In September Hermann Goering was elected president of the *Reichstag* after which Papen received an overwhelming no-confidence vote. Then came the November elections, and the Nazis lost 34 seats. Thinking he now had him at bay, Papen invited Hitler to join with him in a nationalist coalition. When Hitler ignored the offer, Papen suggested a *putsch* based on Article 48, which Hindenburg favoured but the *Reichswehr* did not. It was rejected and Papen was out, replaced by Schleicher as Chancellor. Papen, with Hindenburg's son, Oskar, then met secretly with Hitler to work out a deal for a Hitler cabinet, should the Nazi leader be named to replace Schleicher. It came to pass on 28–29 January. Schleicher resigned after rumours spread that he was planning a *putsch* against Hindenburg, and Papen persuaded the president to offer the chancellorship to Hitler. There seemed no other choice.

HITLER BECOMES CHANCELLOR

On 30 January 1933, Hindenburg received Adolf Hitler at the presidential palace, and officially designated him Chancellor of the Weimar Republic. A few moments later, Hitler came out of the palace, with tears in his eyes claimed one observer, flashed a victory salute to the crowds filling the *platz* and the Wilhelmstrasse. They responded with applause and shouts of acclaim. That night a victory celebration took place, with torch-lights and 25,000 SA and *Stahlhelm* troops marching through the Brandenburger Tor and past the Chancellery, through a window of which could be seen, in Joachim Fest's words, the 'nervous, prancing figure of Hitler.' Goering, Goebbels and Hess were with him.

From a constitutional point of view, Hitler's appointment was no different from that of Papen; in political terms it was the beginning of a revolution. And, one might add, a revolution quite beyond the capacity of the presidential inner circle to foresee. Remarked Papen privately: 'No danger at all. We've hired him for our act.' And, when the formalities had been concluded, Hindenburg said to the newly appointed Chancellor and his cabinet: 'And now, gentlemen, forward with God.'

CHAPTER ELEVEN

Nazi Germany and the Second World War,
1933–1945

Adolf Hitler's term as Chancellor of the Weimar Republic began in January 1933 as 'a change of administrations.' In 1934 he turned his office into that of a totalitarian dictator and initiated the Third *Reich*. It would stand, he assured his subjects and the world, for a thousand years.

The First Days

Hitler's detractors saw him as a 'prisoner' of Alfred Hugenberg, and too much the amateur to deal with Germany's many problems. The people would resist him; and there would be foreign intervention against his regime. They could not have been more wrong. Hitler's objective from the first moment, as Hitler biographer Joachim Fest phrased it, was to 'gather all the threads of power into his own hand by the time the eighty-five-year-old President [Hindenburg] died. And he knew how to go about it. . . .'

THE *REICHSTAG* FIRE

That included exploiting the *Reichstag* Fire. Less than a month after Hitler became Chancellor, the *Reichstag* building was gutted by fire. This occurred one week before the *Reichstag* elections Hitler had called for immediately he was in office. Now, with his cohorts in strategic offices, such as Herman Goering in control of the Prussian police, he was able to launch a 'reign of terror' that effectively sabotaged the election campaigns of opposition parties. It was recorded that upon hearing that the *Reichstag* was ablaze, Hitler exclaimed, 'Now I have them!' The Nazis claimed that Communists set the fire, a claim supported by Marinus van der Lubbe, a Dutch Communist caught in the burning building 'triumphantly babbling, "Protest! Protest!"' He was arrested and charged with arson. The next day, on Hitler's advice, Hindenburg issued a presidential decree for the 'Protection of the Volk and State' on the grounds that the fire was 'the signal for a Communist uprising.' The decree empowered Hitler as Chancellor to arrest Communists and temporarily suspend civil liberties generally. 'Temporary' indeed; civil rights were suspended for the rest of the Hitler regime. Meanwhile, many German Communists fled to Holland, where they held mock trials and 'convicted' Nazi party leaders of setting the fire as an excuse for banning political opposition.

The fire was arson, and evidence presented at van der Lubbe's trial strongly suggests that he acted entirely on his own – though it was a popular claim among historians in the 1950s that the Nazis set the fire as an excuse for ending civil liberties. In any case, the Nazis claimed that the fire was a conspiracy and used Hindenburg's decree to muzzle the left-wing press, arrest hundreds of Communists and Socialists, and

A poster showing Adolf Hitler and von Hindenburg shaking hands

unleash the SA to break up meetings and wound and kill political opponents in street clashes. When the elections took place on 6 March, the Nazis polled more than 17 million votes and secured 288 seats, which was still not quite a party majority; but as the German Nationalists aligned their 52 seats with the Nazis, Hitler had a *Reichstag* majority in fact.

EMPOWERING HITLER

It would never do for Germans to get the idea that the Nazis were not firmly in control. Failure to win an official majority inspired Hitler to stage a propaganda event; Holger Herweg dubbed it a 'patriotic passion play.' The event took place in the Royal Church of the Hohenzollerns in the Berlin suburb of Potsdam, where Frederick Wilhelm I and Frederick II were entombed. The date was 21 March 1933, the 62nd anniversary of Otto von Bismarck opening the first Imperial *Reichstag*. The idea was to show a binding connection between old Prussia and National Socialism. On one side sat admirals and generals of Imperial Germany; on the other men of the SA and SS. An empty chair at the front reminded all of the exiled Wilhelm II. The 'moment of truth' was Hindenburg and Hitler solemnly shaking hands over the royal graves. A choir sang Bach Chorales while outside of the church, artillery rounds were fired. The Hindenburg Myth (the field marshal of the Great War and the symbol of the Prussian Junker tradition) was now wedded to the Hitler Myth (the populist leader and symbol of Aryan supremacy). A poster celebrating the event depicted the handshake with an altar and cross in the background. Interestingly, Hitler's head is bowed while Hindenburg looks straight ahead, and a beam of light from the window illuminates the President's head, but not also the Chancellor's.

On this day, *Völkischer Beobachter*, the Nazi party newspaper, announced the opening of a concentration camp for political dissidents at Dachau, near Munich – it was the first of many to have the phrase *Arbeit Macht Frei* ('Work Liberates') above the entrance. Three days later, at Hitler's request, the *Reichstag* (now meeting in Kroll Opera House) passed the Enabling Act, which gave the emergency powers to set the Nazification of the German state in motion. Only the Social Democrats voted against it, and when the act had passed, the National

Socialist deputies sang 'Horst Wessel,' the party song, in celebration. They were joined by crowds of supporters outside.

NAZIFICATION

Hitler now launched *Gleichschaltung,* Nazi 'synchronization,' to create an ideal *Volksgemeinschaft,* or 'truly integrated society.' Remarked Joseph Goebbels: 'One can say that today history is once more being made in Germany.' Between March and August SA troops cooperated with local police and Nazi supporters in a campaign of political terror: they overthrew non-National Socialist governments in Baden, Bavaria, Hesse, Saxony, Württemberg, Bremen, Hamburg and Lübeck; swastikas were raised over all government buildings, and officials were arrested *en masse* including 25,000 in Prussia alone. By December only one in seven elected mayors remained in office, and two-thirds of Germany's newspapers had been shut down. Millions of Germans stampeded to join National Socialist ranks. Founding party members sneered at this; the party was being 'bourgeoisized.'

In May, strikes, collective bargaining, and indeed unions, were outlawed and all workers were enrolled in Robert Ley's German Labour Front. So too women's organizations, whose members were 'transferred' to others such as the League of German Girls, the National Socialist Housewives' League, and the National Socialist Mothers' service. In June, Pope Pius XI (1857–1939) signed a Concordat with Hitler in which he recognized the regime, in exchange for Hitler's promise that the Vatican would continue to run the Church and its educational and other organizations in Germany – which may explain why the Vatican did not act on Mussolini's recommendation in 1938 that Hitler be excommunicated. Meanwhile, the Social Democrats were outlawed. Some of the leaders went into exile in Prague, while others were sent to concentration camps now springing up across Germany in imitation of Dachau. Other parties were either shut down or dissolved themselves. The National Socialists were declared the only legal political party in Germany, an announcement made, ironically enough, on 14 July.

This was only the beginning. Nazi organizations took over virtually everything: 40,000 agricultural cooperatives joined the National

Socialist Party; the war veterans association, *Stahlhelm* (Steel helmet), merged with the SA; and, led by Adolf Krupp, German industry 'embraced the *Führerprinzip*' and formed the *Reich* Estate of German Industry – controlled, of course, by the Nazi party – and on 1 April ordered a national boycott of Jewish businesses. This coincided with enforcement of the Civil Service Reconstruction Law which purged Socialists, Republicans and Jews from government bureaucracy. By 1934, thousands of Jewish lawyers, doctors, civil servants and cultural leaders such as directors, conductors, musicians, actors, and the like had been driven from their posts, and many from Germany itself. That Thomas Mann 'applauded what he called the "desemitization of justice"' gives his opposition to the Nazi Regime a slightly hollow ring.

Meanwhile, Catholic leaders did not complain when dissident priests were beaten and imprisoned, in exchange for being spared the persecution meted out to other religious groups. These included 'fringe' religious groups such as Jehovah's Witnesses, Anabaptists, Seventh-Day Adventists, the Zionist Community, Free Pentacostalists, Baha'i, Church of the Apostle Job, the Bible Faith Fellowship, the Christian Scientists, and the Salvation Army. Pacifist religions were targeted in 1938 when it was made a capital offence to refuse the military draft. Many Catholics expected Hitler to remember his own Catholic roots and leave them in peace; mainstream Protestants also 'played the game.' In 1932, Pastor Joachim Hossenfelder organized a 'German Christian' movement that regarded itself as the 'SA of Jesus Christ.' Its slogan: 'The swastika on our breast, the Cross in our heart.' In 1933, 700,000 Protestant Youth Group members joined the Hitler Youth, while theology students and young ministers joined the National Socialist party in droves. Also in 1933, Hitler authorized army chaplain Ludwig Müller to create a unified '*Reich* Church.'

'CLEANSING'

Next came the removal of 'decadent' and 'undesirable' elements from German society. In the former instance, academicians, scientists and literati, of which twenty-four were Nobel Laureates, were purged at the instigation of Alfred Rosenberg's Militant League for German Culture: they included Max Horkheimer, Ernst Kantorowicz, Paul

Tillich, Karl Mannheim, Heinrich and Thomas Mann, Alfred Döblin, Ricarda Huch, Albert Einstein, Bertold Brecht, Sigmund Freud, Herbert Marcuse, Karl Popper, among others. The SA, SS and Nazi student groups publically burnt books by such as Brecht, Freud, August Bebel, Carl von Ossietzky, Hugo Preuss, Heinrich Heine, Karl Marx and Erich Marie Remarque, and attacked cinemas scheduled to show the Hollywood film version of Remarque's pacifist novel *All Quiet on the Western Front*. And, of course, American Jazz music was suppressed because many of its composers were black or Jewish: Count Basie, Duke Ellington and Benny Goodman, for example. A flood of *émigrés* to Britain, the United States and elsewhere, began. Meanwhile, 'undesirables,' persons with mental deficiencies, epilepsy, schizophrenia, deafness, blindness, and hereditary physical disabilities, alcoholism, prostitution, drug abuse, criminal behaviour and long-term welfare dependency, were required by law to undergo sterilization. Some 320,000 *Reich* citizens had been treated in this way by 1939.

Hitler's Germany

In July 1933 Hitler claimed that *Gleichschaltung* was complete. What did that mean in practice, beyond the *Reichstag* now being a male-dominated, uniformed National Socialist club, and all power emanating from Berlin?

ORGANIZATION

The new state structure was a bureaucracy of the first order. Germany was divided into *Gaue* (districts), the *Gauleiters* (leaders) of which were appointed by the central administration. By 1935, 35 *Gauleiters* commanded 827 regional and 21,000 local party leaders, and 260,000 block and party cell leaders – such as the 40,000 bureaucrats in the German Labour Front – all paid by Berlin. This appeared to exemplify Teutonic order and efficiency, but in fact was what Holger Herweg termed a state of 'authoritarian anarchy'; a labyrinth of conflicting and redundant state, party and private bureaucracies operating within the system, each vying with others for power and rewards. Only Hitler as *Der Führer* stood above this competition. In the end, this 'anarchy' contributed to the collapse of the regime.

ENFORCING *VOLKSGEMEINSCHAFT*

This was Heinrich Himmler's job as head of the *Gestapo* (Secret State Police) and overseer of all other police agencies, including the *Einsatzgruppen* SS, the concentration camp guards who also searched out 'asocial' elements within the *Reich*. The *Sicherheitsdienst* (Secret Service), headed by Reinhard Heydrich (1904–1942), answered only to Himmler and did 'ideological' intelligence work for party and state. Meanwhile, the Race and Settlement Office was created to supervise maintenance of racial purity.

Himmler also oversaw development of the complex system of more than thirty concentration camps that began with Dachau and expanded to include others such as Oranienburg, Sachsenhausen, Buchenwald, Ravensbrück and Bergen-Belsen. They included all manner of 'social undesirables,' identified by triangular patches on their prison uniforms: red for political, black for 'asocial,' purple for Christian fundamentalist, green for common criminals, blue for would-be *émigrés*, pink for homosexuals, and a double triangular yellow patch for Jews in imitation of the Star of David. Some termed it the '*Pour le Sémite*,' a sardonic take off on *Pour le Mérite*, the most coveted German military award of the First World War. Sardonic wit also greeted Himmler's definition of the 'ideal Aryan' as 'blond, blue-eyed, and physically fit.' Dissident humourists concluded that this meant the 'ideal Aryan was as blond as Hitler, as thin as Goering, as athletic as Goebbels, and as handsome as Himmler.'

NIGHT OF THE LONG KNIVES

Many Nazis began and remained revolutionaries, and were not pleased when Hitler made peace with the wealthy and aristocratic in order to have their support. Ernst Röhm (1887–1934), for example, a *Reichswehr* captain in the First World War, wanted the army subsumed under the SA which, after all, was 'Hitler's Army.' This alarmed old aristocracy *Reichswehr* officers to whom the SA were simply street ruffians. In their view, the *Reichswehr* alone was the German Army, and should be the sole bearer of arms in the National Socialist state. A deal was struck: in return for absolute *Reichswehr* support and loyalty, Hitler would suppress Röhm and the SA.

In late June 1934, Hitler ordered Röhm to take sick leave at Bad Wiessee. On the night of 24–25 June, SS units were put on alert throughout Germany, the word being that dissident SA elements were planning a *putsch*. Blacklists of potential candidates for liquidation, including Röhm, were circulated, the *Reichswehr* provided guns, trucks and barracks for SS units commanded by Sepp Dietrich, and on the morning of 30 June, Hitler, a whip and a revolver in hand, led an SS execution squad into Röhm's quarters where, it is said, he and some of his staff were in bed together. Röhm and some 200 SA leaders were arrested and taken to prison, where he was shot out of hand. It has been argued that Hitler's real problem with Röhm was his homosexuality; that is at best specious, because he had known about Röhm's sexual preference for more than a decade, and it had never bothered him before.

Hitler settled a number of old scores on this 'Night of the Long Knives' as it came to be called: those killed included Father Bernhard Stempfle, editorial assistant for the design and publication of *Mein Kampf* and with whom Hitler had had differences over the volume; Gustav von Kahr, Hitler's fellow-traveller in the beer-hall *putsch* of 1923; General von Schleicher, former Weimar Chancellor, and his confidant, General Kurt von Bredow; and above all, Hitler's former ideological rival within the party and now party exile, Gregor Strasser.

Selling the Reich

President Hindenburg died on 2 August 1934. Hitler abolished the office of President, transferred its powers to himself as Chancellor and *Führer*, and required the military and civil service to swear an oath of loyalty to him personally. He was now absolute ruler of an absolutist state; making certain that everyone understood this was a high priority.

PROPAGANDA

Propaganda was part of Nazi policy from at least 1922, and it was an essential element after 1933 both to secure the support of the German people and persuade the world that the new Germany was the greatest nation on earth. Such events as the carefully orchestrated 1934 Nuremberg Party rally, with 100,000 marching SA, SS and Labour Battalion members, flags, speeches, martial music, and above all the *Führer,* were pure propaganda. Joseph Goebbels, head of the Ministry of People's Enlightenment and Propaganda, combined propaganda with censorship. Newspapers printed what the government told them to, or were shut down. Party newspaper *Völkischer Beobachter* simply promoted the government line on everything, while Julius Streicher's *Der Stürmer* focused on anti-Semitic propaganda. Radio broadcasts included martial music, Hitler speeches, managed news reporting, and during the Second World War, 'Charley and His Orchestra' performed popular American and British songs in English, for audiences outside of Germany. Each song would end with a parody of the original lyrics meant to make fun of Winston Churchill, Franklin D. Roosevelt, or some other aspect of the Allied war effort.

Film also was a central channel for Nazi propaganda dissemination. Like broadcasting, it reached a mass audience. Examples of feature film propaganda between 1933 and 1945 include: *Hitlerjunge Quex* cele- brated the Hitler Youth embracing the concepts of 'race, blood, soil, honour, mission,' and expressing hatred for all that was alien and 'undesirable'; *Jud Süss* misrepresented an actual historic figure in order to promote anti-Semitism; *Carl Peters* made a hero of a German colonialist in Africa who actually was a horror; *Fredericus* extolled the military virtues of Frederick the Great; and the late war-time film *Kolberg* assured the German people that they could stop the advancing Allies. Meanwhile, news reels showed Poles, French and Russians being swept aside by the *Wehrmacht.* Cinemas also screened propaganda documentaries, such as *Tag der Freiheit* (Day of Freedom), *Der Marsch zum Führer* (March to the Leader), *Der ewiege Jude* (The Eternal Jew), and above all, Leni Riefenstahl's film of the Nuremberg rally, *Triumph des Willen.* She opened with a metaphor for the 'Second Coming': Hitler in an airplane descending from the sky to land at Nuremberg aerodrome. And there were posters, art work like Arno Breker's Aryan sculptures, for example, and pageants with uniformed marching soldiers, and book burnings. Hitler's dream of dazzling his subjects with the proposed 250,000 seat Berlin Congress Hall, and an outdoor stadium seating 405,000, remained only that: a dream.

OLYMPICS

The 1936 Summer Olympics in Berlin was the ultimate German propaganda event for the world. This was the 'show of shows' aimed at celebrating a strong and vibrant nation on the march. Important foreign visitors were lavishly entertained. Goebbels treated a thousand guests to a special 'night of lights' on the Pfaueninsel; Foreign Minister Joachim von Ribbentrop (1893–1946) entertained 700 guests under a tent at his Dahlem villa where 'Pommery champagne of the best quality flowed in rivers' – after all, he was a champagne merchant before becoming a Nazi big-wig; Goering amused visitors with a miniature eighteenth-century village constructed in the garden of the Air Ministry; and '*Juden Verboten*' (Jews are forbidden) signs were temporarily removed around the city. Leni Riefenstahl again: her film *Olympia* (released in two parts) for which she was awarded the Mussolini Cup at the 1938 Venice film festival, promoted the Aryan ideal by glorifying physical might and idealizing the human body. The opening scene depicts classic sculptures of Greek athletes coming to life as modern-day Olympians. Of course, African-Americans Jesse Owens and Charles Metcalf dominating sprint events challenged that ideal. Not surprisingly, Hitler refused to be present when their medals were presented. Germany also was host to the Winter Olympics in 1936, at Garmish-Partenkirchen in the German Alps.

EDUCATION

Traditional schools and universities continued with teachers and professors now joining the Nazi party. New non-traditional schools included the SS National-Political Training Institution and the Adolf Hitler Schools for teenage boys, and the *Ordensburgen* (Castles for a Knightly Order) for married top graduates of SS or Adolf Hitler schools. *Ordensburgen* emphasized 'racial hygiene,' biology, leadership, administration and geography, all subjects relevant to the idea of conquering and ruling Europe according to Nazi doctrine. All education included some propaganda elements.

THE REGIME: APPEARANCE

Most Germans accepted the regime. And why not? It offered stability, jobs (in 1938 unemployment was 1.9 per cent, far below that of Great Britain and the United States), an end to the 'humiliation' of defeat in the First World War, clean and safe streets, and well-stocked shops. Standing above it all was *Der Führer*, saviour of *Reich und Volk*, who emphasized equality of educational opportunity, job competition, social mobility and promotion based on merit. Hitler's architect Albert Speer (1905–1981) directed the 'Beauty of Labour Programme' which achieved a better work environment through building inspections, better ventilation, additional washing facilities and clean cafeterias. For relaxation, there was 'Strength through Joy,' including such State-directed leisure activities as concerts, films, theatres, games, exhibitions, sea cruises and pilgrimages to Berchtesgaden, the locale of the Berghof, Hitler's private retreat; and all at reduced prices.

AND REALITY

A reality check reveals serious shortfalls, however. Wages and salaries represented a smaller share of the Gross Domestic Product in 1937 than in 1928, while trade and industry profits claimed a larger share – so much for the Socialist element in National Socialism. By 1940 gross income per taxpayer had declined by 3 per cent, and roughly 50 per cent of a worker's income went to purchase food. Nazi propaganda made much of agriculture, but in reality farmers were, in Holger Herwig's words, 'poor, coarse, dirty, and overworked. Their farms lacked sanitation, efficient use of fertilizer, good bookkeeping, and mechanization. More than half the farmers in Germany had no running water.... The number of university students of agriculture and veterinary science fell by 20 per cent between 1932 and 1939.' Simply put, the emphasis was on rearmament, not food production; between 1933 and 1938 funding for defence expenditure rose from 4 per cent to 50 per cent, including 916,000,000 RMs in 1938 alone for autobahn expansion to improve motorized military deployment.

Also, despite propaganda to the contrary, women were accorded second-class status. They were denied access to the National Socialist executive, the higher levels of the civil service, high political office, the principal professions, including academia, and, until the Second World War changed things, the military. Meanwhile, they were hailed as the most important citizens because their primary role was to have babies, which is to say future soldiers – provided, of course, that they were Aryan, loyal and healthy. The latter point was the theme of the film *Ich Klage An,* in which a wife suffering from multiple sclerosis persuades her husband to kill her. Sex education was readily obtainable and divorce was made easy so that a woman could change partners in the event that babies were not forthcoming. On the other side, abortion was difficult (the opposite being true for Jewish women), contraceptives scarce, and taxes high for childless couples. Single women were encouraged to join the *lebensborn* programme, where SS men, the 'Aryan Ideal,' impregnated them. Most were reluctant to avail themselves of this 'opportunity.'

Did it work? No. The average number of children per marriage remained constant, the average household size actually declined, and as late as 1939, women were 37 per cent of the work force at wages 33 per cent below those of men, of course.

Opposition – of a Sort

It was limited, but it did happen. In 1933 Lutheran Pastor Martin Niemöller (1892–1984), a U-boat officer in the First World War, objected to religious persecution, published 'Sixteen Thesis' denouncing Hossenfelder's 'German Christian Movement,' and took the pulpit in Martin Luther's Wittenberg church to denounce Nazi racial doctrines. The 'German Christians' responded 'with a formal call to abolish the Old Testament and the "Jewish" theology of St Paul, while raising Jesus Christ to full "Aryan" status.' In 1937 Pope Pius XI urged German Catholics to repudiate racism and Hitlerism in the name of Christ, the Church and the Primacy of Rome; the regime responded by razing churches, sending clerical dissenters, including Niemöller, to concentration camps, and denying theologians like Dietrich Bonhoeffer (1906–1945) the right to address the public orally or in writing. Bonhoeffer worked with Allied spy networks against the Nazi Regime, and was caught and executed in 1945, just days before the war in Europe ended.

Also during the war, the aristocratic Kreisau Circle, presided over by Count Helmuth von Moltke, great-grandson of the victor in the Franco–Prussian war, urged an end to the Nazi regime, but opposed an anti-Nazi *putsch*. War hero and aristocrat Colonel Klaus von Stauffenberg (1907–1944) felt differently. He launched 'Operation Valkyrie' in July 1944 to assassinate Hitler and seize control. It failed, and 5,000 German officers and others were executed in revenge, some in the Bendlerstrasse courtyard. And there was *Die Weisse Rose* (the White Rose), a group of devoutly Catholic and Protestant students and at least one professor at Ludwig Maximilian University in Munich, who saw Nazism as the perversion of everything in which they believed. They too paid the ultimate price. The danger inherent in placid acceptance of the Hitler Regime was Niemöller's point in these lines written while he was in a concentration camp:

> When the Nazis came for the Communists, I remained silent, for I was not a Communist. When they incarcerated the Social Democrats, I remained silent, for I was not a Social Democrat. When they came for the Catholics, I did not protest, for I was not a Catholic. When they came for me, no one protested, for there was no one left to protest.

Preparing for War

Hitler's aim was to make Germany dominant in Europe and the world. Historians debate whether or not he planned the war that came with his aim; all the same it happened, and his rearmament policy and foreign policy indicate that he had no qualms about going to war. This was indicated as well at a meeting in Berlin in November 1937 when minutes were taken by Colonel Hossbach in which Hitler and his principal military and diplomatic officials discussed scenarios that might lead to war against, variously, Poland, Czechoslovakia, France and Russia.

FOREIGN POLICY: AIMS

Hitler's policy was to set aside the Versailles Treaty: restore lost territories, remilitarize the Rhineland, and repudiate disarmament and reparations. His belligerence on these issues left Great Britain and France uncertain how to deal with him. Prior to 1935 'Collective Security' prevailed among the western powers; that is, keeping Germany in check through a coalition of major and minor powers extending from Poland to Great Britain. The increasingly sympathetic relationship between Hitler and Italy's dictator Benito Mussolini, and a rising pacifist mind set in both Great Britain and France, made that policy difficult to sustain. The 1934 'Peace Ballot' in Great Britain drew 6 million 'votes' against going to war under any circumstances. Meanwhile, pro-fascist political movements took root there and in France, which further undermined willingness to take a hard line on Hitler's revisionist foreign policy.

AND ACTS

Hitler withdrew from European disarmament talks in 1934; in 1935 Italy invaded Ethiopia as part of Mussolini's aspiration to 'recreate' the Roman Empire. Hitler had no objections, particularly as the occupation of Ethiopia featured 'concentration camps, mass executions, use of gas, and aerial strafing of women and children.' Indeed, *Der Führer* chose the moment to proclaim German rearmament on all fronts. The western powers complained without affect to the League of Nations. In 1936 Hitler ordered the remilitarization of the Rhine west bank; again there was only vocal protest. Mussolini seized the moment to sneer at the Anglo–French 'Hoare–Laval Pact' signed in November 1935, which recognized Italian gains in Ethiopia only if Italy guaranteed no further aggression. By 1937 the 'Stresa front,' an Anglo–French effort started in 1935 to include Italy in a defensive alliance aimed at Germany, had collapsed. Meanwhile, the Spanish Civil War had begun in 1936, complicating international relations even more. Germany and Italy supported General Franco, the Soviet Union gave what support it could to the Republican government, and Britain and France were caught in the middle. Also in 1936, Hitler and Mussolini had signed the 'Rome–Berlin Axis' agreement; the Anglo–French response was Appeasement Policy.

APPEASEMENT

Appeasement was the 'official' policy of British prime minister Neville Chamberlain and supported by French premier Edouard Daladier. The

The growth of Nazi Germany, 1933–39

Germany in 1933
Plebiscite joins Germany in 1935
Remilitarised in 1936
Annexed, 1938–39
Satellite states, March 1939
Annexed, September 1939
Occupied by Germany, Sept 1939
Annexed by USSR, Sept. 1939
Annexed by Hungary, March 1939
International boundaries, 1936

essence of it was the assurance given to Hitler by Lord Halifax in 1937 that issues regarding the Danzig Corridor, Austria and Czechoslovakia could be settled in Germany's favour. And so they were. Germany annexed Austria in March 1938 without western interference. In September, Hitler and Chamberlain met three times, the last in Munich with Mussolini and Daladier, to discuss Germany annexing the Czech Sudetenland. This area lay along the northwestern side of Czechoslovakia and was home to some three and a half million ethnic Germans, including Oskar Schindler who would save more than a thousand Jews from Nazi deathcamps during the Second World War. Annexation was agreed to, and accepted with resignation by Czech president Eduard Beneš. This was the 'Munich Pact' which guaranteed 'peace for our time'; or so Chamberlain proclaimed when he arrived back in London.

And it was – at least for Britain and France. In March 1939 Germany threatened Czechoslovakia with war if it did not deconstruct on German terms. The result was an independent Slovakia (actually a German satellite) and the *Reich* Protectorate of Bohemia and Moravia. Chamberlain felt betrayed, and declared unconditional British support for both Poland and Rumania. France agreed, albeit reluctantly.

SUMMER, 1939

This was the critical time. On 22 May, Germany and Italy formed the 'Pact of Steel,' which bound each to support the other no matter what. In July and August British and Soviet military talks came to nothing; worse than nothing, for on the day they met for the last time, Berlin announced that foreign minister Ribbentrop was invited to Moscow for talks with Soviet foreign minister Molotov. The result was the Hitler's non-aggression pact with Joseph Stalin, signed on 23 August. It made Poland defenceless in the event of an attack from either or both; unless Poland received British and French military support.

The issue was the 'Polish Corridor,' of course, the territories extending south from Danzig that Germany forfeited as part of the Versailles Treaty. Now Hitler had a deal with Stalin, and since neither he nor his advisors believed Great Britain and France would reverse their appeasement policies of the prior several years, Poland was issued an ultimatum: surrender the Corridor or else. Polish foreign minister

Joseph Beck refused, confident of British and French support. That was all Hitler needed – and Stalin, too, as it turned out. Germany attacked Poland on 1 September in a *Blitzkrieg* (lightning war) of combined armour and air forces, and on 17 September, the Soviet Union invaded eastern Poland. It was over in a month; Germany annexed the Polish Corridor and agreed to divide the rest of Poland with the Soviet Union along what was termed the Ribbentrop–Molotov Line, with Warsaw in the German sector. And, when the Soviets invaded Finland in November, Germany looked the other way. Meanwhile, Britain and France had begun their war against Germany – such as it was – on 3 September.

The Second World War

The war first was a limited northern European conflict, then a general European war, and finally a world war involving the United States and Japan.

THE 'PHONEY WAR'

Initially, nothing happened in western Europe save for the occasional allied bombing raid which consisted of dropping leaflets more often than explosives on Germany's forward lines, and the arrival of the British Expeditionary Force (BEF) in France. The French stayed put behind the Maginot line, a fortified barricade that stretched the length of the Franco-German frontier. Then in April 1940, Germany attacked Denmark and Norway. Denmark surrendered without resistance; British and French troops came to the aid of Norway, but had to withdraw. By the end of May, Scandinavia was under German occupation, save for Sweden which was a declared neutral.

THE WESTERN FRONT

Also in May, Hitler launched *Blitzkrieg* simultaneously against Belgium, the Netherlands and Luxembourg, drove French and British forces into retreat, and marched towards Paris. Over 300,000 Allied soldiers, mostly British, were evacuated from the beaches at Dunkirk in June; a defeat, but at least it left an army intact for the future. Italy, neutral despite the 'Rome–Berlin Axis' agreement, now joined forces with Germany, declaring war against the Allies. On 14 June the *Wehrmacht* occupied Paris, and France surrendered; Germany took over northern and western France, while the remainder became Vichy France, self-governing but subject to Germany. Now, save for the four neutral nations of Switzerland, Spain, Portugal and Sweden, continental Europe was largely in German hands, and Great Britain had its back to the wall; the result largely of Hitler listening to *Panzer* (tank) commander General Heinz Guderian (1884–1954), who explained to him that 'powerful concentrations of fast-striking, well-armoured, and heavily armed tanks, closely supported by aircraft and other motorized troops, would determine the outcome of the next conflict.'

Hitler visited occupied Paris on 23 June and saw the Palais Garnier, the Eiffel Tower (in front of which he had his photograph taken), and Les Invalides, where he stood in silent tribute before the tomb of Napoleon. He was driven past such sites as the Palais de Justice and the Louvre. At the end of the day, Hitler concluded that as Berlin would be made the showplace of the world, it would not be necessary to destroy Paris.

'THE BATTLE OF BRITAIN'

In 1940, Hitler ordered an air assault on Britain meant to smash the country into submission. It is said that this was in response to an embarrassment inflicted upon *Der Führer* by the RAF; a bombing raid on Berlin in response to German bombs that accidentally fell on London, after he had promised that no enemy bombs would ever fall on the German capital. The British dug in and fought back as best they could; fortunately, the Spitfire fighter was a superior aircraft to anything the Germans had. Meanwhile, U-Boats (submarines) worked at cutting off supplies shipped from North America to Great Britain, and landing craft were assembled on the French coastline, presumably in anticipation of an actual invasion of Britain. It never happened. Some historians are convinced that it never was intended to; that the British Isles were to be left to the *Luftwaffe* (Air Force) and *Kriegsmarine* (Navy), for the *Wehrmacht* had other fish to fry – namely, the Soviet Union.

Hitler did use ground troops against Britain in North Africa under the command of General Irwin Rommel (1891–1944), sent to aid the failing Italian campaign in Egypt. The 'Desert War,' as it came to be known, featured a German army much smaller than that of Britain, but far more successful. At one point Rommel was within sixty miles of Cairo. Meanwhile, Hitler also came to Mussolini's aid in the Balkans, attacking Yugoslavia and Greece; Bulgaria, Hungary and Romania, already in the German camp, assisted in the campaign. The Axis never fully won in this region. By 1942 the conflict had devolved into a guerilla war that ended only with Germany's defeat in 1945.

RUSSIA

Hitler's ultimate goal was Russia. Joseph Stalin apparently understood this. His war against Finland, annexation of Lithuania, Latvia and Estonia, and taking Bessarabia and Northern Bukovina from Romania (which brought the Red Army within 100 miles of the Ploesti oil fields to which Germany desperately needed access), were intended to create a buffer between the Soviet Union and Germany. However, Germany was now in control of western Europe, save for Britain of course, and on 22 June 1941, Hitler launched Operation Barbarossa against Russia. It was the first of two gigantic mistakes.

WORLD WAR

In the first six months of war against the Soviet Union, Germany took control of western Russia from Leningrad in the north to Moscow in the centre, and Stalingrad in the south. All of the Ukraine, including Kiev, was occupied, as were the Caucasus. Victory seemed just around the corner and it might have been, had Russian winter not intervened to inflict upon the Germans exactly what it had inflicted upon Napoleon 130 years earlier. Also, Hitler declared war on the United States in support of Japan's 7 December attack on Pearl Harbor. That was the second gigantic mistake. From 7 December 1941 onward, Germany was surrounded by enemies: the Russians in the East, and the Americans and British in the West and in Africa. Seen in retrospect, defeat was only a matter of time.

HOLOCAUST

Meanwhile, the Hitler Regime worked to resolve the 'Jewish Question.' The 1935 Nuremberg Laws had denied Jews citizenship, civil rights, legal protection, and a social place, and implied that it would be a good thing if they disappeared altogether. On 7 November 1938, diplomat Ernst vom Rath was murdered in Paris by Hershal Gynszpan, a Polish Jew, which launched *Kristallnacht* ('night of broken glass'), a nationwide anti-Jewish pogrom. On the night of 9–10 November, mobs organized by the SS and SA destroyed 267 synagogues, 844 stores, and 171 private dwellings. Michael Lucas recalled what happened in his village of Hoengen, near Aachen:

> After a while the Storm troops were joined by people who were not in uniform; and suddenly, with one loud cry of, 'Down with the Jews,' the gathering outside produced axes and heavy sledgehammers. They advanced towards the little synagogue ... burst the door open, and the whole crowd, by now shouting and laughing, stormed into the little House of God. ... When the first rays of a cold and pale November sun penetrated the heavy dark clouds, the little synagogue was but a heap of stone, broken glass and smashed-up woodwork.

The next day, some 35,000 Jews – and non-Jews who protested – were dispatched to concentration camps. Jews also paid for the damage done to them. Insurance claims were collected by the government, rather than by those whose property had been destroyed.

'THE FINAL SOLUTION'

Getting Jews out of Germany had been Nazi policy since 1920. A Jewish-made film encouraging Jews to emigrate to Palestine was permitted in 1937, and the SS established the Central Agency for Jewish Emigration in 1939. All the same, only some 170,000 Jews left, largely for Belgium, Czechoslovakia, Denmark, France, Poland and the Netherlands; hardly secure havens once the war was underway. Great Britain accepted 10,000 German Jewish children, but opposed Jewish emigration to British-controlled Palestine. Generally, neither Great Britain nor the United States were particularly open to Jewish refugees either then or during the war.

Jewish emigration was banned altogether in October 1941, and the yellow star was made mandatory for all Jews, in or out of concentration camps. In January 1942, Reinhard Heydrich chaired a secret

The gates of Auschwitz extermination camp

conference at Wannsee near Berlin. Here was coordinated the 'final solution,' that is the planned, mass extermination of the Jewish population of Europe. This was the Holocaust. Jews in Germany and every country its armies had conquered and occupied, were to be sent to such 'death camps' as Sobibor, Majdanek, Treblinka, and above all, Auschwitz. All were in the East, outside of Germany. There inmates were worked to death, gassed or shot, and their bodies incinerated in furnaces. In fact, Wannsee merely reaffirmed and elaborated a programme already in progress; its real importance was making the 'final solution' official. It is estimated that some six million Jews from across Europe were exterminated in this manner; it is also estimated that this was only half of the total number of people killed by the Third *Reich*, including such 'undesirables' as Gypsies, 'asocials' and political dissidents, and any number of captured enemy soldiers.

THE WAR AT HOME

Meanwhile, Hitler maintained a domestic atmosphere that kept morale high, at least as compared to that of the First World War. Rationing existed, but was not extreme, and the availability of consumer goods remained at pre-war levels until 1944. This was in part due to agricultural products being taken to Germany from occupied countries. The Nazi ideal of women as homemakers also was maintained, at least until 1942. Then things changed. The number of women entering the work force – increasingly war-related as opposed to domestic – rose significantly; by 1943, women comprised 61 per cent of university students, and 3,500 women served as concentration camp guards, where 'their behaviour differed little from that of their male colleagues.' By 1944, one in every five workers was foreign, prisoner of war or other, who joined the increased number of female workers to take the place of German men needed to supply the military. It seemed to work. War production increased by 300 per cent between 1942 and 1944, the very time when Anglo-American bombing campaigns were at their height.

And, of course, propaganda was disseminated everywhere to maintain public morale. Propaganda films, news reels, documentaries and features portrayed a Germany guaranteed of victory; posters of invincible Aryans protecting Germany from its enemies decorated signposts and lamp posts; and both Hitler and Goebbels filled the airwaves with encouraging bombast. However, Germany was stretched beyond the limit regarding supplies needed to carry on the war, and early in 1942, war materials planners Albert Speer and Fritz Todt concluded that it was only a matter of time before Germany would be defeated. Needless to say they did not tell Hitler.

AIR WAR

In February 1942, Britain launched a mass bombing campaign supervised by Air Marshal Sir Arthur 'Bomber' Harris. The intent was, in the words of Prime Minister Winston Churchill, to 'destroy the morale of the enemy civilian population and, in particular, of the industrial workers.' Revenge for the havoc the *Luftwaffe* wreaked on London, Coventry and other British cities was also a consideration, and bombing German cities took precedence over attacking industrial and communications facilities. The United States was fully engaged in Europe by 1942, and by May 1945 Anglo-American air forces had dropped an estimated million tonnes of bombs on 1,000 cities, towns and villages, killing 635,000 civilians including children, and destroying 3,500,000 houses which rendered 7,500,000 people homeless. In 1945, 'violent house-to-house and street-to-street fighting by last-ditch fanatical Nazi formations, and wilful destruction of bridges, public buildings, and roads by retreating Nazis' added to the decimation; but bombs were the most destructive element: 69 per cent of Kassel was destroyed, Nuremberg 51 per cent, Bremerhaven 79 per cent, Aachen 59 per cent,

Bonn 83 per cent, Kiel 69 per cent, Stuttgart 46 per cent, Hannover and Bremen 60 per cent, Koblenz 58 per cent, Dresden 59 per cent, Munich 42 per cent, Mainz 61 per cent, Frankfurt 52 per cent, and Berlin only 33 per cent. It seemed even more. Wrote a New York *Herald Tribune* correspondent at war's end: 'Nothing is left of Berlin. There are no homes, no shops, no transportation, no government buildings.... Berlin can now be regarded only as a geographical location heaped with mountainous mounds of debris.' In the words of Jörg Friedrich, the air war wrought 'the biggest catastrophe on German soil since the Thirty Years War.'

The single most extreme attack was against Hamburg on 28 July 1943. Thousands of tonnes of explosive and incendiary bombs were dropped, creating a firestorm that reached a mile into the sky and drove flames across the city at ninety miles per hour, raising temperatures to as much as 1,400 degrees Fahrenheit, and melting glass and asphalt. Also, trees were torn up by their roots, and parts of buildings were thrown into the air. One hundred and twenty miles of streets were utterly destroyed, and tens of thousands of people killed, sometimes simply by being melted into pools of body fat. This was remembered by protesters opposed to raising a statue of 'Bomber' Harris in the Strand in London in the 1980s.

August 1943, the destruction of Hamburg by Allied Forces

D-DAY AND AFTER

Germany could not overcome the numerical superiority of Allied and Soviet forces, its advanced war technology notwithstanding. Step by step Germany was driven out of North Africa and Italy, the latter having overthrown Mussolini and surrendered to the Allies in 1943. Also in 1943, Russia, which never gave up Leningrad, Moscow or Stalingrad, had the *Wehrmacht* in retreat. Germany's position in Europe was slowly but steadily eroding, and on 6 June 1944, with the help of the Free French under General de Gaulle, the Allies landed tens of thousands of troops in France along the Normandy coast. This was 'D-Day' which set in motion Germany's defeat in the West. Paris was liberated in August 1944, and Allied troops crossed the Rhine into Germany in March 1945 and took over southern and western Germany. In the East, the Russians took Warsaw in January, crossed the Oder into Germany in February, and by April were in Berlin. Allied troops would never forget what they found in the concentrations camps. Nor would the Germans; nearby residents were made to come to such camps as Dachau and Bergen-Belsen to see for themselves the true nature of the Hitler Regime.

DIE GÖTTERDÄMMERUNG

In April 1945, the Red Army was capturing Berlin, hunting down and disposing of the last elements of German military resistance. The Berlin Symphony gave its final performance which, appropriately, included the prelude to Wagner's opera, *Die Götterdämmerung*. On 29 April, in his bunker beneath the Berlin Chancellery, Adolf Hitler married his supposed long-time mistress, Eva Braun. The next day both took poison, and their bodies were burned in the Chancellery courtyard. Goebbels also chose death, giving poison to his six children, his wife and himself. Goering, on the other hand, claiming urgent tasks in southern Germany, had left the bunker on 20 April and was accused of treason with a death warrant attached when he telegraphed Hitler offering to take command of the *Wehrmacht*. He later surrendered to the Americans, in full-dress uniform. Meanwhile, Admiral Karl Dönitz, in command of *Reich* forces so far as anyone was, wanted peace with the

West while continuing to fight the Soviets. He had to settle for unconditional surrender instead, which was accepted by the Allies on 7 May in a schoolhouse in Reims, France. The 'Thousand-Year *Reich*' had lasted just over twelve years. Now would come the reckoning for the horrors it had visited upon Western Civilization.

CHAPTER TWELVE

After 1945: The Phoenix Rising From the Ashes

Germany was devastated and divided by the Second World War. Nevertheless, in the decades after 1945 it recovered and became an economic power and leading partner in the European Union. This journey was as difficult, trying and filled with hope and despair as any the Germans had ever taken.

After the War

First, there was the aftermath of war: destroyed cities, occupation, division once again between east and west, and an accounting to be had for the terrible war crimes committed by the Nazi Regime.

DESTRUCTION

At war's end, Germany was a non-functioning pile of rubble effectively in a state of anarchy. Starving and disoriented people begged for food, stole food, and played up to the occupation forces in whatever way they could in order to survive. This was the Germany with which Allied occupation forces had to deal beginning in 1945; they did not, at the same time, have to deal as well with active resistance to the occupation. Germany was too 'physically and morally decimated' for that.

POPULATION REDISTRIBUTION

In 1945 Germany was 'a nation on the march,' though not as the Nazis had meant the phrase. Its population now included eight million non-Germans liberated from concentration camps, and thousands more, including Jews, who had entered from Poland, the USSR, and Soviet-dominated eastern European countries. And ten million ethnic Germans had 'come home' after being expelled from Czechoslovakia, Hungary, Yugoslavia, Rumania, Poland, Silesia and East Prussia – 'ethnic cleansing' in reverse, so to speak. To the 'native' Germans, they were as alien as the non-German *émigrés*. All of these people had in common a desperate need to find food, shelter and some kind of future for themselves. Meanwhile, nearly eight million occupation soldiers and others from major and lesser powers circulated through the country. The affect was chaos.

Occupation

What was to be the future of Germany? Would it be 'de-industrialized' and turned into an agrarian nation as prescribed in the Draconian 'Morgenthau Plan,' proposed by US Treasury Secretary Henry Morganthau? Would the Allies simply destroy Germany, which Soviet intellectual Ilya Ehrenburg preferred?

YALTA AND POTSDAM

In February 1945 Roosevelt, Churchill and Stalin met at Yalta in the Crimea. They formulated a post-war plan for Europe and Germany including that the USSR would occupy the eastern European countries liberated by the Red Army, and that Germany would be divided into four occupation zones, including one for France. Later, Roosevelt was much criticized for the first part, but in fact, he had no choice. The Red Army was already in place from Bulgaria to Poland, and Stalin was not amenable to withdrawal. As to the second, the American zone included Bavaria, Hesse, Württemberg-Baden and the 'enclave of Bremen'; the British occupied the North Rhine: Westphalia, Lower Saxony, Schleswig-Holstein and Hamburg; the French took the Rhineland Palatinate, South Baden, South Württemberg and the Saar (but not Karlsruhe and Stuttgart which they had demanded); and the Soviet zone was Saxony, Thuringia, Mecklenburg-Vorpommern, Saxony-Anhalt and Mark Brandenburg. The British zone was the most populated with twenty-two million, and the French the smallest, with

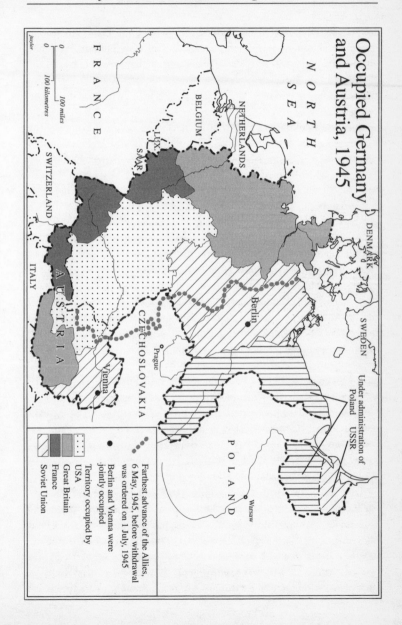

Occupied Germany and Austria, 1945

six million. Austria also was divided for occupation, though treated in the process much more leniently than Germany, much to Soviet annoyance. Yalta also provided for dividing eastern Prussia between the USSR and Poland, and giving eastern Pomerania to Poland; this included Danzig (Gdansk) and Silesia, the capital of which, Breslau, was renamed Wroclaw.

Important cultural and economic cities were also split between the victors: Leipzig, Jena, Dresden, Weimar, Halle and Eisenach under Soviet rule, and Bonn, Marburg, Karlsruhe, Baden–Baden, Düsseldorf, Stuttgart, Mannheim, Essen, Bremen, Nuremberg, Hamburg, Frankfurt and Munich controlled by the western powers. Berlin was the most important of all, and reflected the division of Germany: the USSR had the East Sector, while the West Sector was occupied by France, Britain and the United States. Berlin was located more than 65 miles/100 kilometres inside of the Soviet zone, and soon became a 'microcosm of modern diplomacy,' where over the next thirty years much of the drama of Cold War tensions was played out.

It was agreed at Yalta that occupation policies were to be based on the guiding principles of 'de-Nazification, democratisation, and decentralisation.' In practice, Germany would be totally disarmed, Nazism and militarism destroyed, war criminals tried and punished, all industry capable of military production eliminated or controlled, and that Germany would make compensation in kind (to the value of $20,000,000,000, of which the Soviets would receive half); that is, agricultural and industrial supplies, and forced labour. The Soviets exploited this to the hilt. Wrote historian Dietrich Orlow: 'Russian reparation teams roamed over the Soviet zone dismantling (and shipping to the Soviet Union) everything from scores of factories ... to thousands of bathtubs.'

The Allied leaders met again in June, in Potsdam. Harry Truman sat for Roosevelt, who had died in April, and Clement Attlee represented Britain, Labour having swept to a win in parliamentary elections held after the conference began. While it is said that Truman distrusted Stalin far more than did Roosevelt, Potsdam nevertheless affirmed and spelled out the Yalta agreements; such as that dismantled German industries would include armaments, aircraft, shipping, synthetic gas, oil and rubber, roller bearings, heavy tractors, war chemicals, and radio transmitting equipment, and that crude steel production would be reduced to 30 per cent less than it had been in 1936. Potsdam also provided that Germany would be treated as 'a single economic unit,' though neither the western powers nor the Soviet Union could agree on how that would be achieved. Meanwhile, the Allied Control Council was established, made up of the chief military commanders of each occupying power. Its task was to coordinate – so far as possible – occupation polices as worked out by the Council of Foreign Ministers; a policy of note being the Council order in 1947 to dissolve Prussia, because 'since time immemorial [it] has been the pillar of militarism and reaction in Germany.'

'JUDGMENT AT NUREMBERG'

While the occupying powers did not agree on everything (or even on much of anything), they were together on bringing twenty-one Nazi leaders to trial as war criminals. The Military Tribunal convened at Nuremberg on 20 November 1945 and ran until 1 October 1946, with British justice Sir Geoffrey Lawrence presiding over a panel of jurists representing Great Britain, the United States, the Soviet Union and France. United States Supreme Court Justice Robert Jackson was a principal prosecutor. Nazi leaders conspicuous by their absence were Joseph Goebbels, Heinrich Himmler, and, of course, Adolf Hitler, all of whom had committed suicide. Prominent among those in the dock were Hermann Goering, Joachim von Ribbentrop, Julius Streicher, Franz von Papen, Baldur von Schirach, Rudolf Hess, Admiral Dönitz, General Jodl and Hjalmar Schacht. They were charged with crimes against peace, war crimes and crimes against humanity; participation at any level in the Holocaust was a major factor.

Of these, eleven were sentenced to hang, three were acquitted, three given life sentences, and four lesser terms at Berlin's Spandau Prison. Goering escaped the scaffold by taking cyanide. Hess was the last Spandau inmate, living until 1987 and looked after on a rotating basis by American, Soviet, French and British guards. When he died, the prison was levelled and the grounds turned into a memorial park. Transcripts and volumes of documented evidence indicate that the trials were judicious and fair, and gave ordinary Germans a clear picture of what their former leaders had really been like. Of course, some claimed that the victors had no right to conduct the trials at all; after all, was Nazi behaviour really any worse than Soviet? Never mind that; according to a Soviet-produced propaganda documentary film of the trials, the USSR fought heroically to thwart efforts by the imperialist powers to be lenient with the Nazis.

DE-NAZIFICATION AND RE-EDUCATION

Former Nazis were to be denied administrative or other posts, the object being to rid Germany of the 'poison of National Socialism.' This was opposed even by such committed anti-Nazis as Martin Niemoeller, who called it 'a method for hatred and revenge,' and Eugen Kogon, who claimed that the policy penalized 'those whose only crime was to have made a political error.' Moreover, how could a post-war German administrative system be created using only the relative few who actually had been anti-Nazi? They urged Germans to refuse coopera-tion. Despite protests, the policy was implemented; but differently in each zone. The Soviets regarded as 'de-Nazified and re-educated' anyone who embraced pro-Communist movements and organizations, such as the Socialist Unity Party (SED), or was 'anti-Imperialist,' meaning opposed to America and Britain. It was not uncommon in east Germany to find ex-Nazis holding office, or former Gestapo and *Wehrmacht* officers holding rank in the police and military; Field Marshal von Paulus, captured after the fall of Stalingrad, and General von Seydlitz were a case in point. Junkers came on board, too, as in the case of Bismarck's grandson, Count Heinrich von Einsiedel. In the British zone, political backgrounds were checked only when the person in question had obvious Nazi affiliations; the French simply assumed that all Germans above the age of twelve were beyond redemption, and focused their attention entirely on re-educating the young. That included textbooks for German schools, and a new university in Mainz, 'completely free of Nazi background.'

The Americans tried to live up to the actual policy dictates: extensive background checks and form filing, and the denial of a living to some seven million German families. It proved more harmful than useful. In

1946 they abandoned the process and gave de-Nazification and re-education over to special German tribunals. After 1947, an increasing number of 'ex-Nazis' were in important administrative positions in West German *Länder.*

Restarting Germany

Germany did not lie flattened for long. The German press started again between 1945 and 1950, with such newspapers and journals as *Die Welt, Süddeutsche Zeitung, Frankfurter Hefte* and *Der Monat.* Pro-Communist papers were encouraged in the eastern zone. Broadcasting also resumed, including television in the 1950s, which played an important propaganda role in the east where content was state controlled along ideological lines. Political parties also emerged soon after the war: the Christian Democratic Union (CDU), the Christian Social Union (CSU) and the Free Democratic Party (FPD) in the western zone, and the Socialist Unity Party (SED) in the east. And, with Allied help, the economy began to recover. In 1947, the British and American zones were merged into the 'Bizone' for economic reasons, and the Marshall Plan (European Recovery Program) was launched. The United States poured $4,000,000,000 into western Europe, including West Germany. The amount was only 7 per cent of what was needed, but all the same it provided 'a psychological boost and a catalyst' for economic recovery. The establishment of the *Deutschmark* in 1948 as a 'stable currency' also contributed to economic revival.

THE LIFE OF THE MIND

In East Germany '...[A]rtists, educators, and writers had the task of acting as "engineers of the soul".' Ideological indoctrination was the centrepoint of the school curriculum, and in art and literature, 'Socialist Realism' replaced the abstract, expressionistic and naturalistic. For example, a mural was done for the foyer of the Palace of the Republic in East Berlin, depicting farm equipment and waving fields of grain as the backdrop for starry-eyed, Aryan-looking young men and women gazing into the distance. 'What Socialist youth dream about,' was the legend. Writers were supposed to extol the idealized Proletarian life;

this did not go down well with famous pre-war and pro-Communist writer Bertold Brecht, when his opera libretto *The Trial of Lucullus* was panned because it 'failed to put the working class at the centre of the action.' The Bitterfeld Movement started in 1959 to bring actual factory workers into the literary world as writers. This did not go down well either, and many 'real' writers rebelled against Socialist Realism by stressing conflict between 'the individual's desire for self-realization and society's pressure for conformity.' Such was Wolf Biermann's *Thoughts About Christa T.*, in which a writer and SED Central Committee member commits suicide because she cannot resolve individuality–conformity conflict, and Erwin Strittmatter's *Old Beehead,* where a wily peasant builds his own cooperative farm only to have party bureaucrats destroy it. These works were allowed, albeit grudgingly; Stefan Heym's *Day X,* about the 1953 Berlin uprising, was not, and he had to have it published in West Germany. It is amazing how much the GDR resembled its Third Reich predecessor when it came to mind control.

Meanwhile, many West German writers despaired over Germany's future because they perceived German youth craving American culture. They referred to the end of the war as *Nullpunkt* (point zero), 'total cultural emptiness.' Group 47 was formed in 1947 by writers whose aim was to reckon with the tormented past. Three 1959 novels made the point: in *Billiards at Half Past Nine* Heinrich Böll blamed

Günther Grass, the great writer of post-war Germany

everything on the corrupting influence and hypocrisy of everything from Church to State; in *The Tin Drum* Günther Grass used a boy refusing to grow physically beyond childhood as a symbol of Germany's 'stunted development' during and perhaps before the Nazi era; and in Uwe Johnson's *Speculations About Jacob,* the main character, horrified that he has helped the Soviets put down the 1956 Hungarian uprising, flees to the West only to be disillusioned by its 'crass materialism and unrepentant Nazis.' Other leading writers followed suit: in *The Deputy* Rolf Hochhuth took a crack at Pope Pius XII (1876–1958) for showing moral indifference to Nazi crimes against Jews, while Siegfried Lenz argued in *The German Lesson* that the Nazi era made it impossible for people to lead normal lives.

FILM

West German films, stretching from the immediate postwar to the 1990s, made similar arguments, such as *The Murderers Are Among Us, The Bridge, The Boat* and *The Nasty Girl.* The last features a young woman facing a hostile bureaucracy when she tries to explore the history of her home town during the Nazi era. Reconciliation with a horrific past is never easy, and certainly it was not in the Federal Republic; still, some effort was made. Twenty million West Germans saw at least one episode of the 1979 American television docudrama *Holocaust,* and twenty-five million watched all or part of Edgar Reitz's 1984 saga, *Heimat* (Homeland). This film 'conjured up past associations with the Nazi's vision of "blood and soil" and offered future nightmares of European integrations and cultural homogenization.' Meanwhile, an appetite for quality German films took shape, and the careers of such contemporary film makers as Rainer Werner Fassbinder, Werner Herzog, Wim Wenders, and Margarethe von Trotha, and actors Curt Jurgens, Horst Buchholz, Romy Schneider, Maria Schell, Maximilian Schell, Jürgen Prochnow and Klaus Maria Brandauer took off.

Some critics have claimed that since reunification German film makers have worked to 'catch up' with the popularity of Hollywood films. They have, in film critic Lisbeth Richter Larsen's words, 'chosen to wrench their cultural film heritage off their backs, rejecting that which has labelled German film as heavy and boring.... No reference to history, recent or distant, no environmental descriptions ... and no presenting a problem that has a common German responsibility.' Not necessarily so. Certainly comedy is now a part of German film – for example, Lars Kraume's *Victor Vogel: Commercial Man*, and Martin Walz's *Killer Condom*. However, the 1990s also produced Joseph Vilsmaier's *Stalingrad*, Oliver Storz's *Three Days in April* about the Holocaust, and Ray Mueller's outstanding documentary, *The Wonderful, Horrible Life of Leni Riefenstahl*. And, in February 2003 Berlin staged its 53rd international film festival presenting 300 films from 46 countries over eleven days; the idea, in the words of Culture Minister Christina Weiss, was 'to build bridges between eras, between continents, and between cultures.' While it provided a showcase for 'emerging film makers,' it also paid tribute to the giants of Germany's cinematic past: specifically to F. W. Murnau, the master of German silent cinema.

The Divide

East and West Germany symbolized the Cold War division between the Soviet Union and the United States. 'Iron curtain,' a term coined by Winston Churchill in 1945 to describe Soviet secrecy and dominion over much of eastern Europe, was the Cold War catch-phrase from 1948 to the late 1980s. Germany lay on both sides of it.

BERLIN BLOCKADE

The Soviets accused the Allies of using economic tactics to undercut Soviet control in East Berlin, while the Allies were convinced that Soviet policy was to drive them out of Berlin and incorporate the entire city into East Germany. The crunch came in 1948 when Soviet occupation currency, used throughout Berlin, was replaced in the Western Zone by the new *Deutschmark*. On 22 June the Soviets banned distribution of the new currency in all sectors; the Allies ignored the ban. The next day the Soviets closed all road, water and rail access to Berlin from the West, the routes of supply from West Germany, 'for repairs.' This was supposed to force the Allies to give West Berlin to the Soviet Union.

A military response was out of the question (17,000 Soviet as opposed to only 6,500 Allied soldiers in Berlin), but an airlift was not. The Allies had it in writing from the Soviets, viz. a 1945 agreement, that they could use Soviet airspace to fly between West Germany and Berlin; the Berlin airlift began. Over the next eleven months 212,621 flights – including those of 'Candy Bomber' Gail S. Halvorsen, an American pilot from Utah, who tossed candy to Berlin children as his airplane descended toward Tempelhof Aerodrome – brought 1,700,000 tons of supplies into West Berlin and kept 920,000 families alive. Meanwhile, in April 1949, in response to what the Berlin blockade seemed to threaten, the United States and the major western European powers formed the North Atlantic Treaty Organization (NATO). Apparently the Soviet Union saw this as the 'hand writing on the wall.' In May, Stalin announced that 'repairs' were completed and land routes to Berlin from the west were again open. He also agreed that West Berlin could remain under Allied control, but that there would be no diplomatic relations between the Soviet Union and West Germany.

German Democratic Republic

The Soviet Union proclaimed the German Democratic Republic (GDR) in October 1949, partly in response to the formation of the Federal Republic of Germany (FRG). The GDR was a centrist socialist state run by the Politburo (an elite within the elite), and the SED, which drafted its constitution and ran the People's Congress (later the *Volkskammer*, 'People's Chamber'), a sort of parliament. Forming the GDR assured that Germany would remain divided for the foreseeable future.

WALTER ULBRICHT

The architect of the GDR was Walter Ulbricht (1893–1973). He was from Leipzig, a Communist party member since 1919, and Berlin party leader until forced into exile in Paris, and then Moscow, during the Nazi era. A confirmed Stalinist (he supported the Nazi–Soviet Pact in 1939), Ulbricht returned to Berlin in 1945 to assume leadership of the

SED. He was never technically 'head of state,' but as SED party leader he had the real power in the GDR. By 1952 the SED effectively 'ruled' East Germany, with Ulbricht laying the ground rules for who would be delegates for the *Volkskammer*, and how they would be elected. He also aspired to bring the FRG into the GDR, but gave up on that in 1959 when he symbolically added a hammer and protractor to the black-red-gold flag shared by both Germanies.

A COMMUNIST STATE AND SOCIETY

Meanwhile, Ulbricht created the Ministry for State Security (Stasi) to enforce absolute obedience to the state, and to oversee foreign intelligence operations. The lead East German spy for 30 years was Marcus Wolf, probably the model for Karla, the master spy in novels by John Le Carré. Ulbricht turned 84.2 per cent of the GDR into collectives, established such 'mass' organization as the Free German Youth, headed by future Head of State Erich Honecker, and the Democratic Women's League, regularized GDR relations with Poland, Czechoslovakia and other Communist states, all the while laying the foundations for a GDR more or less independent of the Soviet Union. Moscow went along with that up to a point, and in 1955 invited the GDR to be a founding member and equal partner in the Warsaw Pact, a defensive alliance of eastern European states in opposition to NATO. East Germany's military contribution was the 100,000 man National People's Army, commanded in part by what were termed 'Hitler generals'; that is, former *Wehrmacht* commanders taken prisoner by the Soviet Union at the end of the Second World War.

REVOLT AND REPRISAL

First there was the uprising of 16–17 June 1953, when labourers revolted against the regime in response to the demand for greater productivity at lower wages. They also called for an end to Soviet occupation. It began in Berlin and spread across East Germany. Nearly 500,000 steel, construction, railroad and chemical workers took to the streets, seized 140 government buildings and shut down nearly 600 industrial plants. Ulbricht was 'afraid to face the proletariat,' and stood aside while Soviet tanks and other forces killed hundreds and arrested thousands more. Some were West Germans who had crossed over to join in. When the dust had settled, transportation fees were reduced and pensions and health coverage increased as a sop to the workers.

In 1956 Ulbricht backed Nikita Krushchev's 'liberalizing' of the Stalinist legacy by announcing a five-year plan of 'modernization, mechanization, and automation,' a 30 per cent rise in 'real wages,' and a 40-hour work week for East Germany. However, when the Hungarians rebelled against the Soviet Union, and Krushchev responded with brutality and a complete reversal of 'liberalization' across Eastern Europe, Ulbricht returned to 'hard-line 'normalcy.' He remained there through 1968, when he joined other Warsaw Pact members sending forces into Czechoslovakia to put down the liberalized regime of Alexander Dubček's 'Prague Spring.' This likely was a bad idea: '... the sight of German units invading Czechoslovakia – in the footsteps of Hitler's legions of 1939 – did little to enhance the global image of the German Democratic Republic.'

THE WALL

By December 1960, more than two million East Germans had fled to West Germany, including highly skilled members of the labour force. Between January and March 1961, the number increased by 30,000. Something had to be done to stop the flow. In August, Ulbricht received Warsaw Pact permission to build an 'anti-fascist protective wall' separating East and West Germany, despite having

Willi Brandt with President John F. Kennedy in June 1963 in a divided Berlin

declared publically in June that 'no one has any intention of building a wall.' When completed, 'the Wall' was a wire fence with guard towers across Germany, and in Berlin a cement block, also with guard towers. Two days after building began, Conrad Schumann, an East German soldier, was photographed leaping over a barbed war barricade to escape into the Western Zone. This was pure anti-Wall propaganda, if unintended as such, and simply added to Western determination to prevail in the Cold War. In June 1963 US President John F. Kennedy stood before the Wall and shouted to a cheering crowd of West Berliners: '*Ich bin ein Berliner!*' That '*ein Berliner*' technically was the name for a popular jam doughnut (known in America as the 'Bismarck') was beside the point.

AFTER ULBRICHT

Ulbricht died in 1973, succeeded as State Council Chairman by Erich Honecker (1912–1994), who named his wife, Margot, Minister of Education. Changes occurred under Honecker: more ideological flexibility; a more 'middle-management' bureaucracy; a goose-stepping, Prussian-style army in *Wehrmacht* uniforms which honoured such historic Prussian war heros as General von Scharnhorst, military reformer after 1806; German history 'restored' as in Frederick the Great's statue returned to Unter den Linden, and the 500th anniversary of Martin Luther's birth publically celebrated; and GDR admission into the United Nations in 1973. Honecker's view of East–West German relations also changed. The Stasi cracked down on foreign journalists, and vigorous propaganda programmes were implemented in the schools and the media which emphasized that there no longer was 'one' Germany, nor would there ever be. This was a complete reversal of Ulbricht's long-term perspective.

Honecker also worked to improve the East German economy, which was falling ever further behind that of Western Germany. This included borrowing from West Germany, upwards of 300 billion DM by 1989. Sometimes, West German funds were provided in exchange for the release of East German political prisoners. Needless to say, this did nothing for the East German image, and in the late 1980s a joke making rounds in East Berlin was: 'How have the two German states divided Karl Marx's legacy? *Answer*: The West has the Capital and the East has the Manifesto.'

THE 'DECLINE OF THE EAST'

In the late 1980s, Soviet President Mikhail Gorbachev introduced '*glasnost*' and '*perestroika*' approaches to making a more open and less dogmatically Communist society. He exported the concept across eastern Europe, making his sincerity clear by not interfering when Gdansk union leader Lech Walesa organized a populist uprising against the Polish regime. Honecker resisted Gorbachev's new policy, however, seeking to maintain his centralized authoritarian system. The public backed Gorbachev. In 1989, some 400,000 East Germans left the country for the West, and in Leipzig, more than 100,000 took to the streets each Monday night to demonstrate against the regime. Again, the Soviet Union did not interfere. It was not the best of times for Honecker. He was diagnosed with cancer and left office, succeeded by Egon Krenz (1937–). Krenz lasted forty-six days. He was replaced by Manfred Gerlach (1928–), who remained head of state until reunification in 1990.

Some regretted the passing of East Germany, but by no means all. The regime was nothing if not Orwellian. Stasi records indicate GDR support for the Palestinian Liberation Organization and the Red Army Faction, plotting the assassination of political opponents in West Germany, and detailing citizens to spy and inform on each other. Some GDR leaders ended in prison for their activities, but not Honecker. He was charged in 1993 for having ordered the shooting on sight of would-be escapees from the East, but was let off the hook for reasons of health. He left Germany for exile in Chile, where he died of cancer in 1994.

Federal Republic of Germany

Meanwhile, the Federal Republic was born, grew up, and became an economic and political pillar of strength in western Europe. It began after the constitution, known as the Basic Law, was written in Bonn in September 1948. The Basic Law was not unlike the Weimar constitution. It provided for an elected president, chancellor and bicameral legislature, the latter divided between the *Bundestag,* elected by popular vote, and the *Bundesrat,* elected by *Länder* legislatures.

KONRAD ADENAUER

Konrad Adenauer (1876–1963), patriarchal Catholic and former lord mayor of Cologne, was the first Chancellor, serving from 1949 to 1963. He was architect of the FRG, just as Ulbricht was of the GDR. Adenauer understood that Germany could thrive only by accepting paradigms laid out by the Allies, and looked to the United States as West Germany's best hope for the future. He also played up fear of the Soviet Union as a path to both *rapprochement* with the Allies and support for his policies at home. Indeed, uniting the Allies behind West Germany with the ultimate objective of German reunification was the essence of Adenauer's foreign policy.

FOREIGN POLICY

After 1949, the FRG moved steadily toward European integration. Adenauer concluded the Petersberg Agreement with the Allies, which promised complete German disarmament and cooperation with the West in all matters political and economic, in exchange for the Allies ceasing the demolition of factories left over from the war. The disarmament lasted only a year; distracted by the outbreak of the Korean war in 1950, the Allies agreed that the FRG could conduct its own foreign policy and rearm as a long-term part of European security. Making the *Bundeswehr* (national army) followed, under the command of such former *Wehrmacht* officers as General Hans Speidel (1897–1984), who had served under Irwin Rommel in North Africa. By 1955 the FRG was a NATO member committed to providing a 500,000 man contingent. That year the Soviet Union withdrew from Austria, and Adenauer visited Moscow to improve German–Soviet relations. He sat with Soviet premier Nikolai Bulganin at a performance of the ballet *Romeo and Juliet,* and when the feuding Montagues and Capulets embraced on stage, 'in a highly symbolic gesture ... Adenauer softly placed his hands in those of the Soviet leader....' Thereafter, relations with the Soviet Union were 'normalized.'

Meanwhile, Adenauer and French foreign minister Robert Schumann had opened the door to forming the European Coal and Steel Community by agreeing to place Franco-German coal and steel production 'under a common authority.' This, said Jean Monnet, would 'bind Germany economically and politically in the structure of Western Europe.' In 1956 West Germany regained the Saar in exchange for economic concessions to France; in 1957, it joined France, Italy, Belgium, the Netherlands and Luxembourg in making the Treaty of Rome that founded the European Economic Community. Franco-German relations continued to improve under Charles de Gaulle (signing the Elysée Treaty in 1963, for example), for both he and Adenauer wanted a Europe independent of British and American dominance. *'Der Alte,'* as Adenauer was known, thought the British were 'soft on communism,' and resented US President Kennedy working to improve relations with East Germany and the Soviet Union. The Hallstein Doctrine (the FRG would break relations with any state save Russia that recognized the GDR) was made in 1957, and was immediately implemented against Yugoslavia.

DOMESTIC POLICY

The FRG aimed at getting beyond the recent past, establishing democracy, and reviving the economy. Personal privacy was guaranteed by law, and anti-Semitism was banned. When it occurred, it was dealt with harshly. This pleased Germany's 30,000 remaining Jews; on the other hand, they were displeased that the search for escaped Nazi war criminals was not pursued with efficiency or enthusiasm. Adenauer had embraced a 'forgive and forget' mentality, and employed many former Nazis in his government. All the same, in 1952 he agreed to give 3,500,000,000 DM in Holocaust compensation to the new Israeli State – which did not go down well with many of his countrymen – and later the policy was extended to pay more than 100,000,000,000 DM to individual families by the year 2000. Germany has been attentive to Israel's needs throughout the post-war period. For example, in November 2002, Chancellor Gerhard Schröder (1944–) announced that Germany had a 'moral duty' to protect Israel, and would supply it with anti-missile systems as defence against Iraq. And in the 1990s, a Jewish Museum was added to the Berlin Museum.

Then there was the 'economic miracle,' inspired by the 'psychological boost' of 1,500,000,000 Marshall Plan dollars sent to the FRG where its use was orchestrated by economist Ludwig Erhard (1897–1977). He persuaded Adenauer to end rationing and create a fully free market economy, but without sacrificing generous social programmes. It took time, but it worked. By 1960 unemployment was 1.2 per cent, and by 1985 the GDP had increased a hundredfold, exports were at 537,000,000,000 DM, the trade balanced showed a 112,600,000,000 DM surplus, and disposable family income was 400 per cent more than in 1950. Housing shortages continued as obviously there was a lot to rebuild after the war, but jobs, consumption and exports skyrocketed, the latter including the increasingly popular Volkswagen 'Beetle.' By 1989 the FRG was the leading industrial nation in Europe, with a modernized and high-tech urban society that appealed to both West Germans and tourists.

Meanwhile, universities came back to life, including a dramatic increase in the number of female students. University reform, including 'de-Nazification' of faculty, was a priority. Enrolment spread to include a wider strata of society, and escalated in numbers: 1,300,000 by 1984. The downside of such growth was increased stress for already over-worked researchers and teachers, who sometimes faced seminars with 150 students. New universities, Bochum and Bielefeld, for example, helped to relieve this strain. Efforts to expand the curriculum to fit more modern times enjoyed only limited success; but administration, traditionally exclusively in the hands of tenured professors, was 'democratized' to include junior faculty and students. And, inspired by the student unrest that spread across Germany in the 1960s, power over the universities was shifted from politicians to bureaucrats.

THE *SPIEGEL* AFFAIR

In October 1962, the Hamburg journal *Der Spiegel* published government documents showing the *Bundeswehr* to be well short of being combat-ready. Adenauer ordered arrests and offices searched; the result was widespread demands for his resignation. Actually, Adenauer's popularity had waned well before this event, plus he was getting on, having turned 86 in January. The Chancellor took the hint and retired a year later.

After Adenauer

Ludwig Erhard succeeded '*der Alte*' and began a process of opening contact with the East. This was positive. On the negative side was a downturn in the economy owing to a shift from production to service industry in which electronics and high technology took over the market. Erhard was replaced in 1966 by the 'Grand Coalition' of CDU leader Kurt-Georg Kiesinger (1904–1988), as Chancellor, and SPD leader and former mayor of Berlin Willi Brandt (1913–1992), as Vice-Chancellor. They reversed the economic downturn, but faced student protests (encouraged by the Marxist Frankfurt School of Herbert Marcuse and Wilhelm Reich) against the war in Vietnam and the oppressive Iranian regime of Shah Reza Pahlavi. The *Bundestag* passed emergency legislation strengthening police powers, which inspired still more protests, especially after police shot student radical leader Rudi Dutschke. Meanwhile, feminism also took off, and while some of it sounded bizarre – taking the Marxist class struggle into marriage, for example – major improvements were achieved in women's rights, including abortion rights and publicly funded shelters for battered women. Then, in 1969 the SPD gained control in the *Bundestag*, and Willi Brandt replaced Kiesinger as Chancellor.

WILLI BRANDT

Brandt had much going for him: his success as Berlin mayor, he was anti-Communist and pro-democracy, and he had joined the Norwegian resistance against the Nazis in the Second World War – which, admittedly, did not make him popular with all Germans. Indeed, on the home front, Brandt had much to deal with: spiralling inflation and dependence on imports that slowed the 'economic miracle'; risking major deficit spending because of huge expenditures on education and social programmes; Arab terrorists seizing, and killing, Israeli athletes during the 1972 Munich Olympic games; the 1973 Yom Kippur War

(Israel, Egypt and Syria) which tripled the cost of Middle East oil exports to Germany; and the revelation in 1975 that Günther Guillaume, the Chancellor's personal advisor, was an East German 'mole.' Brandt had been warned of the fact by security services, but had refused to act. He resigned the Chancellorship on 6 May 1974.

OSTPOLITIK

Brandt did much better in foreign policy. His *Ostpolitik* brought the FRG and the Soviet Union closer together by relaxing the Hallstein doctrine, extending loans and steel piping to the Soviet Union in exchange for natural gas piped into West Germany from Siberia, recognizing the Oder–Neisse border between Poland and Germany, establishing formal relations between Poland and West Germany (in 1970 Brandt knelt symbolically before the memorial to the Warsaw Ghetto uprising), and agreeing with the Soviet Union to renounce the use of force in settling outstanding differences.

From Brandt to Reunification

Helmut Schmidt (1918–), Brandt's defence minister, was Chancellor from 1974 to 1982, followed by Helmut Kohl (1930–) from 1982 to 1998. In this era it was business as usual for the most part, regarding the economic problems noted above and concerns over the nuclear arms race, environmental issues – in response to which the Green Party formed in 1978, and elected its first *Bundestag* representatives in 1983 with 5.6 per cent of the national vote – and Germany playing a central role in forming the European Union (EU). New issues came along, however, which were anything but 'usual.'

'BAADER-MEINHOF'

Urban terrorism (with some East German support) was a reality in the 1970s; notably the *Rote Armee Fraktion* (Red Army Faction), founded and led by Gudrun Ensslin, Andreas Baader and Ulrike Meinhof. The mind set was clear: 'You know what kind of pigs we are up against, that is the generation of Auschwitz. . . . We must arm ourselves.' The RAF began in 1968, and its principal leaders were jailed four years later.

From prison, they issued orders to their followers, mostly students, who between 1974 and 1977 murdered at least thirty people, kidnapped others, and bombed US and German government installations and the occasional department store. The objective was to so destabilize German society so that revolution would be inevitable. The RAF was linked to Middle East terrorists, who in 1977 attempted a Lufthansa jetliner hijacking to force the release of jailed RAF leaders. It failed, and by the end of the year, the jailed leaders had followed the example of Ulrike Meinhof and committed suicide in prison. 'Their fatal legacy,' wrote Martin Kitchen, 'was that the authorities were so obsessed with left-wing terrorism that they tended to ignore the sinister activities of extremist right-wing groups.'

'NEO-NAZISM'

There were those who remained convinced that Hitler had been right all along. The German Reich Party, dominated by ex-Nazis, started in 1945. Its most extreme element emerged in 1950 as the Social Reich Party, whose leaders included Werner Naumann (1909–1982), a high official in Goebbels' propaganda ministry. A Federal Constitutional Court outlawed the party just before the 1953 election. A hiatus followed until 1964 when appropriately named 'Adolf' von Thadden (1921–1996) founded the National Democratic Party. Its perspectives included Chauvinism: 'All of Germany is ours,' Xenophobia: 'Throw out all foreigners,' and Holocaust denial. The last was based in part on evidentially unsupported writings by revisionists the likes of David Irving. And, of course, there were 'street-gang' neo-Nazi organizations and movements, including 'skin-heads,' the rank and file of which were largely under-educated, unskilled and often unemployed youths. Their major target was the Turkish, Greek, Spanish and other *Gastarbeiter* (guest-workers), who were recruited first in the 1960s to shore up a labour shortage. After unification, two neo-Nazi organizations, *Der Republikaner* and *Die Deutsche Volksunion,* gained seats in *Länder* legislatures. Whatever role they had played, or would play in the future, neo-Nazi extremists reflected one question central to German identity since 1945: 'how to be a German in the post-war world?'

THE 'FALL OF THE WALL'

The 'uprising' against the East German government in 1989 came to a head on 9 November. On that day a Politburo member announced that the East-West border would be opened, which launched a *Volksfest* (people's festival) with people dancing on top of the wall and smashing at it with sledgehammers. On 10 November the GDR announced it would dismantle the wall, and the FRG promised to make available 'welcome money' to any GDR citizen crossing into the West. Four days later 8,600,000 million East Germans had done precisely that. Mikhail Gorbachev remained committed to no Russian interference in East German affairs, Helmut Kohl seized the opportunity to call for German reunification, and East Germans filled the streets of such cities as Leipzig proclaiming 'We are one people!' A brief GDR government effort at resistance went nowhere, and on 22 December 300,000 Germans celebrated the opening of the Brandenburg Gate. Soon after that the wall began to come down.

UNIFICATION: AGAIN

The Western powers quickly came on board with reunification. After all, a divided Germany had stood in the way of a stable Europe. Moreover, Helmut Kohl had taken well-publicized symbolic steps to gain reconciliation with the post-war Western world. In 1985, he had shaken hands with French President François Mitterand at the site of the 1916 Battle of Verdun, and with US President Ronald Reagan at Bitburg cemetery, where some fifty *Waffen-SS* soldiers were buried. He also visited Israel, where, unfortunately, he spoke of 'the grace of late birth' which was negatively interpreted as a claim that he was too young to have any responsibility for German acts committed between 1933 and 1945. But in time Kohl was forgiven, and US President George Bush assured his European allies that unification posed 'no security problems to Europe.' Meanwhile, Russia also accepted reunification, though Gorbachev had reservations regarding the impact it might have on the NATO defence system. His concerns were eased when Kohl extended a 5,000,000,000 DM 'line of credit' to the Soviet Union in June 1990, and Gorbachev accepted the idea that unified

Germany in NATO posed no threat to Warsaw Pact members. Of course, that became academic when the Soviet Union itself broke up and the Warsaw Pact dissolved. Meanwhile, Britain, France, the United States, the Soviet Union, and the GDR and FRG made a treaty that recognized a unified Germany with full sovereignty and the Oder–Neisse line as its eastern border. This became official on 3 October 1990, and moving the capital from Bonn back to Berlin began in 1992. That was complete by 2000, along with a reconstructed and extended Reichstag building done between 1994 and 1999 by English architect Sir Norman Foster, that featured a controversial accessible glass dome. The reconstruction process was begun, so to speak, by artist Christo's wrapping of the building in white cloth.

Germany Today

Since unification, wrote a reporter for *The Economist*, 'Germany has finally come out of its post-war shell.' That is, with the largest population and economy in western Europe, it has become 'the undisputed giant at the heart of one of the two richest continents in the world,' and looks toward becoming the centre of the European Union; hence the symbolic move of the capital from 'the sleepy little Rhineland town of Bonn . . . to raucous, once-imperial Berlin, just 80 km from the frontier with Poland.'

All well and good, but Germany after unification has had its share of problems: scandals involving prominent political figures, including insider stock trading, vacations paid for by businessmen and charges that Chancellor Kohl used strong-arm tactics to silence his critics; neo-Nazi groups on the rise and Austrian right-wing politician Jörg Haider's claim that Austria should again be a part of Germany – *Anschluss* revisited, so to speak; disastrous environmental conditions left over from the East German regime; and resentment among some in the East that they are part of a state under West German domination – they are Prussians, after all. In other words, 'the more things change, the more they remain the same.'

Germany since reunification has had economic problems, too; nothing new there, either. Between 1995 and 2000, productivity

growth was only 2.8 per cent per annum, and a brief boom in 1999 ended in 2001 when productivity growth was only 0.3 per cent and unemployment was 8.3 per cent, the fourth highest rate in the European Union. The problems were many. A fall-off in investments and a tax structure that, according to some sources, restricted the freedom of industry to expand; the comparatively weak East German economy which strained that of the West; the general economic downturn in the United States and western Europe after 2000: and the enormous cost of cleaning up after the devastating floods that ravaged the Elbe region in 2002. Some blamed economic doldrums on the Euro, the European Union common currency with which Germany replaced the *Deutschmark* in January 2002. The charge was that it caused prices to rise, which resulted in consumer spending cutbacks. Whatever the cause, BBC news analyst Tim Weber opined that 'Chancellor Schröder will have to occupy himself with just one big issue, the economy.'

An SPD–Green coalition carried the 1998 Bundestag elections, and SPD leader Gerhard Schröder (1944–) succeeded Helmut Kohl as Chancellor. He named Green Party leader Joschka Fischer (1948–) as foreign minister. The coalition won again in 2002, but with a narrower margin of victory than in 1998, perhaps because economic doldrums have continued. Nor did it help that some Green supporters have accused the party of 'selling out' to the SPD, perhaps inspired by the

Helmut Kohl with his successor Gerhard Schröder

fact that it was the Green Party Defence Council representative who argued for a German military system restructured into a 'highly professional' German army composed of 'rapidly deployable forces,' an odd position for an essentially pacifist party. 'Selling out' was not connected with the environment, however, a high Green priority. Jürgen Trittan, Environment Minister since 1998, works tirelessly to promote environmental protection nationally and internationally, despite foot dragging by some industrial nations.

While Schröder has connected well with European Union colleagues, a sharp rift appeared in German–American relations. In March 2003, he announced that Germany, France, Russia and some other members of the United Nations Security Council would oppose an Anglo-American war against Saddam Hussein's Iraq. 'I am certain there would have been a different way to disarm the dictator, the United Nations way,' Schröeder said in a speech to the German nation. Foreign Minister Fischer was even more adamant in opposing war in Iraq – 'I am not convinced' was his response to US Defense Secretary Donald Rumsfeld's claim that Iraq was hoarding masses of chemical and biological weapons. However, Schröder had not informed Fischer of his agreement with France, and the two had a shouting match over the issue, with Fischer threatening resignation (which he rescinded) because in his view the Chancellor was doing harm to Germany's international position. Meanwhile, Rumsfeld expressed outrage at the Franco-German stand, publically excoriating them as the 'old Europe' and no longer of any consequence. Many Americans called for a boycott of German and French products. This should have suggested to the CDU an opportunity for political gain; in fact, it has divided the party between CDU leader Angela Merkel who supports the American position, and Bavarian premier Edmund Stoiber, who opposes it.

All this came at a time when Fischer was emphasizing the 'need to strengthen the European pillar of NATO' and Schröder and Jacques Chirac were celebrating the 40th anniversary of the Elysée Treaty by suggesting that the EU establish a dual presidency – divided, by implication, between Germany and France – and not long after Russian President Vladimir Putin had spoken before the *Bundestag* in fluent German. To sceptics across Europe it had the appearance of a special

Franco-German partnership within the EU, to which Russia would not object. And why not? The Union effectively began with the 1991 Maastricht Treaty of which Helmut Kohl and François Mitterand were the principal architects, and in the early 1960s Adenauer and De Gaulle had worked towards a Franco-German special place within Europe. That, after all, was why they signed the Elysée Treaty in the first place. Business as usual.

ASPECTS OF CONTEMPORARY GERMAN CULTURE

German art is both new and not entirely new. Examples of the latter include Franz Ackermann's paintings which combine the external reality of a location with the artist's subjective feelings about that place, and work by Cologne painter Candid Höfer, whose paintings of buildings and gardens have a decidedly traditional flavour. Examples of the former are Günter Förg's photography, sculpture, etching, and painting all of which emphases the experimental, and the photography of Wolfgang Tillmans, born in Remscheid but resident in London, which art critic Carlo McCormick described as 'a warped 90s hybrid of the personal and social, the commodified and ephemeral, the glamorous and prosaic.' His preferred subjects include 'young club kids, DJs, ravers, and punks who live their lives outside, splayed out in the streets, huddled in corners, or dancing ecstatically.' Popular music has taken on much of the character of that which began in Great Britain with the Beatles and evolved in subsequent decades into Punk, Rap and other genres. Classical music is alive and well also: opera companies thrive in most of Germany's major cities, often including performers from outside of Germany; so too major symphony orchestras, such as the Berlin Philharmonic, whose conductor is now Sir Simon Rattle from England.

One implication of *The Economist* report is that Germany today is working at being a part of the world to a degree that it never had been before. That is nowhere more obvious than in sports. In the 1980s and 1990s tennis professionals Boris Becker and Steffi Graf became international icons: Becker took Wimbledon three times, the Australian Open twice, and the US Open once; and Graff won all four Grand Slam tournaments (Wimbledon, the Australian Open, French Open and US Open) in 1990. Meanwhile, Germany hosted the Summer Olympics at Munich in 1972 – besmirched by the tragic kidnapping and murder of Israeli athletes by Arab terrorists – and put forward a bid to host the 2012 summer Olympics in Hamburg. German Olympic athletes have also made their mark. In 2000 at Sydney, Australia, Germans won 13 Gold, 17 Silver and 26 Bronze medals in every category of event, and in the 2002 Winter Olympics in Salt Lake City in the United States, 12 Gold, 16 Silver and 7 Bronze – even better than their total of 29 medals at Nagano, Japan in 1998. And in football, Germany almost won the 2002 World Cup, losing in the final to Brazil by two goals, having won it in 1954, 1974 and 1990. Goal keeper Oliver Kahn (who claimed that the loss was his fault) was named best player. Germany did win its bid to host the 2006 World Cup. Not bad for 'a nation of Tribes'; and, perhaps, a showcase for the new Germany of the new century.

Notes

Notes

List of Rulers

Maximilian II, *1564–1576*
Rudolf, *1576–1612*
Matthias, *1612–1619*
Ferdinand II, *1619–1637*
Ferdinand III, *1637–1657*
Leopold I, *1658–1705*
Joseph I, *1705–1711*
Charles VI, *1711–1740*
Charles VII, *1742–1745*
Francis I, *1745–1765* (Maria Theresa)
Joseph II, *1765–1790*
Leopold II, *1790–1792*
Francis II, *1792–1806*

(Austrian Empire)

Francis I, *1804–1835*
Ferdinand I, *1835–1848*
Franz Joseph, *1848–1916*
Charles I, *1916–1918*

(Brandenburg-Prussia)

Frederick I, Elector, *1417–1440*
Frederick II, *1440–1470*
Albert Achilles, *1460–1486*
Johann Cicero, *1486–1499*
Joachim I, *1499–1535*
Joachim II, *1535–1577*
Johann George, *1571–1598*
Joachim Frederick, *1598–1608*
Johann Sigismund, *1608–1619*
George Wilhelm, *1619–1640*
Frederick Wilhelm, *1640–1688*
Frederick III, Elector, *1688–1701*; King Frederick I, *1701–1713*
Frederick Wilhelm I, *1713–1740*
Frederick II, *1740–1786*
Frederick Wilhelm II, *1786–1797*
Frederick Wilhelm III, *1797–1840*
Frederick Wilhelm IV, *1840–1861*
Wilhelm I, King, *1861–1871*, Emperor, *1871–1888*
Wilhelm II, *1888–1918*

(Bavaria)

Maximilian I Joseph, Elector, *1799–1805*, King, *1805–1825*
Louis I Augustus, *1825–1848*
Maximilian II, *1848–1868*
Louis II, *1864–1886*
Otto, *1886–1918*

Heads of Government

Imperial Chancellors:
Otto von Bismarck, *1871–1890*
Georg Leo von Caprivi, *1890–1894*
Chlodwig zu Hohenlohe-Schillingfürst, *1894–1900*
Bernhard von Bülow, *1900–1909*
Theobald von Bethmann-Hollweg, *1909–1917*
Georg Michaelis, *1917–1918*

WEIMAR REPUBLIC

Presidents:

Friedrich Ebert, *1919–1925*
Paul von Hindenburg, *1925–1934*

Chancellors:
Philipp Scheidemann, *1919*
Gustav Bauer, *1919–1920*
Hermann Müller, *1920*
Konstantin Fehrenbach, *1920–1921*
Joseph Wirth, *1921–1922*
Wilhelm Cuno, *1922–1923*
Gustav Stresemann, *1923*
Wilhelm Marx, *1923–1924*
Hans Luther, *1925–1926*
Wilhelm Marx, *1926–1928*
Hermann Müller, *1928–1930*
Heinrich Brüning, *1930–1932*
Franz von Papen, *1932*
Kurt von Schleicher, *1932–1933*
Adolf Hitler, *1933–1945* (Weimar Republic and Third Reich)

FEDERAL REPUBLIC BEFORE AND AFTER REUNIFICATION

Presidents:

Karl Anold, *1949* (acting)
Theodor Heuss, *1949–1959*
Karl Heinrich Lübke, *1959–1969*
Gustav Heinemann, *1969–1974*
Walter Scheel, *1974–1979*
Karl Carstens, *1979–1984*
Richard von Weizsäcker, *1984–1994*
Roman Herzog, *1994–1999*
Johannes Rau, *1999*–present

Chancellors:
Konrad Adenauer, *1949–1963*
Ludwig Erhard, *1963–1966*
Kurt-Georg Kiesinger, *1966–1969*
Willi Brandt, *1969–1974*
Walter Scheel, *1974* (acting)
Helmut Schmidt, *1974–1982*
Helmut Kohl, *1982–1998*
Gerhard Shröder, *1998*–present

DEMOCRATIC REPUBLIC

Heads of Government:

Johannes Dieckmann, *1949 and 1960* (acting)
Wilhelm Pieck, *1949–1960*
Walter Ulbricht, *1960–1973*
Friedrich Ebert, *1973* (acting)
Willi Stoph, *1973–1976*
Erich Honecker, *1976–1989*
Egon Krenz, *1989*
Manfred Gerlach, *1989–1990*

Chronology of Major Events

BC

Ca. 330   Pytheas of Massilia brings the existence of Germanic peoples to the attention of the Romans

102–01   Roman general Marius annihilates the Teutons at Aquae Sextiae, and the Cimbri at Raudian Fields

AD

9   Arminius (Hermann, 'Wielder of the Terrible Two-handed Sword') defeats the Romans in the Teutoburger forest

341   Bishop Ulfila begins his Christian mission among the Visigoths

496   Clovis (Clodovech), king of the Franks, is converted to Christianity

507   Clovis defeats the Visigoths, unifies the Frank kingdom, and takes control of most of Gaul

590   Columbanus arrives from Ireland with twelve companions to found monasteries and preach Christianity among pagan Franks

687   Pepin of Heristal, Mayor of the Palace, restores the unity of the Frank kingdom

732   Charles Martel, Mayor of the Palace, defeats the Arabs at Poitiers

751   Pepin the Short takes the crown as the first Carolingian King of the Franks

754   St Boniface, 'the Apostle of the Germans,' is killed by pagan Frisians. His remains are buried in the Cathedral of Fulda, in Hesse

785   Widukind, leader of the pagan Saxons, is baptized with Charlemagne (Karl der Grosse), King of the Franks, standing as godfather

800   Charlemagne is crowned the first Holy Roman Emperor by Pope Leo III

843	Treaty of Verdun grants Charlemagne's grandson, Louis, title to the East Frank portion of the Carolingian Empire, which will become Germany
884	Carolingian Empire briefly reunited under Charles the Fat
919	Henry I elected king of the East Franks, begins the Saxon line of German emperors
955	Otto I, the Great, great-grandson of Widukind, crushes the Magyars (Hungarians) at Lechfeld near Augsburg
962	Otto I crowned Roman emperor by Pope Leo VIII, beginning the *Sacrum Romanum Imperium Nationis Germanicae* (Holy Roman Empire of the German Nation), although that name was not applied until the 15th century
1077	Emperor Henry IV ends his controversy with Pope Gregory VII by prostrating himself before Gregory at Canossa
1105	Colonization of eastern Germany begins
1190	Order of the Teutonic Knights founded in connection with the Crusades
1229	Crusades establish the Kingdom of Jerusalem under Hohenstaufen rule
1230	Prussia is given to the Teutonic Order as a papal fief
1250	Berlin and Cölln established as twin towns on the River Spree. They merge into the city of Berlin in 1432
1254	The Federation of Rhenish cities is established in Worms
1280	Hanseatic League is founded in northern Germany; in time it extend east to include Novgorod in Russia
1351	Black Death kills perhaps one-third of the German population; many blame the Plague on the Jews
1410	The Teutonic Knights routed by a Polish–Lithuanian army in the Battle of Tannenberg
1419	Jan Hus is burned at the stake for heresy. His followers launch the Hussite Wars in retaliation
1456	The first Bible is printed on Johannes Gutenberg's movable type press
1519	Martin Luther posts his Ninety-Five Theses on the church door in Wittenberg
1525	Peasants' Rebellion sweeps across Germany, inspired by writings of Martin Luther, who sides with the princes against the peasants
1528	Albrecht Dürer, one of Germany's greatest artists, dies
1536	Desiderus Erasmus, leading critic of the papacy, who stopped short of joining the Reformation, dies
1573	Hans Holbein the Younger, leading German portraitist, dies
1618–48	The Thirty Years War

1648	Peace of Westphalia ends the Thirty Years War
1689–97	War of the League of Augsburg
1701	Frederick William I is crowned the first king of Prussia
1701–14	War of the Spanish Succession
1740–1780	Maria Theresa of Austria
1740	Frederick II becomes king of Prussia; war begins between Austria and Prussia over Silesia
1756–1763	The Seven Years War
1760	Berlin occupied by Austro-Russian forces, royal palaces are ransacked, and the city is forced to pay an indemnity of two million Thaler
1763	Peace of Huburtesburg ends the Seven Years War
1774	Johann Wolfgang von Goethe publishes *Sorrows of Young Werther*
1785	Immanuel Kant publishes *Critique of Reason.*
1792	Austro-Prussian alliance formed against Revolutionary France
1795	Partition of Poland between Russia and Prussia, which began in 1772, is completed
1806	Confederation of the Rhine is formed; Holy Roman Empire is dissolved; Prussia is defeated by the French at Jena and Auerstadt
1808	Johann Gottlieb Fichte publishes *Addresses to the German Nation*
1812	Prussian Jews are emancipated; Napoleon invades Russia
1813	Napoleon defeated in the 'Battle of Nations' at Leipzig
1814	Prussia introduces universal male conscription
1814–15	Congress of Vienna
1815–1866	The German Confederation
1817	German students embrace nationalism in a festival at Wartburg Castle
1819	Austria issues the Karlsbad Decrees to suppress dissent and preserve the traditional quasi-feudal system that characterized the Austrian Empire
1832	The Hambach Festival calls for German nationalism; Austria issues the Six Articles to suppress calls for nationalism and other expressions of dissent, in the Empire and Confederation
1834	The German *Zollverein* (Customs Union) is formed
1835	The first German railroad is opened between Nuremberg and Fürth
1847	Prussian United Diet convened for the first time
1848	Revolution breaks out in Vienna and Berlin; the Frankfort Assembly is convened to create a constitutional German nation; Karl Marx and Friedrich Engels publish *The*

	Communist Manifesto; Franz Joseph ascends the Austrian throne, the last Austrian emperor but one
1849	Frederick Wilhelm IV of Prussia declines a German crown
1850	Frederick Wilhelm IV accepts a Prussian Constitution with voting on a class basis
1859	Austro-Italian War.
1861	Wilhelm I becomes King of Prussia; the Progressive Party formed in Prussia
1862	Otto von Bismarck becomes Minister-President of Prussia
1864	Danish–Prussian War adds Schleswig and Holstein to the German Confederation
1866	Austro-Prussian War ousts Austria as the principal German power, and leads to the restructuring of the Austrian Empire as the Austro-Hungarian Empire
1868	Richard Wagner's opera *Die Meistersinger* premiers
1869	The Social Democratic Party is formed
1870–1871	Franco-Prussian War; France is defeated and the Second German Empire is created with Wilhelm I of Prussia as German Emperor, and Bismarck as Chancellor; the event was announced in a ceremony at Versailles Palace outside of Paris, then under Prussian occupation
1873	The Falk Laws are passed against the Catholic Church as part of the *Kulturkampf*
1875	German railroad nationalization begins; *Reichsbank* is created
1878	Congress of Berlin presided over by Bismarck to resolve territorial disputes in the Balkans
1882	Italy joins Austria and Germany in forming the Triple Alliance
1883–1889	The *Reichstag* pass into law Bismarck's policies on health and accident insurance and old age pensions
1885	Germany establishes colonies in both East and West Africa
1888	Wilhelm II becomes German Emperor
1889	Adolf Hitler is born in Braunau, Austria
1890	Bismarck dismissed as Imperial Chancellor, replaced by General von Caprivi
1891	The Pan-German League is founded to promote German imperialism
1893	Franco-Russian alliance formed
1894	Federation of German Women's Associations is created; Blue Rider art movement begins in Munich
1898	*Sezession* art movement begins in Berlin; the German Navy League is founded; the First Navy Law is passed
1899	*Kyffhäuser* veterans movement started
1899–1902	Boer War in South Africa

1900	A German expedition goes to China to suppress the Boxer Rebellion
1901	Thomas Mann publishes *Buddenbrooks*
1906	The Schlieffen Plan is drafted, which will be the model for Germany's advance into Belgium at the outbreak of the Great War; universal male suffrage is instituted in Austria
1907	Universal suffrage introduced in Austria; Albert Einstein's 'special' theory of relativity is published; Richard Strauss's *Salome* premiers
1908	Austria annexes Bosnia-Herzegovina; Wilhelm II is interviewed by London's *Daily Telegraph*
1913	Lord Haldane disarmament mission to Berlin fails
1914–1918	The First World War, known then as the Great War
1917	Bolshevik Revolution takes Russia out of the war; unrestricted submarine warfare begins
1918	Germany defeated and armistice declared at Compiègne; Wilhelm II abdicates his throne; revolution breaks out in Kiel and spreads across the country including Berlin
1919	Germany signs the Treaty of Versailles; the Weimar constitution creates a German Republic with Friedrich Ebert is its first President
1925	Ebert dies and Field Marshal Paul von Hindenburg is elected President
1933	Hindenburg appoints Adolf Hitler as Chancellor
1935	Full German rearmament declared; Nuremberg Laws lay out persecution of Jews; Saar votes for reunion with Germany
1936	Germany backs General Franco in the Spanish Civil War
1938	Germany annexes Austria; the Munich Pact is signed, giving Germany the Czechoslovakian Sudetenland
1939	Germany makes a non-aggression treaty with Russia; invades Poland
1939–1945	The Second World War
1941	Germany launches 'Operation Barbarossa,' the invasion of Russia
1943	German Sixth Army surrenders at Stalingrad
1944–1945	Most intense period of Allied bombing of Germany
1944	Allies land at Normandy; attempt on Hitler's life fails
1945	Allied leaders meet at Yalta; Hitler commits suicide; the war ends; Nazi leaders indicted for war crimes are put on trial at Nuremberg
1948	Berlin blockaded by Russians in an attempt to force Western Allies to give the city up to the Soviet Union
1949	Both the Federal Republic of Germany and the German

	Democratic Republic are formed, the former sponsored by the Allied occupation authorities, and the latter under the auspices of the Soviet Union
1949–1963	Konrad Adenauer is Chancellor of the FRG (West Germany)
1949–1973	Walter Ulbricht is the principal leader of the DDR (East Germany) in various offices including chairman of the Council of State after 1960
1951	Federal Republic of Germany joins the Council of Europe
1954	Soviet Union recognizes GDR sovereignty
1955	The Federal Republic is recognized as a sovereign state and becomes a member of NATO
1955	Warsaw Pact is established including GDR
1957	Germany signs the Treaty of Rome, which leads to Euratom and the European Economic Community; Saar returns to Germany
1961	The Berlin Wall goes up; East German soldier, Conrad Schumann, becomes famous for leaping over rolled wire to escape into West Berlin
1963	US President John F. Kennedy speaks to a Berlin audience in protest against the Wall; Chancellor Konrad Adenauer and French President Charles de Gaulle lay the foundations for Franco–German cooperation with the signing of the Elysée Treaty
1968–1977	The Red Army Faction (Baader-Meinhof) wage a terrorist war on the FRG
1969	Chancellor Willi Brandt begins *Ostpolitik*
1970	FRG signs a treaty with Poland
1971	Erich Honecker succeeds Ulbricht as DDR leader
1972	Israeli athletes are taken prisoner by terrorists at the Munich Olympics
1973	Both the FRG and DDR join the United Nations
1978	Green Party established
1984	Chancellor Helmut Kohl makes his 'grace of later birth' speech in Israel
1986	The rise of Jörg Haider begins in Austria
1989	A flood of refugees pour into the FRG from GDR via Hungary; the Berlin Wall is torn down, and the Brandenburg Gate is opened
1990	East and West Germany are reunited into a single Germany, with elections in which Germans from both participate; Helmut Kohl and the CDU win the election
1991	Transfer of the German capital from Bonn to Berlin begins
1992	Neo-Nazi violence is greeted by anti-Nazi demonstrations

1995	Artist Christo (Christo Javacheff) wraps the Reichstag Building in Berlin in white cloth to celebrate German reunification
1998	Helmut Kohl and the CDU are defeated by a coalition of the SPD and Green Party; SPD leader Gerhard Schröder becomes Chancellor; Conrad Schumann, East German soldier famous for leaping over barbed wire into West Berlin in 1961, commits suicide; Berlin Wall Memorial opened.
2001	W. G. Sebald, one of Germany's greatest post-war writers, dies
2002	Floods threaten such historic cities as Dresden and Cologne; controversial Nazi period film maker Leni Riefenstahl celebrates her 100th birthday; Sir Simon Rattle 'takes up the baton' as conductor of the Berlin Philharmonic Orchestra.
2003	French President Jacques Chirac and Chancellor Gerhard Schröder commemorate the 40th anniversary of the signing of the Elysée Treaty; Schröder joins Chirac in refusing to vote for a UN Security Council Resolution backing an Anglo-American war against Iraq.

Major Universities and Founding Dates

Charles University (Prague), *1348*
Vienna, *1365*
Heidelberg, *1385*
Cologne, *1388* (closed from 1798 until re-established in 1919)
Erfurt, *1392*
Würzburg, *1402*
Leipzig, *1409*
Rostock, *1419*
Greifswald, *1456*
Freiburg-im-Breisgau, *1457*
Ingolstadt, *1472*
Trier, *1473*
Mainz, *1477* (closed from 1792 until re-established in 1946, under French occupation)
Tübingen, *1477*
Marburg, *1527*
Königsberg, *1544*
Jena, *1558*
Helmstedt, *1574*
Giessen, *1607*
Rintelen, *1621*
Altdorf, *1623*
Kiel, *1665*
Halle, *1694*
Berlin (Humboldt), *1809*
Munich (Ludwig Maximilian), *1826*
Berlin (Free University), *1948*

Select List of Religious Buildings (from the oldest dated remains)

Cathedrals:

AACHEN (North Rhine-Westphalia), Aachener Dom, 9th century
ALTENBERG (North Rhine-Westphalia), Altenberger Dom, 13th century
AUGSBURG (Bavaria), St Maria, 10th century
BAMBERG (Bavaria), Bamberger Dom, 13th century
BARDOWICK (Lower Saxony), SS Peter and Paul, 12th century
BAUTZEN (Saxony), St Peter, 13th century
BERLIN (Brandenburg), Berliner Dom, 19th century
BRANDENBURG (Brandenburg), SS Peter and Paul, 12th century
BRAUNSCHWEIG (Lower Saxony), St Blasius, 12th century
BREMEN (Bremen), St Peter, 11th century
COLOGNE (North Rhine-Westphalia), SS Peter and Mary, 13th century
DRESDEN (Saxony), Hofkirche, 18th century
EICHSTÄTT (Bavaria), Eichstätter Dom, 11th century
ERFURT (Thuringia), St Maria, 8th century
ESSEN (North Rhine-Westphalia), Essener Dom, 9th century
FRANKFURT-AM-MAIN (Hesse), St Bartholomew, 13th century
FREIBERG (Saxony), Freiburg Münster, 15th century
FREIBURG-IM-BREISGAU (Baden-Württemberg), Unsere Liebe Frau, 13th century
FRITZLER (Hesse), St Peter, 11th century
FULDA (Hesse), SS Salvator and Bonifatus, 18th century
GREIFSWALD (Mecklenburg-West Pomerania), St Nicholas, 13th century
GÜSTROW (Mecklenburg-West Pomerania), SS Maria, Johann Evangelist, Cecilia, 13th century
HALBERTSTEDT (Saxony-Anhalt), St Stephen, 13th century
HILDESHEIM (Lower Saxony), St Maria, 11th century
KASSEL (Hesse), St Peter, 12th century
LIMBURG AN DER LAHN (Hesse), Limburger Dom, 13th century
MAGDEBURG (Saxony-Anhalt), St Mauritus and St Katherine, 13th century

MAINZ (Rhineland-Palatinate), SS Martin and Stephen, 11th century
MEISSEN (Saxony), Meissener Dom, 13th century
MERSEBURG (Saxony-Anhalt), Merseburger Dom, 11th century
MINDEN (North Rhine-Westphalia), SS Peter and Gorgonius, 11th century
MUNICH (Bavaria), Frauenkirche, 15th century
MÜNSTER (North Rhine-Westphalia), St Paul, 13th century
NAUMBURG (Saxony-Anhalt), SS Peter and Paul, 13th century
NEUSS (North Rhine-Westphalia), St Quirin, 11th century
OSNABRÜCK (Lower Saxony), St Peter, 8th century
PADERBORN (North Rhine-Westphalia), SS Maria, Liborius, and Kilian, 11th century
PASSAU (Bavaria), St Stephen, 15th century
REGENSBURG (Bavaria), St Stephen, 13th century
SCHLESWIG (Schleswig-Holstein), St Peter, 12th century
SCHWERIN (Mecklenburg-West Pomerania) Schweriner Dom, 14th century
SOEST (North Rhine-Westphalia), St Patroclus, 12th century
SPEYER (Rhineland-Palatinate), SS Maria and Stephen, 11th century
STENDAL (Saxony-Anhalt), St Nikolas, 15th century
TANGERMÜNDE (Saxony-Anhalt), St Maria, 12th century
ULM (Baden-Württemburg), Ulm Münster, 14th century
VERDEN (Lower Saxony), St Maria, 13th century
WORMS (Rhineland-Palatinate), SS Peter and Paul, 11th century
WÜRZBURG (Bavaria), St Kilian, 11th century
XANTEN (North Rhine-Palatinate), St Victor, 12th century
ZWICKAU (Saxony), St Maria, 13th century

Abbeys and Churches:

ALTENBURG (Thuringia), St Bartholomäu, 12th century
AMMERSEE (Bavaria), Andechs Monastery, 12th century
ANNABERG-BUCHHOLZ (Saxony), St Anne, 15th century
ASCHAFTENBURG (Bavaria), SS. Peter and Paul, 12th century
AUGBSBURG (Bavaria), St Anne, 14th century
BAMBERG (Bavaria), St Michael, 15th century
BARTH (Mecklenburg-West Pomerania), St Maria, 14th century
BERLIN:
  Kaiser Wilhelm Memorial, 19th century
  St Maria, 13th century
  St Nickolai, 14th century
  Maria Regina Martyrum, 20th century
BERNBURG (Saxony-Anhaldt), St Agidienschloss, 18th century
BIELEFELD (North Rhine-Westphalia), St Nikoli Alstädter, 14th century
BONN (North Rhine-Westphalia), SS Cassius and Florentius, 11th century

BRANDENBURG (Brandenburg), Lehnin Abbey, 12th century
BRAUNSCHWEIG (Lower Saxony), St Michael, 12th century
CELLE (Lower Saxony), Wienhausen Monastery, 13th century
COBURG-Grunfeld (Bavaria), Vierzehnheiligen, 18th century
COLOGNE (North Rhine-Westphalia):
　St Pantaleon, 10th century
　St Gereonis, 11th century
　Gross St Martin, 12th century
DESSAU (Saxony-Anhalt), St Georg, 18th century
DONAUESCHINGEN (Baden-Württemberg), St Johann, 18th century
DORTMUND (North Rhine-Westphalia), St Reinhold, 13th century
DRESDEN (Saxony), Frauenkirche, 18th century
EBERSWALDE-FINOW (Brandenburg), Chorin Monastery, 13th century
EICHSTÄTT (Bavaria), Rebdorf Monastery, 12th century
EISENACH (Thuringia):
　St Nikolai, 12th century
　St Peter, 15th century
　St Georg, 16th century
EISLEBEN (Saxony-Anhalt), SS Peter and Paul, 15th century
ERFURT (Thuringia):
　St Severus, 12th century
　St Schotten, 12th century
　Augustinian Monastery, 13th century
ERLANGEN (Bavaria):
　Hugenotten, 17th century
　Dreifaltigkeit, 18th century
ESSEN (North Rhine-Westphalia), Werden Abbey, 13th century
ESSLINGEN (Baden-Württemberg):
　St Paul, 13th century
　Frauenkirche, 14th century
ETTAL (Bavaria), Ettal Abbey, 14th century
FORCHHEIM (Bavaria), St Martin, 17th century
FRANKFURT-AM-MAIN (Hesse), St Paul, 18th century
FREIBERG (Saxony), St Nikolai, 14th century
FREIBURG-IM-BREISGAU (Baden-Württemberg), Universitätkirche, 17th
　century
FULDA (Hesse):
　St Michael, 9th century
　St Peter, 12th century
GIFHORN (Lower Saxony), St Nikolai, 18th century
GÖRLITZ (Saxony), SS Peter and Paul, 15th century
GÖTTINGEN (Lower Saxony):
　St Johann, 14th century

St Maria, 14th century
St Jakob, 14th century
GREIFSWALD (Mecklenburg-West Pomerania):
  Hilda Abbey, 12th century
  St Jakob, 13th century
  St Maria, 14th century
HALLE AN DER SAALE (Saxony-Anhalt), St Moritz, 14th century
HAMBURG (Hamburg):
  St Peter, 13th century
  St Katharine, 14th century
HAMM (Hamm (North Rhine-Westphalia), St Paul, 13th century
HEIDELBERG (Baden-Württemberg), Heiliggeistkirche, 15th century
HEILIGENSTADT (Thuringia):
  St Martin, 14th century
  St Giles, 14th century
HELMSTADT (Lower Saxony), St Ludger Monastery, 9th century
HILDERSHEIM (Lower Saxony):
  St Michael, 11th century
  St Mauritius, 11th century
  MagdaleneKirche, 13th century
HÖXTER (North Rhine-Westphalia):
  Cover Abbey, 9th century
  St Kalian, 12th century
KAIMANS (Saxony), St Just, 14th century
KIRCHHEIM UNTER TECK (Baden-Württemberg), St Martin, 7th century
KLEVE (North Rhine-Westphalia), St Mariae Himmelfahrt, 14th century
KOBLENZ (Rhineland-Palatinate):
  St Kastor, 9th century
  Liebfrauenkirche, 12th century
LANDSBERG AM LECH (Bavaria), Heiligkreuzkirche, 18th century
LEIPZIG (Saxony):
  St Nikolai, 12th century
  St Thomas, 13th century
LINDAU (Bavaria), St. Peter, 11th century
LÜBECK (Schleswig-Holstein):
  St Maria, 13th century
  St Katharine, 14th century
LÜNEBURG (Lower Saxony), St Michael, 14th century
MAULBRONN (Baden-Württemberg), Maulbronn Abbey, 12th century
MARBURG (Hesse), St Elisabeth, 14th century
MEISSEN (Saxony), St Afraen, 13th century
MINDEN (North Rhine-Westphalia), St Maria, 11th century
MÜHLHAUSEN (Thuringia):

St Blaisius, 11th century
St Maria, 14th century
MUNICH (Bavaria), St Peter, 11th century
MÜNSTER (North Rhine-Westphalia), St Lambert, 14th century
NAUMBURG (Saxony-Anhalt), St Wenzel, 13th century
NERESHEIM (Bavaria), Neresheim Abbey, 17th century
NEUBRANDENBURG (Mecklenburg-West Pomerania), St Johannes
    Monastery, 13th century
NORDHAUSEN (Thuringia), St Blaise, 15th century
NUREMBERG (Bavaria):
St Lorenz, 13th century
St Sebaldus, 13th century
OFFENBURG (Baden-Württemberg), Heiligkruezkirche, 17th century
PADERBORN (North Rhine-Westphalia), St Ulrich, 12th century
PLAUEN (Saxony):
St Johann, 12th century,
Luther, 17th century
PRENZLAU (Brandenburg):
St Maria, 13th century
Trinity, 13th century
QUEDLINBURG (Saxony-Anhalt), St Wiperi Cloister, 12th century
RAVENSBURG (Baden-Württemberg), St Jodok, 14th century
REGENSBURG (Bavaria):
St Emmeram Cloister, 7th century
St Ulrich, 11th century
REUTLINGEN (Baden-Württemberg), St Maria, 13th century
SAALFELD (Thuringia), St Johann, 14th century
SCHLESWIG (Schleswig-Holstein), St Johannis Cloister, 12th century
SCHNEEBERG (Saxony), St Wolfgang, 16th century
SIEGEN (North Rhine-Westphalia), St Martin, 10th century
SOEST (North Rhine-Westphalia):
St Maria zur Höhe, 13th century
St Maria zur Wiese, 14th century
STRALSUND (Mecklenburg-West Pomerania), St Katharine Cloister, 13th
    century
STUTTGART (Baden-Württemberg), Heiligkreuzkirche, 12th century
TANGERMÜNDE (Saxony-Anhalt):
St Nikolai, 14th century
Dominican Cloister, 15th century
TRIER (Rhineland-Palatinate):
St Matthias, 12th century
Liebfrauekirche, 13th century
ULM (Baden-Württemberg), Wiblingen Monastery, 11th century

WEIMAR (Thuringia), SS Peter and Paul, 15th century
WITTENBERG (Saxony-Anhalt):
  St Maria, 13th century
  Schloss Church (Reformation Memorial Church), 16th century
ZWICKAU (Saxony), St Katharine, 13th century

Selected Readings on German History

Annals of Fulda, The, trans. and annot. Timothy Reuter (Manchester, 1992)

ASPREY, ROBERT B., *Frederick the Great: the Magnificent Enigma* (New York, 1986)

BARRACLOUGH, GEOFFREY, *The Origins of Modern Germany* (Oxford, 1957)

BRYCE, JAMES, *The Holy Roman Empire* (London, 1904)

CARSTEN, F. L., *The Origins of Prussia* (Oxford, 1954)

DAVIDSON, EUGENE, *The Trial of the Germans: An Account of Twenty-Two Defendants before the International Military Tribunal at Nuremberg* (New York, 1966)

FEUCHTWANGER, E. J., *Prussia: Myth and Reality* (London, 1970)

FLECKENSTEIN, JOSEF (trans. Bernard S. Smith), *Early Medieval Germany* (Amsterdam, London, New York, 1978)

FULBROOK, MARY, *History of Germany, 1918–2000: The Divided Nation* (Oxford, 2002)

HERWIG, HOLGER, *Hammer or Anvil? Modern Germany, 1649–Present* (Lexington, MA: D.C. Heath, 1994)

JAMES, EDWARD, *The Franks* (London, 1988)

KITCHEN, MARTIN, *The Cambridge Illustrated History of Germany* (Cambridge, 2000)

KOCH, H. W., *A History of Prussia* (New York, 1978)

KRACAUER, SIEGFRIED, *From Caligary to Hitler: A Psychological Study of The German Film* (Princeton, 1947)

LAQUEUR, WALTER, *Weimar: A Cultural History, 1918–1933* (New York, 1974)

MADDOCKS, FIONA, *Hildegard of Bingen* (New York, 2001)

MALLORY, J. P., *In Search of the Europeans* (London, 1989)

MANCHESTER, WILLIAM, *The Arms of Krupp, 1587–1968* (New York, 1968)

OWEN, FRANCIS, *The Germanic People: Their Origin, Expansion & Culture* (New York, 1960)

PINSON, KOPPEL S., *Modern Germany: Its History and Civilization*, 2nd edition (New York, 1989)

REINHARDT, KURT F., *Germany, 2000 Years*, 2 vols. (New York, 1961)

ROY, JAMES CHARLES, *The Vanished Kingdom: Travels Through the History of Prussia* (Oxford and Boulder, Colo., 1999)

TAYLOR, A. J. P., *The Course of German History* (New York, 1961)

TAYLOR, RONALD, *Berlin and Its Culture* (New Haven, Conn., and London, 1997)

TENBROCK, ROBERT-HERMAN (trans. Paul J. Dine), *A History of Germany* (Munich, 1965)

THOMPSON, E. A., *The Early Germans* (Oxford, 1965)

VALENTIN, VEIT, *The German People: Their History and Civilization from the Holy Roman Empire to the Third Reich* (New York, 1946)

WELCH, DAVID, *Propaganda and the German Cinema, 1933–1945* (Oxford, 1983)

WIERUSZOWSKI, HELENE, *The Medieval University* (Princeton, New Jersey, 1966)

Historical Gazetteer

Numbers in bold refer to the main text

Aachen The Rhenish city from which Charles the Great ruled his empire. It came to be known also as Aix-la-Chapelle. **22, 25, 26, 33, 43, 58, 87, 89, 135, 249, 251**

Augsburg A major trading centre with Roman origins, which was the headquarters of the Fugger trade and banking empire beginning in the 15th century. The Fuggers, raised to noble status, became the principal financiers and suppliers of Habsburg political and military ambitions. It also was the seat of an Imperial Diet which played a central role in opposing the Protestant Refor-

The cathedral in Aachen built by Charles the Great

mation. **7, 32 46, 48, 52, 65–6, 97, 125**

Bamberg One of the oldest imperial cities, and an ecclesiastical centre since the 11th century. The cathedral is famous for its 13th century 'knight of Bamberg' equestrian statue, which represents an unidentified king, thought by some to be St Stephen of Hungary, brother-in-law to Emperor Henry II whose tomb stands in the centre of the nave. Bamberg's Cathedral school was organized to educate the clergy in the ways of imperial administration. **35**

BATTLES

ACRE (Palestine), 1190: Crusaders laid siege to this city, and one side effect was formation of the Order of Teutonic Knights, both to do battle and care for the sick and wounded. **41**

BREITENFELD (Saxony), 1631: Swedish king Gustavus Adolphus defeated an Imperial army under General Tilly in the first major battle of the 'Swedish Phase' of the Thirty Years War. **94**

CHÂLONS (France), 451: Roman general Aëtius, in alliance with Visigoth King Theodoric I, defeated Attila the Hun. **8**

DUNKIRK (France), 1940: Having been routed by advancing German forces, more than 300,000 Anglo-French forces were evacuated from the beaches near this city and carried across the English Channel to Britain. **246**

DURBEN (Prussia), 1260: The Lithuanians defeated the Teutonic Knights on this occasion, which inspired a Prussian rebellion against

them. It was put down with Polish aid. **119**

FEHRBELLIN (Prussia) 1675: Frederick Wilhelm, the Great Elector of Prussia, defeated the Swedes in this battle, after which he drove them out of East Prussia. **124**

FRANKENHAUSEN (Thuringia), 1525: Imperial forces destroyed a rebel army led by Thomas Müntzer, effectively ending the Peasants' Rebellion. **85**

JENA AND AUERSTADT (Prussia), 1806: Napoleon's forces routed the Prussians, after which the Prussian king was forced to move his seat eastward from Berlin to Königsberg. **143**

KÖNIGGRÄTZ (Bohemia), 1866: Prussian forces overwhelmed an Austrian army, which brought Bismarck one step closer to bringing about the unification of Germany under Prussian dominance. **160**

LECHFELD (Bavaria), 955: Otto the Great led an army drawn from all German tribes to defeat a Hungarian army; the result was the conversion of Hungary to Christianity. **32**

LEIPZIG (Saxony) 1813: This was the 'Battle of the Nations' in which an army drawn from various German states, though dominated by the Prussians, defeated Napoleon and paved the way for the fall of his French empire. **143**

LENINGRAD and STALINGRAD (Russia), 1943: German forces were defeated by the USSR in their attempts to capture these two key Russian cities, and put on the defensive as a result. These defeats marked the beginning of the end for Germany on the Eastern Front in the Second World War. **248, 253**

LOBOSITZ (Saxony), 1756: Frederick II of Prussia's first major victory, against the Austrians, in the Seven Years War. **136**

LÜTZEN (Saxony) 1632: In this Thirty Years War battle, King Gustavus Adolphus of Sweden was killed, but his army then routed the Imperial army led by Albrecht von Wallenstein. **94–5**

MARNE (France), 1914: The German advance towards Paris was stopped, and the German line fell back toward Verdun. This was as close as Germany came to Paris in the First World War. **145**

NÄFELS (Switzerland), 1388: The third major victory of the 14th century for the Swiss League over the Habsburgs, which greatly enhanced Switzerland's expansion. **64**

NORMANDY (France), 1944: Allied forces – British, French, American – landed on several beaches along the Norman coast, established a foothold, and began the long process of defeating Germany. It was the single most important event of the Second World War in the European theatre. **253**

RONCESVALLES (Pyrénnés), 779: Basque warriors ambushed a Frank rearguard led by Roland, Count of Breton and related to Charles the Great. They were killed to the last man, and became the subject of folklore, as in the *Rolandslied,* the German version of Song of Roland. **23**

SOISSONS (France), 486: Clovis defeated Syagrius, the last Gallo-Roman king, and the set the course for Frank domination of what in time would become the Carolingian Empire. **13**

TANNENBERG (Poland) 1410: The Poles soundly defeated the Teutonic Knights and set in motion their decline as a force in northeastern Europe. **119**

TEUTOBURG FOREST (Rhineland), 9: Hermann (Arminius) defeated three Roman Legions and halted Roman penetration beyond the Rhine River. **7**

TOURS AND POITIER (France), 732: Charles Martel stopped the Muslim advance into the kingdom of the Franks. **19**

VALMY (France), 1791: A French revolutionary army met and defeated an imperial army including Prussians, under the command of the duke of Brunswick. **141**

VERDEN (Lower Saxony), 782: Franks slaughtered some 4,000 Saxons who had been betrayed to the Franks by their own nobility. **22**

VIENNA (Austria), 1683: Fighting for the Habsburg emperor, a Polish army commanded by King Jan Sobieski lifted the Turkish siege of Vienna which had been imposed with French support. Viennese bakers celebrated lifting the siege by baking buns replicating the Crescent of Islam. In time these buns came to be known as 'croissant,' most commonly associated with France. **104**

WATERLOO (Belgium), 1815: The tide of this battle between a British army under the Duke of Wellington and the French forces of Napoleon Bonaparte, was likely turned when a Prussian army under Marshall Blücher came to Wellington's aid. **143**

WEISSBERG (Bohemia), 1620: This is the famous Battle of White Mountain, in which Bohemian rebels against the Holy Roman Empire were defeated. It marked the beginning of the Thirty Years War. **92**

Bayreuth Every four years, the four operas of Wagner's Ring Cycle are performed at the Bayreuth Festival. Wagner himself chose the site in 1872, with the support of King Ludwig II of Bavaria, and had the festival hall built to his own design. Both Wagner and Frederick Liszt, his father-in-law, are buried in Bayreuth. **179**

Berchtesgaden The place most famously known as Hitler's Alpine mountain-top retreat. It also was a salt-mining site beginning in the 16th century. **240**

Berlin

BENDLERSTRASSE (Stauffenbergstrasse): The location of the Hitler's War Ministry. Colonel Stauffenberg and others were executed by firing squad in the courtyard after a failed attempt to overthrow the Nazi Regime in July 1944. The street is now named Stauffenbergstrasse in his memory, and the former Ministry is a war museum. **242**

BERLIN WALL MEMORIAL: A memorial opened in 1998 to remind Berliners and all others of the inhumanity that the Berlin Wall represented. **267–8**

BRANDENBURGER TOR: A triumphal arch at the west end of Unter den Linden, toped by the Victory Quadriga (four horses pulling a chariot) statue. The Tor was built in 1789 with the assent of King Frederick Wilhelm III; the statue was added in 1793. Napoleon took the statue to Paris after 1806, and it was returned in 1814. **146–7, 194**

GRUNEWALD: A park in western Berlin which originally was the hunting ground with lodge for the Electors of Brandenburg.

HUMBOLDT-UNIVERSITY: This university opened in 1809 in what had once been the palace of Frederick II's brother, Prince Heinrich. It is named for its principal founder, the intellectual, writer, and diplomat, Wilhelm von Humboldt. **143**

KURFÜRSTENDAMM: This street has existed since the 16th century, when it was the path connecting the Electors to their hunting lodge in the Grunewald; during the age of Bismarck, it was transformed into the cultural and commercial centre of a rapidly expanding city, its sidewalks lined with Berlin's best restaurants, cafés, night clubs, galleries, hotels, and fashionable shops.

OLYMPIC STADIUM: Built with 100,000 seats for the XIth Olympic Games in 1936. The Nazis expected the games to be an advertisement for Aryan racial supremacy; in fact, Jesse Owens and Charles Metcalf, two African-Americans, dominated sprint events and the broad jump, and their names are inscribed on a commemorative plaque at the Olympic stadium. Leni Riefenstahl's film documentary on the Olympics was from start to finish a propaganda piece devoted to the Aryan ideal among both men and women. The Berlin football (soccer) club now makes its home in the stadium. **239**

ORANIENBURG: Some 19 miles north of Berlin, this was the site of the infamous Sachsenhausen Concentration Camp. The Camp is now a museum and memorial in memory of those who died there. **236**

REICHSTAG: Where the Bundestag is based. It was built in the 1880s and served as the seat first of the Imperial parliament, and then of the Weimar Republican parliament. It was gutted by fire in 1933, rebuilt, and then virtually destroyed again during the Second World War by Allied bombing. Repairs were made, but it stood largely unused until Berlin was again made the German capital following reunification in 1990. Now it once again is home to the German parliament. **277**

SCHAUSPIELHAUS: One of Berlin's principal concert halls, built originally as a theatre by Karl Frederick Schinkel in 1818–21, and designed in the Greek Classic mode. It was the site for the premier of Carl Maria von Weber's opera *Freischutz*. **146**

SCHLOSS CHARLOTTEN-BURG: An elaborate urban castle built in 1695 for Queen Sophie-Charlotte, wife of Frederick I. Additions were made over the 18th century until it reached its present proportions. It is now one of Berlin's principal art museums. **125**

SPANDAU: A suburb of Berlin which became famous as the prison for convicted Nazi war criminals who were not sentenced to death. Rudolf Hess outlived all other life-sentenced prisoners, and in his last years was the only inmate. He was guarded in turn by Americans, British, French, and Russians, and when he died, the prison was razed and the site turned into a garden-park. **259**

TEMPELHOF AIRFIELD: The Tempelhofer Feld was the parade ground for the Berlin Regiment beginning in the 18th century. In the 20th it became the location for Berlin's principal airport, the landing site for the Berlin Airlift. Tegel replaced it in 1976 as the principal airport for civil air traffic. **265**

TIERGARTEN: Berlin's oldest park, stretching west from the Brandenburger Tor to Ernst-Reuter-Platz. It was a royal hunting reserve, transformed in the 19th century into an English-style garden by landscape architect Peter Joseph Lenné. **161**

UNTER DEN LINDEN: This great avenue, translated as 'under the lime trees,' was the idea of Frederick Wilhelm, the Great Elector, in 1647. Many historic sites lie along this avenue, including Humboldt-Universität. **125, 194**

WANNSEE: A beautiful lake in the Zehlendorf district, near which in 1942 was held the secret Wannsee Conference, which laid out the ground rules for how the Holocaust would be conducted in German-occupied eastern European countries. Reinhard Heydrich chaired the conference. **250**

Bingen Hildegard von Bingen, whose religious music was an inspiration to all European Christians, founded a convent here in 1150. **49–50**

Bonn Known as the 'gateway' top the Middle Rhine and remembered as the birthplace of Ludwig van Beethoven. It began as a Roman army camp and in the 16th century emerged as the official residence of Archbishops and Electors of Cologne. Bonn's importance expanded even more in 1949 when it became capital of the West German Federal Republic. (Bad) Godesberg, where Hitler and Chamberlain had their second meeting to resolve the Sudeten Crisis, is now part of Bonn. **215, 252, 258, 269, 277**

Braunau am Inn The town in Austria where Adolf Hitler was born. **223**

Braunschweig Known in English as Brunswick, this was the birthplace of court jester and wag Till Eulenspiegel, celebrated in story and song since the 16th century, including an orchestral piece by Richard Strauss in 1894. It also was the centre of Guelf power under Henry the Lion, and the site of the first football (soccer) match played on the European continent. **42, 142**

Bremen One of the premier German maritime cities with trade rights since 965. It joined the Hanseatic League in 1358, was declared an Imperial Free City in 1646, and stood on a par with Liverpool in England as a Cotton Exchange in the 19th century. **34, 46, 170, 201, 233, 252, 256, 258**

Canossa Here in the Italian Alps, an outwardly repentant Emperor Henry IV met with Pope Gregory VII in 1077, and they resolved their differences – at least in appearance – over Henry's objection to the concept of absolute power in the hands of the papacy. **39**

Cologne (Köln) Agrippa, mother of Roman Emperor Nero, was born here. Emperor Constantine made it a bishopric in the 4th century, and Charles the Great upgraded it to an archbishopric in the 9th century. It has been a centre of intellectual life from Albertus Magnus, Meister Eckhart, and Duns Scotus in the Middle Ages, to Heinrich Böll after the Second World War. **7, 17, 34, 46, 48, 51, 59, 65–66, 89, 162, 270**

Dessau This medieval trading city and princely seat of power also was where Hugo Junkers developed gas engines and heating equipment, and the first all-metal aircraft in the world. His name was associated with many types of German military aircraft in the Second World War. In 1926 the world-famous Bauhaus School of Design moved here from Weimar. **220-1**

Dresden This city was a German cultural centre from the 17th century on. It was a monument to Baroque and Rococo architecture. Heinrich Schütz, Germany's first great composer, was *kapellemeister* there, Wagner was a staple at the Opera House, and it was home to Wild West novelist Karl May. 59% of the city was destroyed by Allied bombs in the Second World War. **98, 113, 125, 136, 201, 252, 258**

Düsseldorf The city first achieved fame as an electoral and ducal residence. It was taken over by France in the Napoleonic era and ruled by the likes of Jerome Bonaparte, when it came to be known as a 'minor Paris.' In the nineteenth century it became known for its artistic qualities. Heinrich Heine grew up here, Robert Schumann was conductor in residence of the municipal orchestra, and Felix Mendelssohn-Bartholdy directed the city's Rhine Festival. **86**

Eisenach The medieval *Minnesängers* who engaged in jousting tournaments here inspired Wagner's opera *Tannhäuser*. Martin Luther studied in Eisenach, and J. S. Bach was born here. It also is the site of the Wartburg, the medieval castle where in 1817 students staged a festival to promote the idea of the German nation, to which Imperial Chancellor Metternich was diametrically opposed. **77, 115, 148, 258**

Eisleben The town where Luther was both born and died, a fact celebrated at Lutherstrasse 16, his birthplace, by a display of documents that recall his life and work. **77**

Ems The spa in the North Rhine-Westphalia region from which a dispatch was sent to Bismarck in 1870, concerning a meeting between Prussian King Wilhelm I and French ambassador Count Benedetti. Bismarck turned the dispatch into an excuse for the war against France that made possible the unification of Germany in 1871. **161**

Erfurt A historical centre of German spiritualism and mysticism, home to Meister Eckhart in the 14th century, and where Luther became an Augustinian monk. He celebrated his first Mass in Erfurt in 1507. **54, 77**

Essen Effectively the hub of Germany's industrial revolution in the 19th century, and the the centre of the Krupp industrial cartel, one of the largest arms manufacturers in the world from the 18th century through 1945. The power and prestige of the Krupp family was symbolized by their 269-room Villa Hügel, built in 1870–1873. Villa Hügel was larger even than the major Hohenzollern castles. **163, 258**

Frankfurt-am-Main This city was important in both the Roman and Carolingian eras, where first German kings and then Holy Roman Emperors were crowned. It was a major commercial and financial centre beginning with trade fairs in the 13th century, and was where the 1848 Revolution parliament sat. The Paulskirche is preserved today as a memorial to the democratic striving symbolized by that revolution. So too is the family home of Goethe, who was born in Frankfurt. **52, 58, 98, 102, 111, 144, 154, 163, 252, 258**

Freiburg-im-Breisgau Founded in the 12th century, it has been ruled by both princes and Habsburg emperors. Marie Antoinette bade farewell to Austria here on her way to Paris as the future bride of Louis XVI of France. It has been a university city since 1457. **33, 48**

Fulda The site for the annual German bishops' convention because it is the final resting place of St. Boniface, the 'Apostle of the Germans,' who was murdered by pagan Frisians in 754. **19, 70**

Garmish-Partenkirchen Germany's best-known Alpine ski resort is located here. It was the site of the 1936 Winter Olympics. Richard Strauss lived there for many years, and died there in 1949. **1, 239**

Göttingen The university here is unique in Germany because it was founded by George II of England. It has produced 40 Nobel Prize winners, including Max Planck, who developed Quantum Theory in Physics, and is buried here. Bismarck was a student at the university, though not a particularly good one. **156**

Halle The birthplace of Georg Friedrich Händel, which is celebrated with the annual Händel Festival of baroque music. **77, 107–8, 115, 258**

Hamburg Historically one of Germany's most important seaports and a major city of the Hanseatic League. It also was the site of Germany's first Stock Exchange in 1558, and as a strictly neutral city, it managed to stay out of the Thirty Years War. Hamburg was designated a Free Imperial City in 1618. **46, 52, 103, 115, 170, 201, 233, 252, 256, 258, 282**

Hannover In 1714, the Elector Georg-Ludwig of Hannover (Hanover in English) succeeded to the throne of England as George I, the long-term result of a Hannoverian-Stuart marriage union in 1658. Hannover was annexed to Prussia in 1866. **32, 42, 47, 100, 104, 136, 142, 201, 252**

Heidelberg The political centre of the Palatinate for centuries. Its university is one of Germany's oldest and most famous. The city was sacked and laid waste by the French in 1689, and was destroyed by fire in 1693. The present architectural style dates from the rebuilding that followed. **59, 79, 154**

Hildesheim Legend has it that the town began in 1815 when Louis the Pious hid his reliquary in a rose bush before lying down to sleep after a long day of hunting. When he awoke the reliquary could not be found, and, taking this as a heavenly sign, Louis founded a chapel that soon led to a bishopric, and then the town itself.

St Michael's church, Hildesheim

The city was the centre of Romanesque art throughout the Ottonian dynasty. **34, 47–8**

Kiel A port city and former Hanseatic League member which became important only in 1871 when it was selected to be Germany's principal naval base. A canal was then built to connect the port directly to the North Sea, which upset the British and helped generate the Anglo-German naval race of 1896–1908. It also inspired Erskine Childers' *The Riddle of the Sands* (1903), considered to be the first English spy novel ever written. **159, 188, 195–6, 200, 252**

Königsburg (Kaliningrad) Founded by the Teutonic Knights, this was the principal city of East Prussia until the region was absorbed into the Soviet Union after the Second World War. It served as the Prussian capital after Napoleon occupied Berlin in 1807. **45, 119, 122, 125–6, 143**

Kyffhäuser A range of hills in Thuringia where lies the *Barbarossahöhle*, a cave in which, according to legend, Frederick Barbarossa lies sleeping. He waits to someday return and bring Germany to glory. **42**

Leipzig A major trade and fair (including books in later times) centre beginning in the 12th century. One of the first printed books, *Glossa Super Apocalipsim,* was made here in 1481. It was a musical centre as well, featuring over time such prominent composer-performers as J. S. Bach, Mendolssohn-Bartoldy, and Clara and Robert Schumann. **106, 115, 143, 163, 226, 258, 269, 276**

Magdeburg Founded as a fortress in the reign of Charles the Great, it became a major trade, and later industrial, centre. The city was a place of refuge during the Reformation, but did not do so well in the Thirty Years War, during which it was besieged ten times. Baroque composer Georg Philipp Telemann spent much of his life here. **32, 34, 54, 77, 87, 95, 201**

Mainz Among the oldest trading centres, episcopal and university cities on the Rhine. Charles the Great built a bridge across the Rhine there, Johannes Gutenberg lived and worked in Mainz when he invented the moveable type printing press that revolutionized printing across Europe, and Matthias Grünewald the artist worked in Mainz as well as other Rhenish cities. **3, 7, 25, 34, 46–8, 51, 59, 69, 76, 98, 215, 252**

Marburg One of Germany's great pilgrimage centres to pay homage to the remains of St Elizabeth of Hungary, entombed in the Elizabethkirche. That is, until one of her descendants, Landgrave Philip the Magnanimous, converted to Protestantism and had her bones removed to a cemetery. He also founded Marburg University which became a leading centre of Protestant theological scholarship. Marburg outdid Magdeburg in the Thirty Years War by being besieged *eleven* times. **25, 95, 258**

Munich

DACHAU: The first Nazi concentration camp for political prisoners opened in 1933, some ten miles outside of Munich. Some 32,000 people died there (it is now a memorial site in their memory) in the course of its existence. **232**

LUDWIG-MAXIMILIAN UNI-VERSITY: Founded by King Ludwig I as a Catholic rival to the Protestant Humboldt University in Berlin. One of its most important contribution to Germany history was the White Rose student resistance movement that opposed the Nazi Regime during the Second World War. **143**

OLYMPIC STADIUM: In 1972, the Games came to Germany for the second time, in part to show the world that Germany's Second World War history was behind it. This made the tragedy that came with the Games even worse. Arab terrorists took Israeli athletes hostage in an attempt to force concessions from the Israeli govern-ment over Palestine. Eleven athletes were killed along with the terrorists before it was finally over. **273**

RATHAUS: The city hall on the Marienplatz is where, on 8 Novem-ber 1923, Hitler led SA units, hung a Swastika flag and claimed to be taking control over the Bavarian govern-ment. Bavarian state police broke up the attempt with gunfire. This was the failed 'beer-hall *putsch*', so named because Hitler had launched it at the Bürgerbräukeller, where he waved a pistol and called for an overthrow of the Bavarian government followed by a march on 'red' Berlin. **215**

Nuremberg (Nürnberg) First, it was a beautiful medieval city; then it was a major trade centre and home to artists the like of Michael Wolgemut and his student, Albrecht Dürer; and in the 20th century, it became the ideolo-gical showplace of the Nazi move-ment. Anti-Jewish legislation was the corps of the Nuremberg Laws (1935) and elaborate party rallies were held there of which Leni Riefenstahl made her propaganda film *Triumph des Willens*. It was the Nazi factor that decided the victorious powers in 1945 to make Nuremberg the site for trying war criminals. **46, 52, 54, 59, 65–7, 86, 125, 150, 179, 238, 251, 258–9**

Oberammergau Site of the some-times controversial Passion Play depicting the life of Christ, first per-formed in 1634 in fulfilment of a vow made the year before in response to an outbreak of plague. It has been performed every ten years since, most recently in 2000. **106**

Potsdam The Berlin suburb that became the seat of the Prussian kings in the 18th century. Sans Souci was built as the royal palace, soon gaining for Potsdam the reputation of a 'Prussian Versailles.' The Cecilienhof Palace was the location for the 1945 Potsdam Conference where the vic-torious allies decided the fate of post-war Germany. **97, 130, 232, 258–9**

Prague Bohemia's principal city that has played an important part in German history since the early Middle Ages, including being the starting point for the Thirty Years War. Its occupation by Germany in March 1939 alerted Britain and France that Hitler's guarantees at the 1938 Munich Conference were a hollow promise. **33, 57, 59, 65, 68, 91, 152, 233**

Regensburg A Celtic village that became a Roman garrison which emerged as a centre of religious life in the Middle Ages, and was the seat of the Wittelsbachs as dukes of Bavaria until the 13th century. It also was an

Index